D0345509

The MARKET MASTERS

The MARKET MASTERS

Wall Street's Top Investment Pros
Reveal How to Make Money
in Both Bull and Bear Markets

KIRK KAZANJIAN

WILEY

John Wiley & Sons, Inc.

Published by John Wiley & Sons, Inc., Hoboken, New Jersey.

Published simultaneously in Canada.

For general information on our other products and services, please contact our Customer Care Department within the United States at 800-762-2974, outside the United States at 317-572-3993 or fax 317-572-4002.

Wiley also publishes its books in a variety of electronic formats. Some content that appears in print may not be available in electronic books. For more information about Wiley products, visit our web site at www.wiley.com.

Library of Congress Cataloging-in-Publication Data:

Kazanjian, Kirk.
    The market masters : Wall Street's top investment pros reveal how to make money in both bull and bear markets / Kirk Kazanjian.
      p.   cm.
    Includes index.
    ISBN-13 978-0-471-69865-4 (cloth)
    ISBN-10 0-471-69865-2
    1. Investment analysis. 2. Investments—United States. 3. Investment advisors—New York (State)—New York—Interviews. 4. Stockbrokers—New York (State)—New York—Interviews. 5. Stock exchanges—New York (State)—New York. I. Title.
    HG4529.K387   2005
    332.67'8—dc22

                                   2004028128

Printed in the United States of America.

10 9 8 7 6 5 4 3 2 1

CONTENTS

PART FOUR THE SECTOR SPECIALISTS

PART FIVE THE FIXED-INCOME WIZARDS

PART SIX INVESTING LIKE THE MASTERS

INTRODUCTION

There was a time when making money in the stock market looked pretty easy. For a short period, especially in the late 1990s, it seemed you could buy just about any company—even one with little operating history, no profits, and inexperienced management—and make a small fortune literally overnight. But once the bubble burst, and many of these high-flying stocks went down to zero, the truth became apparent: Making money in the market is hard work. True wealth is built over time through disciplined investing using techniques and strategies that have been proven successful over the long haul.

While it's easy to look like a genius when the market goes straight up, it's in the more difficult times, such as those we've experienced over the last few years, that the truly great investment pros emerge head and shoulders above the rest of the pack. Without question, managers able to stay ahead of the crowd in both bull and bear markets are extremely rare. They have a keen sense of knowing when and what to buy and—just as importantly—when to sell. They avoid following trends, learn from their mistakes, and stick with a winning strategy through thick and thin. Indeed, these men and women are *The Market Masters*.

In the pages that follow, you will meet 18 managers who are clearly at the top of their game. All have trounced the competition over time and emerged from the recent brutal bear market relatively unscathed. Indeed, to be crowned a "Master," each manager must have outperformed both their peer index and the overall market for at least the last five years preceding our interview. Most have done it for much longer.

Some managers, including Samuel Stewart, Daniel Fuss, and Andy Pilara, have decades of experience. Others, including David Chan, John C. Thompson, and Riad Younes, represent the new generation of great Wall Street investment minds (though each still has worked in the business for more than 10 years).

The Market Masters takes you one-on-one with all of these gurus to uncover their strategies for beating the market in both good and bad times. In addition to collectively managing tens of billions of dollars for institutions and other well-heeled investors, all of the Masters run publicly traded mutual funds, which serves a dual purpose. First, it means they have demonstrated and easily quantifiable track records, so you know their strategies work. Second, for those who prefer funds over individual stocks, it gives you a chance to meet some of the industry's best managers whom you can actually hire, should you find their philosophy matches up with your own.

As a result, regardless of whether you're looking for some top-notch funds to add to your portfolio, or simply want to discover how to select winning stocks and bonds from some of the leading minds in the business, you'll enjoy and profit from every page of *The Market Masters*.

Each profile follows a similar path. We begin by discussing the manager's background and how he or she got into the business. We then move into the Master's investment process and uncover the secrets of his or her success. The interviews generally wrap up by talking about each expert's current observations of the world and the market, along with some of the most important lessons they've learned along the way.

The book is divided into six parts, and features managers who specialize in a variety of styles and market sectors both in the United States and abroad. In Part One, you'll meet five growth gurus—Manu Daftary, Whit Gardner, Janna Sampson, Sam Stewart, and John C. Thompson—all of whom look for stocks with growing profitability and earnings using a variety of techniques.

Part Two features five managers built in the mold of value investing legends Benjamin Graham, David Dodd, and even Warren Buffett. These experts—Rob Lyon, Andy Pilara, Rich Pzena, John Schneider, and Susan Suvall—are on the prowl for stocks that Wall Street has put on sale, and especially like to buy when everyone else wants to sell.

In Part Three, you'll meet two managers—Sarah Ketterer and Riad Younes—who invest the bulk of their money in overseas companies. They not only tell you how they find these stocks, but also why international investing makes sense for at least part of your overall portfolio.

Part Four will introduce you to four managers who specialize in specific market sectors. David Chan follows healthcare, Andrew Davis has made a name for himself investing in real estate investment trusts, David Ellison is a long-time financial services analyst, and Paul Wick is about the most seasoned technology manager in the business.

Finally, since many portfolios are comprised of both stocks and bonds,

Part Five features two of the best fixed-income managers on Wall Street today. Daniel Fuss is widely considered to be the dean of bond investing (he's been doing it for more than 45 years), while Margie Patel is clearly tops in the area of high-yield securities.

While all of the Masters have slightly different ways of choosing their investments, they do share many traits in common. Part Six sums this up with a chapter on the "Ten Keys to Beating the Market." This last section also includes a helpful glossary of frequently used investment terms, in case you run across any terminology within the interviews that you're not familiar with.

I'd like to personally thank all of the Masters for all of their help in putting this book together and for being so generous with their time and knowledge. Thanks also go out to my expert transcriber, Darla McDavid, who always does excellent work, along with the entire team at John Wiley & Sons, including Debra Englander, Joan O'Neil, Kim Craven, and Peter Knapp.

As always, I welcome your comments and feedback about the book. You can write to me at kirk@kirkkazanjian.com.

With that, it's time to start learning how to make money in the markets around the world from those who really know how to do it. I'm sure you'll find these conversations to be both enlightening and entertaining, and wish you much success with your future investment endeavors.

PART ONE

The GROWTH GURUS

MANU DAFTARY

DG Capital Management

When Manu Daftary arrived in the United States from his native India in the 1980s, he never imagined he'd one day be overseeing huge sums of money. After several years of analyzing and selecting investment managers to run college endowments, Daftary was handed a stock portfolio to run on his own. Since he had long observed the styles and techniques of the country's leading money managers, he brought what he considered to be their best practices together in forming the foundation of an investment strategy he continues to follow today.

Daftary, 47, ultimately started his own investment firm in Boston in 1996. He is also subadvisor to the top-performing Quaker Aggressive

Growth Fund. Daftary's core beliefs are that earnings drive stock prices, companies with earnings surprises tend to outperform the general market, and avoiding downside volatility is the key to long-term outperformance.

Daftary is an opportunistic investor and enjoys wide discretion when it comes to running his fund. For instance, he is allowed to raise as much cash as he wants, is free to buy companies of all sizes, and can even short stocks as he sees fit. As a result, Quaker Aggressive Growth is often compared to a hedge fund, since it's definitely not for the faint of heart.

As you'll learn, Daftary looks at stocks through a variety of glasses. When it comes to analyzing bigger companies, valuation is of utmost importance. For the smaller names, value is important, but earnings momentum is king. Above all, diversification is crucial since, as Daftary puts it, despite your best efforts, you never truly know which stocks will become your biggest winners.

Kazanjian: *I know you grew up in Bombay, India. What originally brought you to the United States?*

Daftary: When I graduated from college in India, there wasn't much opportunity there other than joining the family business and I really didn't want to do that. The MBA programs in India were very underdeveloped, so I decided to go overseas to study. I had the choice of going to either London or the United States. My brother was at Long Beach State in California and suggested I apply there. I redid my bachelor's in business and then entered the MBA program at Long Beach State. Quite honestly, it wasn't a great school and I was bored. So before completing my MBA, I applied to a blind ad asking for a financial analyst, assuming it was something related to cost accounting. It turned out to be a position at Cal Tech helping to run the school's endowment program. I got the job and came in as a trainee. At Cal Tech I learned the ropes of the investment business, and ultimately finished my MBA while working there.

Kazanjian: *Were you picking stocks at Cal Tech?*

Daftary: No. I did plan sponsor work, which included asset allocation studies and the hiring and selecting of managers to run the money. By 1983, I thought about moving on, and considered relocating to New York, since there really wasn't much of an investment community in Los Angeles. I was packing my bags one day and saw an ad in the *Wall Street Journal* from the University of Southern California looking for someone with my capabilities. I interviewed with the treasurer of the university who was very dynamic and I liked her right away. She called me following the interview and said I was hired. I was still planning to leave for New York, but she persuaded me to come in as the number-two person there. I worked with her for three years on the same sort of plan sponsor projects, picking managers and such.

Kazanjian: *When did you actually get to start managing money yourself?*

Daftary: In 1985. That year, the treasurer of USC got approval to actually manage a stock portfolio internally, instead of just farming it out to other managers. Once we got the approval, she gave me the portfolio to manage. I didn't have to work with committees or anyone else. It was really great.

Kazanjian: *How did you go about choosing stocks, given that this was all new to you?*

Daftary: I was learning on the job. The funny thing is I had spent three years at USC thinking a lot about stocks because I was interviewing managers to run money for the university. In that process, I was learning about how to pick stocks from very smart people. We liked to hire managers who were just starting out. Many had left larger management firms and were young and hungry. A lot of them are still friends today. But when I took over the portfolio, I knew the first thing I needed was a Quotron machine. We didn't have one in the office. Then I had to worry about getting accounting systems and establishing relationships with brokers. Since we had none, I called up USC's alumni office and asked whether they had any graduates who had gone on to become brokers. We found three. It was a real bootstrap operation. When I started my own firm in 1996, it was truly my second startup. At USC, we started out managing around $5 or $10 million. That was up to $200 million by the time I left. And we did it all with a very skeletal staff. I had only two assistants.

Kazanjian: *You left USC in 1988 and worked at two other firms before going out on your own in 1996. What made you ultimately start your own company?*

Daftary: In 1996, I was recruited to help run an investment firm in Boston. But it was clear that the gentleman who brought me in to take it over was never going to leave. Personality-wise we just didn't get along. About a year and a half into the job I decided I had to get out of there. At that point, an old friend of mine called. Jeff King, who had started the Quaker family of funds, said to me, "You're very unemployable right now. You need to go out on your own." He knew I wanted to do it and really egged me on to make that move. He had enough faith in me to hire me to start the Quaker Aggressive Growth Fund, even though I didn't have a track record. But the question was how to raise money. Jeff took me around and I was able to raise about $7 million from an offshore investor as seed money for a hedge fund. So I left my job and started the firm, without much in hand. There was a lot of panic at first, but I felt I didn't have any choice. For the first two years, it was hard growing the firm because we didn't have a track record. Plus, the $7 million we had was hedge fund money with high expectations that could leave any day.

Kazanjian: *When did the Quaker Aggressive Growth Fund start?*

Daftary: DG Capital, my firm, was incorporated in July 1996 to manage hedge fund money initially. The Quaker Aggressive Growth Fund began operations in November of the same year.

Kazanjian: *Your firm now runs about $650 million. That's some pretty good growth.*

Daftary: Yes. A little more than half of that is in the Quaker mutual fund. The rest of the money is run for institutional clients like endowments and foundations.

Kazanjian: *When it comes to managing money, you seem to have a go-anywhere investment approach.*

Daftary: I've always felt that a big problem in the industry is that there is a lot of compartmentalization going on, where managers are hired by plan sponsors for a very specific reason.

Kazanjian: *You mean to specifically buy growth or value stocks and the like?*

Daftary: Growth, value, small-cap, mid-cap—I philosophically have never believed in that. I feel that a money manager who is on the leading edge of everything that happens in the stock market should be given all flexibility to adjust the profile of the portfolio based on an evaluation of the risk level of the overall market. Even back in the 1980s, I felt that a lot of plan sponsors didn't realize the risk that they were taking in hiring certain managers because they didn't understand the risk level. They just saw the returns. They said, "Okay, we see the returns, and know you have higher risk, but we'll put you in this efficient portfolio and it will all work out." That looks great on paper, but in reality it just does not work over time. Our philosophy as managers is you should enable us to evaluate what risk to take for the assets we are managing, in our case stocks. In order to do so, you basically have to be a multicap manager and have an opportunistic approach.

Kazanjian: *So you have the freedom to buy anything you like?*

Daftary: Yes. We will go where we think it's necessary based on the risk that we need to take. That is the philosophy. We won't be typecast. The bottom line for all managers is that you have to beat the S&P or you'll be fired. It's interesting. When I started managing money, all I knew was Graham and Dodd and Warren Buffett. I had just read *The Intelligent Investor* and John Templeton was an idol. So I was really a value manager back in the 1980s. As we diversified the portfolio at USC, we realized we needed to run some of the money as growth. When I looked at the growth sector, I realized that earnings drive stock prices over time and if earnings go up, stocks go up. The problem I had with the growth universe was that it tended to be extremely volatile, especially on the downside. Given that growth managers tended to underperform over time, I wondered why one would hire people in this area. My belief was that the only way you can effectively manage money in the growth area is by avoiding disasters.

Most growth managers are very good stock pickers. Unfortunately they tend to have a lot of blowups in the portfolio, which really kills the performance. The reason they have all these blowups is twofold: First, the U.S. equity markets are mostly value-oriented, because the economy only grows 2 to 3 percent over time. Second, it's very difficult to find a classic growth stock, and when growth managers spot it, they all jam into the stock together. When the trend reverses, they all blow up together. That's the reason the whole growth sector goes out of favor.

I believe the only way you can outperform in the growth universe is to avoid negative surprises and downside volatility. If you go down 40 percent, you must go up 67 percent to break even again. If you can truncate the downside, you'll have all the money to play on the upside, which is where all the money is made in the stock market.

Kazanjian: *That's an admirable goal, but how do you achieve it?*

Daftary: We are very concerned about buying companies that could have negative earning surprises. We actually spend more time making sure we avoid the losers than finding the winners. We put great care into figuring out supply–demand characteristics, meaning that we avoid stocks where there are a large number of institutional owners of the stock who will most likely be sellers over time. We want to be very early investors in our companies. I should also point out that we look at large-caps differently than mid-caps and small-caps. Large-caps tend to be more efficient, meaning that everyone is looking at and following them.

Kazanjian: *Do you take a look at the market and other macroeconomic factors when making this evaluation?*

Daftary: Yes. We look at what's going on in the overall economy. One really has no choice, especially if you're a growth manager. For example, we pay close attention to interest rates. We also look at money flows, meaning we want to know whether dollars are going into the market or not. That's a supply-demand characteristic we monitor. The direction of the dollar is important, especially for large-caps with sales overseas. We also look at valuations. For example, in early 2004 I told clients we were getting negative on small- and mid-cap stocks because their valuations were unsustainable, especially if interest rates kept going higher. We look at overall valuations for the various sectors as well.

I've always said that you can be the biggest crackerjack analyst, but after doing all your work on the company, will people care about it? We want to look at stocks people care about. The only reason people care about stocks is because they're either going to blow their earnings numbers away or they're totally undiscovered and will eventually be owned by others.

Kazanjian: *You're also not afraid to raise cash when you're negative on the market. In 2000, your fund had 80 percent of its portfolio parked in cash. What led you to make that tactical decision?*

Daftary: It wasn't an instant decision. Back in 1998 we had the Russian crisis, the global financial markets were getting killed, and everyone was extremely negative. Luckily for us, in the summer of that year we had raised cash and avoided the severe market decline that had occurred. However, by the end of that year, we began to buy companies that were growing 25 to 30 percent a year, especially in the technology area, but which traded at 10 to 11 times earnings. So we were very early back in October 1996 to take positions in companies that did extremely well in 1999. By the summer of 1999, however, we raised the cash level up to 40 percent. Some of the companies we had bought at 10 to 12 times earnings were now trading at 40 times earnings. I get very concerned when stocks are trading at 30 to 40 times earnings, regardless of what the growth rate is. That's when your risk really starts to ratchet up. While we moved back into the market in September 1999, by February 2000, the same thing started happening again. We had stocks going up 10 to 15 percent a day. I know from past experience that money doesn't grow on trees. When they start doing this, you know there's a problem. We started raising cash into February and March, which is why the cash level got so high. When you see

IPOs doubling and tripling on a daily basis, you have to stop and see what's going on. We did not get caught up in the fever of that time. People call this market timing. I say it's risk control. I like being invested. In fact, I think most of the money is made in the market on the long side (being fully invested), not by making these tactical moves that can mess you up mentally. I'd rather be fully invested. The problem is there are certain periods of time where that's not prudent.

Kazanjian: *Eventually you were right, but you were a bit early on the move to cash.*

Daftary: Yes, and I kind of wish we had moved into some of the more value-oriented stocks, instead of selling out altogether. I didn't realize how effective Greenspan would be in cutting rates and pumping up consumers. I wish I had owned more consumer and housing stocks back then.

Kazanjian: *Given the tremendous latitude when putting your portfolios together, how do you begin the process of finding individual stocks?*

Daftary: We're really opportunistic in our stock selection. We get ideas from all over. Given that we're multicap in focus, we can look at many ideas. As I previously noted, we look at large-caps differently than small-caps and mid-caps. Most of our performance attribution over time has come from our mid- to small-cap ideas, because that's where you get your triples and quadruples. On the other had, we have very modest expectations for our large-cap ideas. While we don't think we add any long-term value by investing in IBM, there are certain points in time when IBM, on a risk-adjusted basis, can give you 15 to 20 percent rates of return.

Kazanjian: *So let's start there. Where do you find, and how do you evaluate, your large-cap ideas?*

Daftary: We do screens to see what looks reasonable in this space on a valuation basis. We rely on information from Wall Street for the large-cap names. We talk to specific analysts on a company and look at earnings estimates. For large-caps, we let the Street do the work for us. We don't need to do primary research on these companies. In the large-cap space, we like to buy companies that are out of favor. We realize that when you start buying momentum, you're really playing with fire. There's no downside protection if you buy a stock that's run up 40 to 50 percent and the multiple's expanded but nothing else has changed. We want to own large-cap stocks that have come down to a reasonable historical valuation. We then check the cash flows and balance sheet. If we can buy something at 12 to 13 times forward earnings with a dividend yield, it probably makes sense to own it. Even though valuation is important, these are classic growth stocks we're looking for, meaning we're not buying aluminum or iron ore. We want companies with a very high ROE (return on equity), good growth characteristics, good cash flows, and a good management team in place.

Kazanjian: *In other words, you want to snatch up growth stocks when they hit a trouble patch.*

Daftary: That's a great way to look at it. I do believe that over time large-cap growth managers don't tend to add much value because it's a very efficient market. They tend to buy momentum and ultimately blow up. That's why we want to own those classic growth stocks when they come down to a reasonable valuation because of a temporary glitch.

Kazanjian: *The trick is making sure the glitch is only temporary.*

Daftary: That's why we don't get into what we call a "value trap." A very recent example of a value trap, in my opinion, is Tenet Healthcare. Tenet's stock is under a lot of pressure. A lot of value managers own it because they think it's got a good franchise. Yet the balance sheet keeps deteriorating, the CFO resigned, and earnings keep blowing up. The value guys keep buying on the way down because they think it looks cheap. It's a value trap because the company doesn't have a catalyst in place. Sure, it looks cheap, but the earnings aren't there anymore because of all the bad debts. We won't buy a company like Tenet until there's a catalyst and maybe some inflection point on the horizon. We're looking for companies with a potential earnings surprise coming out in the next two quarters. That is very important for us. And perhaps also a management change. That's what happened to Tyco. As soon as they hired a new CEO, the stock started outperforming. We don't want to be buying a stock just because it's going down and it looks cheap. That is a no-no for us. I always say you find one cockroach in your room, you'll find another one.

Kazanjian: *How is your analysis different for small- and mid-cap stocks, and where do you find these companies?*

Daftary: Those stocks tend to move more on earnings momentum. We find them from many sources. We do run earnings surprise screens internally. We scan to see if there's anything interesting. But it's rare to find a good company just by doing a screen. We go to investment conferences to find out what's going on. We go to trade shows. We have a person here who goes to a lot of technology trade shows to test the latest gadgets. And we see companies one on one. Boston is a good place to be, just like San Francisco and New York, since a lot of management teams come through town. The management teams give you a bit of color on the company and sector. We take that information and generate an earnings model and a balance sheet model, and do some additional primary research on the companies. We then talk to contacts in the industry to find out what's going on. The information you get is somewhat random, but when you start digging into a company, you keep digging and digging until you find the pot of gold. We do a lot of digging around. We also talk to others in the investment business to see what they're looking at.

Kazanjian: *So once you've found an idea, what's the deciding factor on whether you buy the stock?*

Daftary: Once we get the information or we've seen the company, we prepare an income statement. If there is no analyst on the Street or regional brokerage firm that follows the company, we'll also do a primary research report. We then do an earnings estimate going out for the next year and come up with a number. Let's say we have a company trading at 15 times earnings with really good cash flow. We'll then look at the demand–supply characteristics of the stock to check whether other institutions own it. If it's not followed very well, that makes us even more interested because we know money tends to eventually gravitate to companies that perform well. If the stock is cheap now, over time the big guys will find it. Once this work is done and everything looks good, we will start buying. In some cases, we will take a minor position in the beginning, and then wait for more of our valuation thesis to occur before buying more. If, on the other hand, the earnings of a company fail to meet our expectations, it is gone. We are very, very ruthless. Then we say, "Shame on us! It was our fault because we messed up on the earnings forecast and therefore did sloppy work."

Kazanjian: *It almost sounds like your approach for small- and mid-caps is the exact opposite of your approach for large-cap stocks. You're trying to buy the small names as they go up, and the bigger ones on the way down.*

Daftary: It's true. The reason is that in the small- and mid-cap space, these companies tend to be more one-product specific, and the news tends to get better as the market share gets bigger for the company. The earnings that we project out tend to be very conservative compared to what the company usually does. If they're on a roll, they can really get going and beat the numbers, to where momentum buyers start moving in. You have to be more of a momentum player in this space. Still, the best thing is to be a little more proactive and buy these stocks when prices are coming down and hopefully add more as people start getting excited about it.

Kazanjian: *You said you sell the smaller stocks when they don't meet earnings expectations. What are some other reasons to pull the trigger?*

Daftary: Valuation is one. Stock returns are based on earnings growth and multiple expansion. Sometimes a stock goes up because its multiple expands and people get more excited about it. If the earnings don't go up as the multiple expands and the target price doesn't change, we'll sell when it hits our target price. Clearly if the company disappoints us, we'll also sell. The third reason is if we get a little concerned about earnings going forward, maybe because the economy doesn't look great. If the outlook gets too bad, we may even think of shorting the stock.

Kazanjian: *Speaking of which, unlike most fund managers, you have the freedom to short stocks in your portfolio. How do you find ideas to short, and when do you decide to follow this course of action?*

Daftary: Shorting is one of the most difficult investment processes around. Generally people don't like to short, so you're kind of trying to swim upstream most of the time. The short side is really the reverse of the long side. All we're doing on the short side is looking for potential earnings disappointments. We're looking for companies on the short side with fundamental problems and balance sheet deterioration. A lot of growth managers spend time on income statements, earnings, margins, and all that stuff. But if a company is just making its numbers by deteriorating the balance sheet, which happens frequently, you can really get into trouble. Balance sheets tell you a lot. They tell you whether receivables have gone up too much and whether this could be a real problem for earnings going forward. The process really is reversed on the short side. If we figure out that a company is going to miss its numbers, or know the estimates are coming down while the valuation looks expensive, we get very interested. The problem with many of these high expectation stocks is they're so expensive, even when they miss estimates and get cut by 30 percent, they still look expensive. People get frozen and wait to keep selling. Therefore, we look for situations to short where we think the supply available to sell could be greater than the demand as more people start getting out.

Kazanjian: *Shorting can be quite costly when you're wrong. At what point do you decide to cover shorts that go the wrong way for you?*

Daftary: We have a stop-loss for 15 to 20 percent on the other side. You've got to be quick on that, because stocks are volatile and can go right through that level in no time.

Kazanjian: *What's the highest percentage of your portfolio you'll short?*

Daftary: In the mutual fund we have a 25 percent restriction. Over the history of the fund, our shorts have on average been in the 7 to 8 percent range.

Kazanjian: *Have you done analysis to see whether the shorts have actually enhanced your fund's performance over time?*

Daftary: A lot of clients ask for that. In 2003 the shorts hurt us. But over longer periods, we have actually made money. I look at short selling really for two reasons. The most important is to make money. The second is to hedge my long positions. But that's not as important as trying to make money.

Kazanjian: *Shorting stocks can be very tricky. Do you recommend that individuals try this approach for their own portfolios?*

Daftary: No. I would say that individuals have to be very careful. Most individual investors try to do conceptual shorts. That is the kiss of death. In other words, they say, "I think eBay is expensive, so I'm going to short it." The logical question is, "Why is it expensive?" Unless there is a fundamental reason the stock is likely to miss a number and the supply and demand characteristics are adverse, you should avoid shorting.

Kazanjian: *Back to the long side, is there a set percentage of the portfolio you like to keep in large-caps, versus small- and mid-caps?*

Daftary: We really do believe in building the portfolio from the bottom up. The way the weightings get into the portfolio is really based on the best ideas being generated and put in there. The market weightings fall into place based on the stocks that we're buying.

Kazanjian: *How many stocks do you tend to own?*

Daftary: Anywhere from 40 to 75, depending on whether we're more heavily in small- and mid-caps or large-caps. For large-cap names, we'll take up to a 5 percent position. We won't go that high for smaller stocks. One reason for diversification is that out of 10 growth stocks, six tend to blow up, according to a study done by an ex-boss of mine. Therefore, I don't believe that growth managers should own 20 names. They should own 40 to 50 names. You don't know which stocks will be the ultimate winners. The random stock that goes up 100 or more percent is just that: random. It's pure luck.

Kazanjian: *You have said before that you felt the United States was the best place in the world for people to invest their money. Of course, we have some international*

managers in this book who would disagree. But do you believe people in the United
States should own any foreign securities?

Daftary: No, I don't. Remember, I come from India, so sometimes you
have to listen to the natives, right? Maybe back in the 1970s there was a
noncorrelation with the world markets. But the world has become a lot
smaller now and the correlations are a lot higher. If that's the case, one of
the main foundations of the argument for investing overseas is gone. Second, people don't realize the risks you have in these overseas markets, including political risks. While I was a little shaken after September 11, I've
always said that the United States has great natural resources and a great
defense system. As a result, I feel there should be a premium for investing
here. I still believe that. There's also fraud in many of these international
markets. I don't own any international stocks.

Kazanjian: *What are your overall expectations for the U.S. market over the next*
several years?

Daftary: Over time, I still think 7 to 10 percent annualized rates of return
are feasible. I do think investor expectations remain too high. People are
expecting 20 percent rates of return. You're not going to get them. I think
the thing to pay attention to over time is risk. Not losing your money is
going to be very important going forward.

One reason Daftary believes risk management is so important now is
because we haven't had a true systemic recession since the early 1990s.
Sure, things have been tough economically for the last few years, but it has
been nothing like some of the downturns of the past. That's why Daftary
feels his flexible style is such an advantage. It allows him to adjust to the
current economic environment, be it by raising cash, switching more
heavily into lower valuation securities, or even shorting stocks to profit
from a potential decline in the overall market.

W. WHITFIELD GARDNER

Gardner Lewis Asset Management

Thanks to a risk-free offer from his dad, Whit Gardner learned a valuable lesson about the stock market early on that enabled him to earn enough money to buy his own car when he turned 16. That interest in equities carried on through high school and college, and he's never looked back.

After working in several supportive roles within the brokerage industry, Gardner got experience analyzing private companies at a Netherlands-based venture capital firm. Through contacts gathered at this job, he landed a portfolio manager position at Friess Associates, an earnings momentum-driven growth shop. In 1990, Gardner and one of his fellow managers at Friess struck out on their own, founding Gardner Lewis Asset Management. Today, in addition to running institutional money across all market capitalizations, they manage the Chesapeake Core Growth Fund, which concentrates on larger companies.

While the 41-year-old manager's approach combines elements of both growth and value, he emphasizes that growth is the real driver. Beyond all else, he prides himself in doing his own homework to find something exciting happening in every potential holding that will surprise the rest of Wall Street, and therefore drive the underlying stock price much higher.

Kazanjian: *When did you first develop an interest in investing?*

Gardner: When I was about 12, I had some money in a savings account earning around $5\frac{1}{4}$ percent. My father asked me what I planned to do with that money. I said I was saving up to buy a boat by the time I was 16 or 17. I delivered newspapers in a residential neighborhood in Wilmington, Delaware, which had a big retirement building. Dad said, "I'll tell you what. Why don't you buy stock in that company (the one that owned the retirement building) you deliver newspapers to." When I asked why, he said, "Because your money will grow much faster." He then agreed to guarantee the principal—about $325—plus the interest if it fell below what I would get from keeping it in the passbook savings account. I didn't realize what he was doing at the time. My father wasn't involved in the investment business at all. He worked for the DuPont Company. From that day forward I read the *Wall Street Journal* every day. I wanted to see what the stock was doing.

Kazanjian: *How did it do?*

Gardner: It's one of those things that only happens a few times in a career. It was taken over, and then that company was taken over, and the surviving company was taken over a third time. I probably made five or six times on my money the first time and then came close to doing it again. It was amazing.

Kazanjian: *Did you make enough to buy that boat?*

Gardner: I did, although I actually bought a car instead when I turned 16.

Kazanjian: *What was the name of the company you bought back then?*

Gardner: It was called Retirement Living. It was right at the beginning of that whole retirement community movement. It was acquired by Forum Group, and later Hospital Corporation of America, and finally Marriott.

Kazanjian: *Did you carry your interest in stocks with you to high school?*

Gardner: In high school, I worked for a broker at Merrill Lynch as a go-pher. I answered his telephone and did research on companies he was interested in. I also started building a little portfolio of my own. When I went to college, I knew exactly what I wanted to do. I actually started a small fund when I was in high school that included savings from my brothers and parents. I carried that into college.

I went to Southern Methodist University specifically because it was located in Dallas. I had never even visited the campus before. At the time, Dallas/Fort Worth had a massive population influx. I figured I could be hired while still in school because of the demand in the area. I went to school with the intention of trying to work somewhere on the sell-side and was hired by Lehman to do everything from opening mail to cold calling and technical analysis. I literally started in the mailroom. I soon moved from Lehman to Drexel. Then I felt like I really needed some more formal training. When I got out of school, I went into a financial analysis training program so that I could better understand how financial statement analysis ought to be performed. I then entered a venture capital training program and went to work for Orange Nassau, a Netherlands-based venture capital firm. My rationale was that I should learn how to do the fundamental bottom-up tire kicking that's required for private investment. Then, as now, you had no liquidity if you were wrong about an investment decision that you made, and were therefore taking on extreme risk. I thought that would be a great place to start and learn best practices relative to due diligence. Frankly, I also felt that public company investors weren't very good at this.

This was back in 1986. I was under the belief that the best investors were investors in private companies. I was representing the interests of the venture capital firm I worked for at the board meetings of some of our portfolio companies. At one point I got a call from John Lewis, who worked for Friess Associates, an investment management firm that also runs the Brandywine Fund. He wanted to get my understanding of what was occurring in the rent-to-own industry. I met John at a meeting where I represented my firm's interest regarding a company in our portfolio called Remco. John's call really sparked my interest because he was a public company investor using a process that was very similar to mine.

Kazanjian: *Is this call what ultimately led to a job offer at Friess Associates?*

Gardner: John said his boss, Foster Friess, would like to meet with me. I did so and about eight months later, I was working at Friess. I was there until

1990, when I got an offer to run the money management division of an investment bank. I thought that was an interesting opportunity and seriously considered it. At the last minute, I decided I didn't want to work at this firm for a couple of reasons, including the massive conflict of interest that exists between the sell-side's construct and its ultimate investors. The bottom line is that I've always felt the distribution structure of Wall Street is inherently flawed in that it creates a mechanism whereby sell-side firms can sell products that aren't necessarily in the best interest of those looking to make a profit. I figured why not go out and create a pure, unbiased, untainted opportunity to ferret out information and perform fundamental work. So I asked John Lewis to join me and we went out on our own in 1990.

Kazanjian: *I take it you're not a big fan of sell-side research.*

Gardner: To do research right, you need to go directly to the companies themselves and talk with their customers, competitors, and suppliers. You need to understand from and through the eyes and ears of the CEO, CFO, and head of marketing what's creating change within the business that hasn't been properly perceived or priced into the stock. We've always felt the best way to do that was by doing the work ourselves. That way you avoid the conflict that might arise out of contact with Wall Street, which may be biased or simply be information that's being disseminated to many others, making it less meaningful.

Kazanjian: *There has been a lot of criticism leveled over sell-side research over the past few years, especially as it relates to the conflicts of interest at these Wall Street firms. A number of steps have supposedly been taken to improve the quality of this research and lessen these conflicts of interest. Do you think the research is getting any better as a result?*

Gardner: Not at all. It's ironic because if we sat down 10 years ago, I would have said exactly the same thing. The reality is that Wall Street continues to be structured in such a way that its most profitable transactions are investment banking deals. Yes, there have been steps taken to try to create this Chinese wall to divorce the sell-side from this conflict that exists. The problem is that research budgets are dramatically compromised because of the relative inability of these firms to cover the costs associated with carrying it out. Thus, you've seen dramatic cutbacks in the research efforts on the part of these firms because they don't have the revenues to cover the expense.

Kazanjian: *Let's talk about this homegrown process of yours. How do you go about finding companies for the portfolio?*

Gardner: The factors we initially look for are fairly basic. We want earnings growth of approximately 15 percent if not better, given our growth orientation. This could be cash flow growth as well. We also look for companies with valuations that have an opportunity to expand. Thus, we want to invest in a company when earnings are growing and the price-to-earnings ratio afforded those earnings can expand based on a positive change taking place in the business, like a new product, management, or distribution strategy, or manufacturing technology. We also try to get protection on the downside by making sure we haven't paid too much for the stock.

Kazanjian: *Is that what some people refer to as GARP, or growth at a reasonable price?*

Gardner: It's not really GARP. Our portfolio is more growth oriented. GARP guys often invest in cyclical growth companies that they perceive as being growth companies simply because they're in the upswing of a cycle. The other thing that happens is that GARP guys invest in companies growing at very low rates with low multiples, which they rationalize as being inexpensive. GARP has a tendency to lean more toward valuation and less toward the company's growth characteristics.

Kazanjian: *Is earnings growth the number-one thing you look at?*

Gardner: It is important, as is valuation, but even more important is the change taking place in the business that others haven't perceived that will drive earnings beyond that which is expected. We also check to see how strong the company's balance sheet is, with a focus on low indebtedness or strong cash flows. We'd rather our companies go to the bank with their arms crossed than their arms outstretched. The last factor we look at is the company's sensitivity to the macroeconomic environment. We're trying to invest in companies with destinies controlled more by that which they are attempting to execute rather than that which they can't control, such as aluminum prices, oil prices, or interest rates. These outside factors can derail the opportunity for earnings growth, and a company cannot influence them in any way, shape, or form.

Kazanjian: *So the overall macroeconomic outlook is important to you in making this fundamental assessment?*

Gardner: More important is how sensitive the company is to the macro outlook. We want to invest in companies that are less sensitive. The whole idea is to let management put its hands on the wheel and control the vehicle in the direction of their choosing. Then we can monitor how well they are doing as it relates to our expectations for the company. But if you were to put all these factors down in terms of priority for us, I'd say first we want to find a positive change in the business that is different from that which people expect. Second we want to see how fast the company is growing, and third is how the company is valued.

Kazanjian: *Given that your most important variable is of a more qualitative nature, and not something you can simply punch up on a computer screen, how do you find these companies to begin with?*

Gardner: The three things that make our process different are how we source ideas, how we construct the portfolio, and how we organize ourselves to attack the research itself. Going to your point, the last thing that we would do is utilize some form of computer screening. When I started in this business, the PC was not yet available and we used charts that were three months old. Today somebody could go on Yahoo! Finance and perform screens that people back when I started out spent millions of dollars on equipment to perform. The point is that anyone can do these screens now, so it doesn't provide any unique information. Again, what drives our stocks is change that is not already reflected in expectations. Even if we were to screen for earnings estimates, these changes wouldn't be reflected in what we think a company could ultimately earn. All of our calls are proactive calls. We literally pick up the telephone or go visit with those companies we believe can meet the criteria we talked about. It's a proactive process, not a reactive one.

Kazanjian: *But how do you find them, given that there are so many possible choices out there?*

Gardner: If I were to narrow down the universe to those likely to approach a 15 percent growth rate, selling at two times their growth rate or less, and not heavily sensitive to macroeconomic factors, you'd have around 600 companies. From here, we start making proactive calls to the management teams within those various organizations. Most importantly, we use the bias we get from these calls to figure out where we should go next. We call them contact webs. Let's say we're on the phone with Teradyne, which does backend semiconductor tests. We know that Power One is among Teradyne's suppliers. It's very likely that after we talk with Teradyne, we'll phone Power One to find out exactly what's going on with the company and whether business into Teradyne is improving, declining, or status quo. From that conversation, we learn not only what's happening to Teradyne, but also where Power One's own business is strong and weak. That call to Power One might cause us to become more interested in Cisco if Power One's business with them is strong (Cisco is Power One's largest customer). These calls help us to find pockets of strength in these companies that aren't understood or well perceived by others. We also keep an eye out for companies that announce positive earnings, to make sure we're up to date with what's going on and to see whether there's something we've missed. One thing that's unusual is that we assign analysts at the firm companies to research randomly, sometimes even alphabetically, not based on sector, market cap, or anything like that. The intent is to maintain a process that insures we do our research work in a way that isn't myopic, in terms of our view of a company or industry.

Kazanjian: *On the valuation side, can you expand more on what you think a reasonable price is to pay for a stock?*

Gardner: Typically we like to use the growth rate as some sort of valuation barometer. If you're dealing with small-cap stocks, which are obviously riskier, we want to pay a significant fraction of the growth rate. Usually we're looking for a PE that's less than the growth rate.

Kazanjian: *So if a stock is growing at 30 percent a year, you want to buy it at a PE below 30?*

Gardner: Correct. In that scenario, with 30 percent growth, we'd ideally be looking for a PE between 19 and 22, especially for smaller companies.

Kazanjian: *What about larger companies? How do you value those differently?*

Gardner: As companies become larger, the earnings become more sustainable. We'd like to invest in large companies at PEs below their growth rates as well. However, where the growth rate is very strong, and highly recurring, we're willing to go slightly above the growth rate. You won't see us pay 40 times earnings for a 20 percent grower, though we might pay 25 times for a 20 percent growth rate in a large-cap company, compared to 15 times for the same 20 percent growth in a small-cap company. It's really not that simple, but the idea is that we want to adjust for the risks associated with the company's business and its ability to meet Wall Street's expectations. Once we get there, we can assign a multiple accordingly, with the idea being that we still want room for it to expand.

Kazanjian: *It's interesting that you're willing to pay up for large-caps. Most investors would rather pay more for small-caps, on the belief that they can sustain higher rates of growth.*

Gardner: It really has to do with the sustainability of earnings. If we felt that high growth rates in small-cap companies were sustainable, we'd pay more for them. There are cases where Wall Street thinks a stock's growing at 30 percent, yet we think it's growing at 40 percent, so we'll gladly pay 30 times Wall Street's expectations.

Kazanjian: *What makes you decide to sell a stock?*

Gardner: We take our earnings estimate and estimated multiple to give us a target price. All things being equal, we're going to exit a stock when it reaches this price target. But the reality is that it usually doesn't happen that way. We're always out there making contact with a large number of companies, trying to become aware of things that are occurring that others are unaware of. We call it building the mosaic. We get an idea of what's working and grow to understand how it will affect companies financially. If something we own is not working out, we'll sell. But most importantly, we maintain no more than 50 names in our large-cap portfolio and no more than 65 names in our small-cap portfolio. Therefore, a sale is most often made as a result of a new opportunity that exists that we perceive to be better than one currently in the portfolio. Let's say we invest in a company and have a 40 percent projected appreciation target for that particular name. If the idea works out and only has 15 percent potential appreciation remaining, it is likely we'll replace it to make room for another holding that has the full 40 percent appreciation potential. Indeed, the number-one reason we sell a stock is to displace it with something else we like more. This keeps us out of trouble, and creates a constant competition within the portfolio for the best possible companies. As a result, all of our holdings have to be firing on all cylinders.

Kazanjian: *For ideas that aren't really pulling their weight in terms of appreciation, yet still look attractive from a valuation perspective, how patient will you be to see a stock work out?*

Gardner: We set price targets and have expectations regarding what we expect to occur in the business to receive the appreciation we project. Provided a company stays on a track that is either consistent with or explainable within our expectations, we'll stay with it. A lot of the momentum guys are too focused on whether companies beat the quarter by a penny. That's not investing to us. We think investing is about understanding the changes taking place and the opportunity for a company to gain market share and thrive in a space that's been misunderstood, undiscovered, or unexploited. A lot of times it takes years, not days. If a company is hitting our expectations, we continue to own it. But if there's a fundamental disappointment, perhaps the product is leapfrogged by another one or doesn't gain the traction we expect, we'll sell under the recognition that we were wrong about our premise from the start.

Kazanjian: *What's your average holding period?*

Gardner: Although we shoot to own a stock for three to five years, our forced displacement methodology results in an average holding period of a little over one year.

Kazanjian: *You described your process as being bottom-up, and said you try to keep a consistent number of stocks in the portfolio. Do you pay attention to sector diversification?*

Gardner: Yes, that's another part of the construct. We want to win through stock selection and we don't want to put ourselves in a position where we derive returns through some unintended bet within the portfolio. We find new ideas from the bottom up and they enter the portfolio until such time as we're 10 percent either overweighted or underweighted to a particular sector compared to the overall market. For instance, if finance is 20 percent of the market, we couldn't have more than 30 percent or less than 10 percent in that sector. We think timing markets and rotating sectors is ultimately a loser's game. The reason is simple. There are issues or events that occur from left field that can't be controlled. If you overexpose yourself to those issues or events, it can be highly detrimental.

Think back to 1994 when the Clinton administration was in its first term. At that point HMOs were the fastest growing singular segment we could find in our universe of companies. Many were growing at 30 to 50 percent, and HMO penetration in this country was minimal. It's almost impossible to believe, because if you look at the industry now, almost everyone's in an HMO. The opportunity for that industry was enormous, and valuations were generally low. In a single hour, there was a speech that proposed the nationalization of the U.S. healthcare system. That sent incredible shockwaves through these stocks. If you had been overexposed to the sector, you probably wouldn't have recovered from it for a long time. The point is that events or issues can emerge that never affect the fundamentals of a company, yet can dramatically derail its stock price. We don't want to succumb to that kind of risk. Thus, we do not want to be beholden to any one sector.

Kazanjian: *The portfolio of Chesapeake Core Growth, the large-cap fund you manage, looks like a potpourri of companies. As we speak, such pure growth stocks as Cisco and Dell sit beside more traditional value names as Boeing and Tyco. How can such divergent companies coexist in the same portfolio?*

Gardner: I think eclecticism is part of the opportunity and the advantage. It really comes down to the point at which we capture these companies for the portfolio. The reality is that growth is what drives us. We let our companies bubble up from our bottom-up work but actually control risk from the top. We look at the interrelationships of the companies we own to understand whether we are controlling risk as we should. So yes, the portfolio looks very eclectic, but this eclecticism should provide the upside and control the volatility. Also, a lot depends on when we bought the stock. For instance, Amazon.com is clearly a growth stock. We would have never owned it in 1999. We visited with the company and thought highly of its prospects, but couldn't get our arms around the valuation Wall Street had placed on it back then. We went through a phase where Amazon sold for more than $110 per share. About three years ago, Amazon had fallen to around $15 per share. I visited with Jeff Bezos and realized they had made some really significant changes related to the stability of the company. This meeting also tempered some of the concerns I had relating to its competition. Amazon was trying to deploy its technology in a way that could expand its businesses beyond books, music, and video. While execution was strong, Wall Street had become unenamored with dot-coms in general, particularly those that weren't yet profitable. Our analysis suggested that Amazon would not only be cash flow positive shortly, but also would soon become profitable and see earnings grow very rapidly. We bought our stock over the course of a year with our last purchase in July 2002. At that point Street estimates for Amazon were a loss of something like 2 cents a share. We thought the company could make around 15 cents. The stock was around $15. As a multiple of earnings relative to that short stub period, that was really a high stock price. But we thought it would earn 60 cents the following year, while Wall Street was forecasting 20 cents. It was a huge disparity. We felt like we were buying the stock at $15 divided by .60, not $15 divided by .20.

Kazanjian: *What made you see 60 cents when everyone else saw 20 cents?*

Gardner: A couple of things. First, the fact that the company was incredibly focused on operational efficiency. Wall Street had criticized the company for its lack of focus in that area. From talking with Bezos, I realized that fixed costs were being overcome by the ability of the company to generate revenues above those fixed costs, which meant the incremental profitability was huge. Also, economies of scale were growing and they were broadly diversifying, including creating storefronts for mom-and-pop businesses. These were all drivers for us.

Kazanjian: *So, taking your estimate of 60 cents, you were buying the stock for around 16.5 times your anticipated earnings.*

Gardner: Exactly. But if you looked at the stock simply on that six-month period, it was much more expensive. You have to look at where the company is going to be, not just where it is today. We thought that 60 cents would go to $1, which is exactly what happened. Granted, not all of our decisions work out this well. But this is a classic example of our process in motion.

Kazanjian: *Do you still own Amazon today?*

Gardner: We sold almost all of our position when the stock got up to the $55 level because we felt the valuation was stretched.

Kazanjian: *Given that the process isn't perfect, what's the most common reason stocks don't work out?*

Gardner: It's usually because companies don't deliver on the profit margins we expect. Normally what happens is that the company isn't able to sell a product at the price it expected, it is unable to sustain its margins because of competitive pressure, or the item costs more to produce than originally thought.

Kazanjian: *Do you have a stop-loss rule to cap your potential downside?*

Gardner: We don't have a specific price at which we're absolutely going to sell, but we do have a sort of wakeup number. Back in the 1980s we used to say that if a stock moved $1 either way we would be on the phone finding out what was going on. We obviously had to change that. We now follow a 20 percent rule. Basically, if a stock is down over 15 percent but less than 20 percent, we try to make sure we understand what happened to cause this. We then decide whether it's an opportunity to add to our position, or whether we should leave.

Given that early on Gardner spent time studying the more technical aspects of stock analysis, I asked what he thought of technical analysis. This is the art of reading stock charts to analyze and predict stock directions, which is a technique often used by momentum investors. Gardner admits technical analysis is helpful in telling him about the psychology surrounding a company, but it's not a driver in deciding whether he purchases a stock. "We do the fundamental work first," he insists, "and if the technical indicators confirm it, that's wonderful. For us, the fundamentals override everything else."

JANNA SAMPSON

OakBrook Investments

Although Janna Sampson spent the early part of her career at the investment division of a bank that specialized in indexing, she has always believed that the right active manager can outperform the market. The best way to do that, in her mind, is by owning brand-name companies with what she calls "market power." Simply put, she wants to own businesses with large market shares and definable barriers in place to protect them from the competition.

As you might guess, the universe of companies with such a solid standing is relatively small. Sampson therefore keeps a fairly concentrated portfolio of around 20 to 25 names. She looks to buy these growth-oriented stocks when they fall out of favor for what she considers to be an unjusti-fied reason. While Sampson admits these are the kinds of companies one could arguably buy and hold for the long term, she contends that snatch-ing them up at cheap prices and selling them when things turn around produces higher returns over the long haul.

In addition to managing money for a variety of institutional clients, Sampson and her colleagues at OakBrook Investments run the AmSouth Select Equity Fund using this market power approach. Harking back to her banking days, she also manages an enhanced index portfolio that's de-signed to slightly outperform a given stock index (such as the S&P 500) by overweighting what she considers to be the most attractive stocks. As you'll discover, that's no easy task. Yet, sticking with a smaller portfolio of market power stocks has indeed been a profitable strategy for this 47-year-old manager over time.

Kazanjian: *I understand you originally planned to become a lawyer, not an invest-ment manager.*

Sampson: That's absolutely true. I started out majoring in political science at the University of Denver. Late in my college career, I took an econom-ics class from the head of the economics department. She had a tremen-dous influence on me. I ended up double majoring in economics and political science. It changed my whole focus. I became interested in the money and banking side of economics. Instead of going to law school, I wound up getting a master's degree in economics from Georgia State.

Kazanjian: *What was your first job out of college?*

Sampson: I took a job working for a bank economist. I went from there to a small boutique investment firm in the western suburbs of Chicago. That's where my investment background started. I was doing currency trading in the futures market, and worked on developing analytical models for determining which futures were over- and undervalued. We sold our services to big corporate clients that had currency exposures they needed to hedge. We also hedged interest rate exposures for the treasury departments of big corporations.

Kazanjian: *When did you make the transition over to money management?*

Sampson: That firm was having some financial difficulties around 1983 and I feared it was going bankrupt. I started looking around and ended up

going to work in downtown Chicago for what at the time was American
National Bank of Chicago. The bank's investment management division,
which was spun off in 1987 as ANB Investment Management & Trust, was
a big index shop. This is disputed by some, but American National claimed
to have had the first commingled S&P 500 index product in 1974. I went
to work as a portfolio manager in their active investment area. I was there
for 15 years. The firm eventually became a subsidiary of First Chicago
Corporation, which is now Bank One.

Kazanjian: *Is that where you began doing enhanced index investing?*

Sampson: That's one of the things I did. We did enhanced indexing with a
quantitative model, and I worked with the group that developed that
model. This was a bit later on, since that product didn't come to market until 1994. I worked for the chief investment officer, who is now our president at OakBrook. He was in charge of what we now call our Select Equity
strategy. Back then it was known as the Market Power strategy. Three of us
from ANB Investment Management founded OakBrook in February 1998.

Kazanjian: *What made you decide to go out on your own?*

Sampson: First Chicago sold ANB Investment Management to the Northern Trust Company in Chicago. My partners and I felt that Northern Trust
was basically interested in the index business, which had about $30 billion
under management, compared to around $2 billion in our active products.
I was senior portfolio manager for the active side. We decided that, rather
than starting over at another bank, we'd prefer to do it on our own. I spent
years giving presentations to people, trying to market our active products,
and I can't tell you how many times people said to me, "Banks don't do active management well. Come back and talk to us when you're not a bank."
We decided that rather than become part of Northern Trust, we would
step out and form own firm. That's what we did.

Kazanjian: *Are you mostly an institutional manager?*

Sampson: The majority of our $1.3 billion in assets are institutional. We
subadvise three mutual funds for AmSouth Bank in Birmingham, Alabama,
including AmSouth Select Equity. That's the only mutual fund work we
do. Most of our customers are pension plans, foundations, or endowments.

Kazanjian: *Do you buy stocks of all sizes?*

Sampson: We're looking for mid- and large-caps. We don't buy any small
stocks.

Kazanjian: *I want to focus most of our discussion on your select equity strategy, but I'd like to spend a few moments on your enhanced indexing product. I trust you're trying to beat the index while still looking a lot like it. How are you attempting to add value with that product?*

Sampson: We're over- and underweighting stocks relative to their index weightings. There are a number of ways to do enhanced indexing. Some managers use derivatives, which we don't. We have built a quantitative model that tracks such technical data as volume changes, price changes, and short interest, among others. We combine all this information and rank the stocks accordingly. We are attempting to use what's known as auction theory in the field of economics. Our view is that the stock market is an auction market. Some people think of it as a consensus market because there are so many traders. But at any given point in time, the people buying any given stock represent only a small piece of the total investing public. Most people are not trading a particular stock on any given day. Those buying tend to be the most optimistic about the future for the stock. Auction theory tells us that those people tend to overpay for stocks. This is true in art auctions, auctions for oil well leases, and most anything else. A number of studies have shown that whoever wins an auction tends to have paid too much. It's a phenomenon known as "winner's curse." You won the auction, but actually ended up overpaying for whatever you were bidding on.

We believe that phenomenon applies to the stock market as well. We've built a quantitative model to estimate the range of expectations about the value of each stock. This range of expectations changes over time. It can be narrow or really wide. There's a normal range for each stock. We're trying to underweight stocks with very wide ranges because our research says they will come back to normal, meaning the stock price will fall relative to the market. Conversely, we try to overweight stocks with very narrow ranges, relative to their history. It's kind of a complicated thought process, but we're trying to over- and underweight stocks based on this range of expectations. Since we really can't measure expectations precisely, we've built a quantitative model to serve as a proxy.

Kazanjian: *How often do you review the list and make changes to the portfolio?*

Sampson: We typically look at the data and rebalance portfolios once a month. A lot of the information we use in the model, such as short interest, is available only monthly. Plus, there's an awful lot of noise in the daily volume and price change activity. You get more information, I think, when you look at the bigger picture, instead of more frequent changes.

Kazanjian: *You launched this product in a mutual fund format benchmarked to the S&P 500 on September 1, 1998. Judging by the performance of your fund, you've actually underperformed the S&P by a little less than the management fee. So, while you've added a slight bit of value, that's been more than eaten up by the management fee. Does this prove that it really is hard to beat the index? After all, most of these enhanced indexing products do underperform, especially over long periods of time.*

Sampson: Our goal is to add about 1 percent a year on average. Unfortunately, that's not enough to overcome the management fee in the mutual fund. We have the ability to dial that outperformance percentage up or down a bit for our institutional clients. If you're willing to tolerate more risk, we can give you more outperformance. The real market for this product is with big pension funds that have large cores of their portfolios in index funds and are willing to pay an extra 20 to 30 basis points (far less than the mutual fund charges) to outperform the index by 50 to 150 basis points a year. Unfortunately, mutual funds have so many layers of fees, it makes it more difficult when you're shooting for such modest goals.

Kazanjian: *You have, however, been able to outperform the S&P 500 by a wide margin with your select equity strategy. You are on the hunt for what you call "market power" stocks. Tell us what you mean by that.*

Sampson: Market power is an economic concept. Anybody who has had a graduate-level economics course has probably come across it. It simply means having a large market share and a barrier to protect that market share from the competition. Having that barrier is the key. A large market share in and of itself does not get you market power. This economic concept has been around quite a while. We've done a lot of research on companies like this. Our research shows stocks with market power have some unique properties that make them attractive for investing in over the long run. They tend to have higher return on equity, a higher return on assets, and they bounce back much better from disappointments than the average stock. They also have much steadier and more stable earnings growth. You don't get the roller coaster ride that you would with some of the higher growth stocks. These are growth stocks, but not the highest flying newly in vogue growth stocks. They represent quality growth. We like to call it stable growth. These companies tend to be better capitalized and have stronger cash flows than the average company.

Most economists coming out of school today trained in the field of market power go to work for the Federal Trade Commission. That's because market power stocks often run into antitrust problems because of their barriers that prevent competition.

Kazanjian: *Based on what you just said, Microsoft is a company that immediately comes to mind. Is that an example of a market power stock?*

Sampson: Absolutely. Microsoft definitely has market power and has gotten into trouble over how it has built its barriers. The companies most likely to get sued for antitrust violations are those that have market power. These companies also tend to be expensive in the marketplace. People pay up for good, steady, long-term earnings growth, not to mention all of the other favorable characteristics, such as stronger cash flows and a high return on equity. On average, stocks with market power tend to trade at about a 50 percent premium to the broad market, like the S&P 500. We apply a valuation overlay to these stocks and look to buy them when their valuation premium has lessened or dissipated. Perhaps they miss an earnings number by a penny, or have invested in growing the business for the future, causing higher expenses, which the market doesn't value. We look to buy these companies when they have lost their normal premium price, and plan to hold them for an average of two to three years. We wait for the stocks to bounce back to their normal market premium before selling. It's this ability to bounce back that is the key to what we're doing. We know from our research that these stocks are much more likely to bounce back than the average stock.

You always have to do your homework on the fundamentals of any company to understand what's bothering the market when the share price is depressed. When we identify a company that's lost its valuation premium, we then spend a lot of time tearing the balance sheet apart and going back to the most basic fundamentals of stock market analysis. We build our own earnings models and look for what we call true earnings as opposed to published earnings. We want to get rid of earnings from pension funds and other noncontinuing operations. We then adjust for option payouts and other things that can really distort operating earnings.

Kazanjian: *Of the universe of equities out there, how many are considered to be market power stocks?*

Sampson: In the United States, there are about 150.

Kazanjian: *Are these identified by you, or can I find them on some readily available list?*

Sampson: We maintain our own list. Morningstar has a similar concept, which they call having a moat. At the margin, the real issue is determining what constitutes a barrier for the company. Market share is pretty easy to get and measure. I've learned over the last 20 years that there are some interesting things that can provide barriers that you may not have thought about. They are things much less obvious than, say, a patent, which is a classic barrier. One of the largest holdings in our portfolio today is Pitney Bowes, which makes postage meters. Pitney Bowes owns all of the encryption patents used for postage meters and online postage. Those patents provide a lot of protection. Brand name can also be a barrier. McDonald's is a wonderful example of a stock like that. It fairly recently went through a loss of premium and has been coming back. A huge dollar investment for a new competitor to enter the business can be another barrier, although you see that less than you used to. I guess money's not as hard to raise now as it was 50 years ago.

Sometimes the market share isn't obviously large. We own Sysco, which is a food distributor. Sysco only has about an 11 to 13 percent share of the market, although its share is much bigger than its next largest competitor. What gives the company its advantage is that it has a strong brand name in restaurant circles, along with a unique business model for folding out and growing that market share. As the company has used this model to open up new territories, it continues to grow, and its competitors find it difficult to keep up. Sysco has the smallest share of any company we own.

Another barrier is a method of doing business or mode of operation that is so superior that it gives a company protection from competition. Whatever the barrier, it is the key to determining whether a stock has market power and therefore has the ability to bounce back from a temporary price setback. If a stock loses its price premium, but its barrier is damaged, you've got trouble. Classic examples of this are Xerox and Kodak. When Xerox lost the patent on its technology, the stock began a long downward trend that it has never recovered from. I believe Kodak is going through something similar now given the change to digital photography, where Kodak isn't the leader and is somewhat behind the envelope on changing over to that new technology.

Kazanjian: *Are there certain industries where it's basically impossible for any one company to have market power?*

Sampson: Yes. Commodities are probably the best example—for instance, the steel industry or any other basic building material where you're competing only on price. If your principal way of competing is price, you don't have market power. If you compete by differentiating yourself from your closest competitor, you probably have market power. You must differentiate yourself to have market power, although you don't necessarily have market power just because you differentiate yourself. There aren't very many banks, for instance, with market power. It's not difficult to start a bank. In the end, they're all competing on price, and to some degree service, as opposed to having some barrier or patent.

Kazanjian: *What about Internet stocks? It seems like the barrier to entry is so small. Is it possible for an Internet company to be a market power stock?*

Sampson: EBay is probably the best example of a market power stock in the Internet world. It's got the classic economies of scale going for it. In an auction you must have a lot of people bidding. The bigger eBay gets, the harder it is for anybody else to come in and set up an auction site that will be an effective competitor. EBay has market power, although it's a pretty expensive stock currently. Most other Internet companies don't. Either they haven't been around long enough to truly have built a brand name, or there's no other type of barrier. It's possible that some day Yahoo!, Amazon.com, or Google might have market power. I think they're all too young to have it now. They haven't developed that kind of brand name cachet yet that would give them market power.

Kazanjian: *With the exception of Microsoft, wouldn't most technology companies fall into the commodity area?*

Sampson: Certainly hardware companies would. Software companies can be somewhat different, because you can trademark and copyright your software. In the hardware area, it's simply who has the next greatest invention. Even a company as large as Intel is questionable. Intel has done a wonderful job of branding its name and has a very large share, but if a competitor were to make the next great leap in chip technology, it could wipe out Intel's advantage. If your advantage can be wiped out like that, with the click of your fingers, you don't have market power.

Kazanjian: *You have 150 market power companies to choose from, yet you typically keep a fairly concentrated portfolio of 18 to 25 names. How do you decide which stocks to own? Is that based solely on valuation?*

Sampson: Valuation is absolutely the first cut. We run a computer model that goes out and looks at price/earnings (PE) ratios and return changes over the past 3 to 6 months. It spits out ranked lists, showing where the PE for a stock is relative to the market and where it normally would be. We're looking for cases where the premiums have been washed out.

When we see a stock that has lost its premium, we'll sit down and tear the stock apart. What's bothering investors? Is it something that is critical to the market power? Philip Morris, now Altria Group, is an example of a stock with market power that has an attractive valuation, but the threat of lawsuits makes it unattractive as an investment. That stock's return is more dependent on the outcome of a lawsuit than next quarter's earnings.

Kazanjian: *Does the PE have to be lower than overall market PE, or just lower than its own historic PE?*

Sampson: Lower than its historic PE, relative to the market. If its normal premium to the market is 50 percent, and it's now down to a 10 percent premium, it's probably attractive from a valuation perspective. It definitely doesn't need to be cheap like a typical value stock would be.

Kazanjian: *Do you also take cyclical variables into consideration, when looking at these PE ratios?*

Sampson: There are definitely issues with some of the more cyclical stocks. A PE may not be the best measure in these cases because the stock's PE may be lower at the peak of a cyclical boom if investors are expecting the cycle to slow down. A low PE at the apex of a cycle for a cyclical stock is probably not attractive. That's why you have to apply some common sense to where you are in the cycle for the stock itself. Many stocks in the market power universe are not cyclical. They tend to be much more stable. But certainly some of them are cyclical, so you do have to pay attention to that. You also need to be aware of lawsuits and whether the earnings are real. There was a period in the late 1990s where pensions inflated earnings and some stocks looked cheaper on a PE basis than they really were if you adjusted for those pension earnings. We make adjustments and wash out items like pension fund earnings and the cost of options in companies that don't expense them. At any given time, there generally aren't more than 15 to 25 stocks that are attractive for purchase.

Kazanjian: *Judging by the makeup of your portfolio as we speak, healthcare seems to be the industry with the most concentrated market power. Why is that?*

Sampson: Because of patents, all of the pharmaceutical stocks have market power to some degree or another. It just depends on how close those patents are to expiring, and you have to consider the impact of those expiring patents when evaluating these stocks. But certainly from a universe standpoint, a large number of market power stocks are in the pharmaceutical area. Most of the rest of the healthcare industry, such as hospital or managed care providers, do not have market power.

Kazanjian: *Home Depot is one of the companies on your list. In some ways, I wonder whether the company really has much market power, given all the competition in the retail building supply industry.*

Sampson: Home Depot has market power because of its brand name and its purchasing power. For years, Home Depot didn't do much centralized purchasing, but it has moved in that direction in the last few years. Coupled with its brand name, we think that's where Home Depot gets its barrier. Purchasing power for a retailer is a critical part of having market power. We first bought Home Depot in July 2002 when the market thought Lowe's was making inroads in taking away some of Home Depot's market share. Lowe's appeared to be growing relative to Home Depot because Lowe's sales are more cyclically sensitive than Home Depot. In fact, Home Depot has not lost market share at all.

Kazanjian: *What type of growth characteristics do market power companies tend to show?*

Sampson: These are stable and consistent growers in the 10 to 20 percent range. There are occasional stocks with growth rates of 50 to 100 percent or more in brand new industries, but those don't tend to have market power because the industry hasn't been around long enough for them to develop any kind of barrier.

Kazanjian: *What makes you decide to sell a stock?*

Sampson: The sell decision is principally based on valuation, or when stocks get back to trading at that historic premium. The other reason we'll sell a stock is for some kind of outside problem, like a lawsuit. We owned Emerson Electric for a couple of years, and sold it after becoming aware it had more than 250 pending asbestos lawsuits. When we called management, the company didn't really want to talk about the issue. That's not a good thing. We found reference to the lawsuits in a footnote to the company's SEC filing. All they have to do is lose one asbestos lawsuit and they're in bankruptcy. In a concentrated portfolio where you're taking large positions, you can't afford to have a company go bankrupt.

The other thing, and this will get us to sell a stock quickly, is if something happens to the barrier. To use a simplified example, if a company only has one patent that is successfully challenged and lost through a court action, all of a sudden that barrier is gone and we would sell the stock. Stocks that lose their barriers generally don't recover, at least not in any reasonable timeframe. We will also sell companies that start divesting themselves of their market power businesses. Sometimes companies don't understand the attractive attributes of a market power business and seek to diversify their revenue stream.

Kazanjian: *What's your average holding period?*

Sampson: Close to three years. That's how long it generally takes to have the valuation bounce back to its normal premium.

Kazanjian: *How does your assessment of the overall economy and stock market fit into your decision-making process?*

Sampson: It fits into the analysis of individual stocks. If a stock is cyclical, you must be aware of where it is in the cycle. But we're mostly evaluating stocks on their own merits.

Kazanjian: *Almost all of the stocks you own are well-known brand names. These are the kind of companies that some might argue you could just buy and hold forever, given that they'll likely be around for a long time.*

Sampson: I think that many of these companies can be bought and held for a long time, but I believe you'll get a higher return by being somewhat more selective. I don't think if you just buy and hold a basket of market power stocks you'll necessarily get a return that's 4 to 5 percent above the market over a five-year period.

Kazanjian: *Is that because the prices fluctuate so much?*

Sampson: Yes, even market power stocks will have disappointments along the way just like every other stock, which is what we're trying to take advantage of. If you hold them through the downturn, you can be reasonably certain they'll come back. But you won't get the same return as if you buy low and sell high. This is really basic investment sense. Also, there are some stocks you wouldn't want to own at all at certain points because of litigation or some other problem.

Incidentally, one of the unique things about our approach, compared to value investors, is that we don't need a catalyst for buying because the barrier tends to provide that bounce-back without requiring any catalyst per se.

Kazanjian: *Is there anything else about your investment process you'd like to add?*

Sampson: One of the things I want to stress is that it's not as simplistic as simply saying a company has market power and looks reasonably priced. You have to do the fundamental work—tear the balance sheet apart and read the footnotes in the annual report. There's no getting away from that down-and-dirty fundamental stock analysis before deciding what you really want to buy. Sometimes people hear what we do and think it sounds real easy. However, the average person can't tear apart a corporate balance sheet or income statement, or do a cash flow analysis to find potential problems or warning signs. When we identify an opportunity, that's really when the real work starts.

Away from the office, Sampson says she loves to ski. She harkens back to her days growing up in Colorado where, for a time in high school, they used to have "snow days," where the school closed down and kids were bussed up the mountain for a free day of skiing. Sampson also describes skiing as the one family activity her teenage son and daughter actually enjoy doing together with Mom and Dad.

SAMUEL STEWART

Wasatch Advisors

$\int$am Stewart has had a golden touch for picking winning small-cap companies for more than 50 years. After all, the first stock he picked at the
age of 12 turned into a huge winner in only 18 months. Stewart originally
came to the investment business through academia. After getting his MBA
and Ph.D. at Stanford, he taught at Columbia for three years and used the
university's vast resources to refine his investment technique. After a subsequent stint as a financial analyst with the Securities and Exchange Commission, he returned to his hometown of Salt Lake City in the mid-1970s
to teach at the University of Utah.

While the collegiate view has long been that the markets are efficient, Stewart was convinced this just wasn't true, especially for the smaller, more underfollowed stocks. To prove his thesis, he started Wasatch Advisors in 1975 and ran it on the side while also teaching at the University of Utah. Within six years, he was having so much success, he decided to devote his full-time attention to money management.

Today Wasatch Advisors is widely regarded as the premier investment firm specializing in small-cap stocks. As the chief investment officer for Wasatch, Stewart oversees all of the firm's funds, many of which are currently closed to both new and existing investors. Wasatch believes it's important to control portfolio size in the small-cap area of the market, even if that means less business for the firm.

The 62-year-old manager and father of nine describes himself as an inherent growth investor who searches for stocks fitting the acronym ABGC, which stands for America's Best Growth Companies. Among other things, he seeks companies with a persistent competitive advantage and plenty of room to grow. Unlike many small-cap managers, Stewart also believes in sticking with his stocks for the long haul, as long as the fundamentals remain in place.

Kazanjian: *Is it true that you bought your first stock when you were about 12 years old?*

Stewart: It is. My Dad worked for Merrill Lynch for many years. That was the source of my attraction and interest in the market. My first stock purchase was American Motors. I bought the stock in the early 1950s after being impressed with the Rambler car. It went from $5 to $90 in less than two years. This experience obviously whetted my appetite for investing, although I didn't really know what I was doing.

Kazanjian: *But rather than getting into the investment business right away, you began your career in academia. How did that happen?*

Stewart: When I graduated from undergraduate school at Northwestern, I both looked around for jobs and applied to graduate school. Based on what I wrote in my application, Stanford University said that if I had an interest in teaching, it would admit me to the Ph.D. program. That's the route I decided to take. I went from there into academia. I actually got an undergraduate degree in business, and an MBA and Ph.D. at Stanford.

Kazanjian: *What exactly did you do after leaving Stanford?*

Stewart: I taught corporate finance at Columbia for three years. Then I went to the University of Utah for a year, followed by the Securities and Exchange Commission for a year, and then back to the University of Utah for another six years.

Kazanjian: *What was your role at the SEC?*

Stewart: I was a chief financial analyst in the division of investment management regulations.

Kazanjian: *You'd be awfully busy working in that department today.*

Stewart: Yes. The rage at the time was money market funds. The first fund had just been created and the SEC was trying to get its hands around what they were all about.

Kazanjian: *What do you think of how the SEC has done as far as regulating mutual funds and responding to some of the recent improprieties in the industry?*

Stewart: I think it's basically been disastrous to small funds and small investors. Regulations always favor the big entrenched competition. Should this stuff (including market timing and other charges leveled at several fund firms beginning in 2003) have been happening? No. Were there some bad guys in the fund industry? Yes. How serious was the problem? About as serious as a pimple on your body. You don't like it, and you try to deal with it. But in terms of the overall picture, it's not that serious. All these new regulations from the SEC are certainly going to increase costs for the average investor, but they don't provide any real investor protection.

Kazanjian: *I realize you're a bit biased since you run a fund company of your own, but given what you just said, how should investors evaluate a mutual fund in deciding whether it makes sense to own?*

Stewart: I've always liked to use the analogy of a marriage partner. Everybody is always going to look at the past track record. Then you have to follow with a disclaimer that the past record is not an indication of future performance, and I believe that. But you've got to take the time to read what the management is saying. If you've been in the business like me, the number-one thing I do is look at the portfolios to see what's in there. It might be hard for the average investor because they don't have a good feel for the stocks, but they should do as much as they can. Read what they have to say in the commentaries. Does this look like a company with which you want to be associated, or do you say I don't get any of this? The thing that is going to kill you with fund investments is buying high and selling low. The reality is funds, unlike individual stocks, seldom go out of business. There are some exceptions, but most of them just don't spiral down. The best time to buy a fund is usually when its performance numbers look the worst. The best time to sell is usually when its performance numbers look the best. That means you always have to be cutting against the grain to be a successful investor.

Kazanjian: *When did you decide to start your own investment firm?*

Stewart: It was almost immediately after coming to Utah following my post at the SEC in 1975. Probably the most important motivator for starting Wasatch is that in academia at the time, the notion of efficient markets was really front and center. This theory says that nobody can ever beat the market at any time for any reason because all information about the company is already reflected in stock prices. That just didn't make sense to me and wasn't in accord with my experiences in the stock market. So I decided to conduct my own little experiment and show that you can beat the market.

Kazanjian: *Thirty years later, do you still believe the efficient market theorists have it wrong?*

Stewart: I think the more widely covered a company is, the more likely it is to be efficiently priced. The less widely covered a company is, the less likely it is to be efficiently priced. So what correlates with coverage more than anything else in the world is capitalization size. Therefore, the smaller-cap world is less efficient and has more opportunity. Having said that, most of the stuff that really drives stock prices, and most analytical work, is very short-term focused. Everybody looks at what companies are going to earn this quarter or this year. Not many step back to see where the company is going over the next 5 or 10 years. Those who make a lot of money in the stock market tend to talk about 5- and 10-year horizons. My guess is the longer the time horizon, the less likely the market is to be efficient with respect to any particular piece of information.

Kazanjian: *This long-term perspective goes against the grain of how many of your small-cap peers do business. A lot of small-cap managers say you need to trade around these names frequently because they are such volatile securities.*

Stewart: That just doesn't make any sense at all to me. Arguably a well-informed smart small-cap investor could trade around. Because it's a less efficient market, you'll find more cases of over- and undervaluation. The problem is that the liquidity in small-caps is so low, anybody with sizable assets under management just can't trade efficiently like that.

Kazanjian: *Your firm is focused almost exclusively on smaller companies. Is that because of your belief that this area of the market is more inefficient, and therefore the place you can add the most value?*

Stewart: To some degree. One of the very first founding principles of Wasatch is the idea that earnings growth drives stock prices. If you're trying to find out which stocks are going to go up, you've got to focus on which companies will be able to grow earnings. We concluded that small companies in general are better positioned to grow earnings than large companies because most big companies get so diverse and subjected to the law of large numbers that it's harder for them to grow. So our decision to focus on small-caps was mainly based on the idea that small companies could potentially grow faster than big companies.

Kazanjian: *That probably explains why small-cap stocks have outperformed all other equity classes over time. What role do you feel small-caps play in an investor's portfolio? What percentage of a stock portfolio should you keep in this part of the market?*

Stewart: The dominating factor is the investor's time horizon. The longer your time horizon, the more you should be investing in small-caps. For me, my exposure is 100 percent, assuming it's money I can afford to leave invested for five or more years. For the average investor, my guess is 100 percent is too high. But for the average 20- or 30-year-old trying to figure out what to do with a 401(k), I would recommend that you have at least half of your assets in some sort of small-cap category.

Kazanjian: *What's your definition of small-cap, in terms of market capitalization?*

Stewart: It's a little fuzzy in today's market, but I'd say $1 billion and below is small-cap, and under $2.5 billion is on the border. Once you get to $3 or $4 billion, you've probably crossed into mid-cap territory. Micro-caps, of course, are even smaller.

Kazanjian: *If you buy a stock and it goes from a $1 billion to a $5 billion market capitalization, will you automatically sell just because it's grown too big?*

Stewart: By and large, valuation tends to make most market cap driven decisions moot. In other words, if a company's doing really well and getting bigger, often the price will be driven up. If we buy a company at 20 times earnings that's now at 40 times earnings, we'll probably either reduce or eliminate our exposure. In the background we may notice it went from a

$1.5 billion to a $3 billion market cap, but valuation drives the decision. You saw some of this in action during the Internet bubble, where small companies with minimal sales and profit were valued at $5, $10, $15 billion. That was all about valuation. People were willing to pay a lot of money for those companies so they got to be big caps, though the underlying operations were small-cap. So usually valuation will drive us out of a company before market cap will. But there are occasions when we just say, "This is too big, and we're moving on."

Kazanjian: *You've closed all of your small-cap funds to new and, in many cases, even existing investors. What makes you decide it's time to close off inflows to a fund?*

Stewart: It's really style driven. Our rule of thumb tends to be that you can manage about as much money as the weighted average market caps of the stocks in your portfolio. So if the average market cap of the companies in your portfolio is $300 million, then $300 million is probably all you can manage effectively in that asset class.

Kazanjian: *How many stocks do you have to choose from in the small-cap universe? It must be in the thousands, since most stocks fall into this category.*

Stewart: Yes. In our early marketing materials we had a curve that plotted market capitalization against the number of overall stocks, and it's amazingly close to being a right angle. You pull off the top 250 stocks, and most of the rest are in our universe.

Kazanjian: *With thousands of potential ideas out there, how do you narrow down the list enough to find quality stocks for your portfolios?*

Stewart: The thing that caused me to found Wasatch and make me believe I could add value was when I started playing around with different income statements and balance sheet variables looking at whether any consistently led to high returns. I found the best predictor was in those companies with improving returns on capital. So if you focused on companies improving the return on capital, you tended to get good subsequent returns. Therefore, we start off by screening for companies with improving or attractive financial characteristics. Then we start our due diligence. Another way we find them is if we're visiting a company in a particular area, we'll screen to see who else is interesting in that area and has pretty good financial numbers. A lot of times you ask companies who their top competitors are and who's doing well. But screening for improving returns on capital as a start is very important.

Kazanjian: *Once you've found some potential ideas through screening, what kind of deeper digging do you do?*

Stewart: The very first thing, which is almost another kind of screen, is what we call a DuPont Analysis. We lay out a company's financial statements and quarterly data over the past five years, including an array of ratios. You use this to find companies generating good cash flow, earning high returns on capital, and growing sales. But the point is to look over the financial statements and see whether everything fits together. The initial screen might give you an idea based on one or two variables. That's when you go into a more thorough analysis of the financial statements. If the company still looks interesting, the next thing you do is either call management and talk over the phone or go visit them in person to hear their story.

Kazanjian: *What are you looking out for most when speaking with management?*

Stewart: Most importantly you're trying to get a feel for who they are. Do you like management? Do they seem competent and capable? If you have to put that in two words, you're trying to find a management with both *vision* and *execution*. Sometimes those are hard to find in the same person. If so, you want management to understand that and have both visionary people and executors on board. It's pretty easy for a company that's all vision and no execution to get waylaid, just as it is for a company that's all execution and no vision. Beyond that you're trying to understand what their competitive strengths and weaknesses are and, in particular, whether they have any enduring or sustainable competitive advantages.

Kazanjian: *Some of the Masters in this book say they don't bother to talk to management because they can't believe what they say and, besides, the numbers speak for themselves.*

Stewart: If you're a more trading-oriented manager, that approach probably makes a lot of sense, particularly as information has become more widely available and as computers have grown more powerful. But at Wasatch we're trying to get on board early and stay the course. That means holding onto a company through road bumps. Because every company on the face of the earth has setbacks, you've got to figure out whether they're hitting a U-turn or just a chuckhole. To do that, you need to talk to management. The other thing is we always try to have three or four people at these meetings so we get different perspectives. Three people in a room might be eating up the management's story, but the fourth might say, "Yeah, but did you see those gold chains?" If there's a negative vibration, hopefully at least one person will pick up on it. Alternatively, if almost everybody is negative and one person is positive and suggests you put it into perspective, it might keep you from missing a good idea. We also use some investigative reporters to follow up on things that don't tend to come out in the direct management meeting, such as what former employees have to say. We try to trust but verify. That's a good model for the way we approach things.

Kazanjian: *So you've done your screenings and met with management. What comes next?*

Stewart: We're continually doing what I call onion peeling. We might buy a company after a meeting, but we'll continue to push and might decide to move on. But if we like everything we've seen thus far, we'll call the company an ABGC, which is an acronym for America's Best Growth Company. We use that as a way to keep us from getting distracted from worrying about whether they'll have a strong earnings report next quarter or a hot new product coming out. It keeps us focused on the company's long-term prospects and management quality. Having said that, the final step before diving in is always valuation. We might see a company and love it, but if it's selling at an outrageous multiple, we won't buy it. It's hard to define outrageous, since it depends on the company's growth prospects. But if it's selling at 40 or 50 times earnings, that's usually too expensive. If it's too richly priced, we might instead put it on a watch list to buy at a later point. But even after we've bought the stock the journey doesn't end. It's really just beginning.

Kazanjian: *Can you delve into valuation a bit more? For instance, if a company is growing at 40 percent a year and selling at 40 times earnings, is that reasonable to you?*

Stewart: We rely pretty heavily on PE to G (price/earnings to growth). In general, you'd like to buy a company in the neighborhood of a ratio of 1. So if the company is selling at 40 times earnings and growing at 40 percent, that would be a buyable company. But if it's only growing at 30 percent, you might just nibble a bit. If it's only growing at 20 percent, you'd probably say that's too expensive.

Kazanjian: *The trick is figuring out whether that 40 percent growth is sustainable.*

Stewart: Right, and that's part of what you're to get from meeting with management.

Kazanjian: *How many stocks do you generally keep in a small-cap portfolio?*

Stewart: More than you need to diversify. It differs by product, but the Core Growth Fund generally has 50 names, while the micro-cap funds might have around 100.

Kazanjian: *Do you diversify among industries and sectors?*

Stewart: Yes, but I'd like to emphasize that we're really bottom-up driven. A top-down guy would look at the economy and maybe say he thinks interest rates will rise, which would hurt homebuilders, so he won't own any homebuilders, or vice versa. We don't do it that way. We assemble the portfolio company by company. Then we look to see what we have. If we find we've got a 50 percent overweighting in technology, we'll ask whether it makes sense. If it does, we'll run with it. If not, we might lighten up a bit.

Kazanjian: *What's the highest percentage of the portfolio you'll put in a single holding?*

Stewart: Again, that varies by product. We've been known to go as high as 10 percent, but it's generally going to be 3 to 5 percent across the board.

Kazanjian: *You said that once you buy a stock, that's when the journey begins. Given your long-term focus, how closely do you watch your holdings?*

Stewart: Closely. As Bernard Baruch said, "Put all your eggs in the same basket and keep your eye on the basket." Once we own a company, we work even harder than we did while we were just investigating it. We are continually talking to management and competitors, and doing a lot of due diligence. We also hold our feet to the fire internally by something we call captured earnings growth, or how much our companies have grown since we bought them. Every quarter we measured the captured earnings growth of the portfolio as a way of seeing whether we're doing a good job as investors.

Kazanjian: *Given your relative patience, what makes you decide to sell a stock?*

Stewart: I'm going to give you a statement, followed by an example. The statement is we sell if we determine that the company is no longer ABGC, or that our original thesis was wrong. Now here's an example of this. About five years ago, we invested in Sykes, which is a company that runs call centers. This was before call centers in India became so popular. We thought it was an interesting business and went down and visited management. On a subsequent visit, the CEO started talking about some crazy visionary stuff, which made us uncomfortable. Companies that succeed at running call centers are execution heavy, and this guy seemed to be long on vision and short on execution. We decided to sell because our original assessment of management changed. If there's one single thing that gets us out more often than anything else, it's managers who aren't who we thought they were.

Kazanjian: *Even more so than the price of the stock going up or down?*

Stewart: That's a good point. Partly because of the illiquid nature of the small-cap market, if the price moves up and our position gets a little heavier, we'll likely peel back shares in increments. Indeed, 99 percent of our daily trades are valuation driven. But as far as what would get us out of a stock completely once we owned it, it's a change in management that we aren't comfortable with.

Kazanjian: *Of those companies that tend to be unsuccessful investments for you, and I would assume in the small-cap world there are many, what's the common reason they don't work out?*

Stewart: Many small companies are the length and shadow of one person. Even though a number of important people may be involved in the operation, it's easy for a smaller company to be dominated by a single individual. So I'd say it's because we misread management or management makes a dumb move.

Kazanjian: *Is the corollary also true, that your most successful companies are ones due to good execution by management?*

Stewart: Yes, that's exactly true. I'm sure you've gathered by now that management is pretty critical when you're talking about these smaller companies.

Kazanjian: *While your funds all have excellent long-term track records, they underperformed the competition on a relative basis in the late 1990s. Why was that? Did you avoid the hot-performing stocks that fueled the performance of so many other small-cap funds during that time?*

Stewart: That's exactly right and let me tie it back to some of the other things we've discussed. Remember, a lot of these high-flying Internet companies had two things in common. One is they were very immature business models that weren't sustainable. Two, they were being sold at expensive valuations. In doing our due diligence, we would take a look at these companies and say there's really not that much there. We couldn't see anything that looked like a sustainable competitive advantage. In a lot of cases the managers had very little background. We tried to find interesting ideas, and uncovered a few things around the edges, but by and large our basic discipline kept us out of those companies. Since these stocks were driving returns, our performance only looked okay. If you're doing 15 or 20 percent, and everyone else is doing 90 or 100 percent or more, you look relatively bad. That's where we were in the late 1990s.

Kazanjian: *Of course, over the last few years it's been just the opposite. Is that because the other guys suffered when those former high flyers blew up, while your unloved stocks finally found favor?*

Stewart: Yes, and it reminds me of something interesting. At the height of the bubble, I was at a conference and a guy commented to his buddy, "That's just a 20 percent grower. We can always come back for that." This was a very common feeling. At the peak of the bubble, the 20 percent growers were selling for 10 or 12 times earnings. So we were sitting there with these great companies, and it really propelled us when the fast-growing dot-coms fell apart and people realized they weren't a very good idea to begin with. We don't see this kind of opportunity out there now. I would say by and large valuations today are a lot more rational. Anything that is really good tends to be quite expensive, and if you find something that's pretty cheap there's usually a reason why.

Kazanjian: *Small-cap stocks have had several good years. Some say the cycle for small-caps is over, and the place to be going forward is in the larger names. Where do you come out on that one?*

Stewart: You're right. Virtually anybody who pays attention says we've been in the small-cap cycle for quite a while, and if history is a guide, it's got to end soon. But we're small-cap players beyond the small-cap cycle. If we get an adverse movement in small-cap stocks, it just means we'll have to work harder and run faster. I wouldn't disagree that the small-cap cycle is at a minimum long in the tooth. I'd also say that going forward, I don't expect the markets to be as good as they've been going backward. We've been in a very virtuous cycle for stocks. I think 10 or 15 years from now, the Dow may still be at 10,000. My colleagues at Wasatch are a little more upbeat, but I think we're going to be in a flatter spot going forward both for the economy and from the perspective of the stock market.

Kazanjian: *Given that bearish scenario, how should someone invest their money now?*

Stewart: I think it's the time for the professionals, not the amateurs. I think those who succeed at investing over the next 5 or 10 years are those who stick to their knitting, follow their disciplines, and grind it out. If you're an amateur listening to tips in the clubhouse, it's going to be tough. Success going forward might be a low double-digit or high single-digit return. If someone has a 10 percent track record over the next five years, that might look darn good.

Kazanjian: *Your firm has certainly benefited from the rise in small-cap stocks. After all, assets have gone from around $1 billion in 2000 to $9 billion today. Unlike most fund firms, you've closed most of your funds, and stopped accepting any more assets. That's costly to your bottom line, because running more money would bring in more management fees. Why did you make the decision to cut off asset flows to such a large degree?*

Stewart: Strong asset flows are a short-run thing. The reason I founded Wasatch was to show you can beat the market. It's still about beating the market. If we let our funds balloon, we wouldn't beat the market. Yes, we might collect some more money in the meantime, but sooner or later asset levels would go down. It's happened time and again to other shops. I'd rather not experience the downhill side. I'd rather have a firm that can grow steadily, or even plateau steadily. It's about beating the market, not growing assets.

Kazanjian: *Do you worry that a lot of the investors who have come to you over the last few years because of your great performance are buying high, and will wind up selling out once they see returns either moderate or become negative?*

Stewart: Absolutely. There's no doubt that many of our investors, maybe more than half, have not been with us a long time. The newer investors don't tend to stay put and they don't have a reason to stay put. We'd like to give them a reason to stay put, and that's really what our focus is on.

You might say Stewart is starting to expand his horizons a bit. In mid-2004, his firm opened Wasatch Heritage Growth, which invests in mid- and large-cap companies. He fondly describes it as a portfolio for "Wasatch graduates," or stocks that have outgrown his other broad-base small-cap funds, all of which are closed to most investors as this book goes to press. "We had the idea for the Wasatch Heritage Growth Fund a few years ago," Stewart says, noting that it will buy stocks with market caps between $3 and $20 billion. "We developed and ran a 'paper portfolio' for two years to test the theory prior to moving forward with a mutual fund." Unlike most of the other Wasatch funds, Stewart says Heritage's broader market capitalization mandate will prevent the firm from having to close the portfolio any time soon.

JOHN C. THOMPSON

Thompson Investment Management

For John C. Thompson, investing has long been a family affair. His dad ran the investment division of a Wisconsin bank for many years before starting his own firm with several partners in 1984. While Thompson has also spent most of his own career in the investment business, he started out on a completely different track.

Thompson majored in engineering and worked with a large consulting firm after college. It didn't take long to realize that the investment business was much more interesting to him. Ultimately Thompson wound up joining his father's firm as a research analyst in 1993. In no time, he moved into managing money, earning an MBA from the University of Chicago along the way.

Today, he runs Thompson Plumb Growth, a fund his father started in 1992. Thompson has called most of the shots since 1995, though Dad is still around to help out as needed. Although only 35, Thompson has built an impressive track record in his own right, with only one losing year so far (in 2002, although he still beat the S&P 500).

One reason for his success is that, while clearly a growth manager, Thompson pays close attention to valuations. While that keeps him out of some of the high-flyers that post standout gains in roaring bull markets, it also tempers volatility and allows him to generate consistent returns over the long haul.

Kazanjian: *Given that your dad was in the business, I gather you've been exposed to the world of investing your entire life.*

Thompson: Yes, it's always been a family business. Dad talked to me about stocks as a boy, and I used to go to conferences with him. Our family vacation was going to what used to be called the Dain Bosworth Conference in Vail, where company management teams would speak.

Kazanjian: *What did your dad do at the time?*

Thompson: He ran the investment division of what is now U.S. Bank in Madison, Wisconsin. It was called First Wisconsin Bank when he was there. At the time they had about $1 billion, which was a fair amount of money back in the early 1980s.

Kazanjian: *When did he go out on his own, starting what was originally known as Thompson Plumb?*

Thompson: In 1984. There were actually four partners in the beginning. The final partner (Thomas Plumb) left in January 2004. More precisely, we split the Thompson and Plumb operations into two separate companies, although we still brand the funds as Thompson Plumb for consistency.

Kazanjian: *You're now in charge of the Thompson Plumb Growth Fund. Was that fund originally run solely by your dad?*

Thompson: Actually, it was run by a committee until late 1993. We found the committee system didn't work very well.

Kazanjian: *Why not?*

Thompson: What ended up happening is if they bought a stock like Dow Chemical, and one person liked it better than the other two, the other two would still sort of go along with it. When some bad news came out on Dow Chemical and the stock dropped, the other two had this human tendency to say, "I told you so. Let's get rid of it." The one who came up with the idea of the stock in the first place would say, "No, let's wait." But since that person was outvoted, the stock would often be sold at the wrong time for the wrong reasons. Given that no two people have exactly the same ideas on stocks, it's very difficult, in my opinion, to run strictly as a committee where things get voted on. In addition, committees are very slow. Assembling numerous opinions on a certain stock when one guy's on vacation in Florida and the other's at a conference in San Francisco makes the logistics of acting quickly a nightmare.

Kazanjian: *There are some decent funds run by committee. Do you think the process can work well for some firms?*

Thompson: It was a bad idea for us, but it may be a great idea for other organizations with other personalities. If you look at corporate America, how many companies are run by two people? The two that come to mind—Charles Schwab and Kraft—didn't stay with that structure for long. I think you need a single person in charge of any entity.

Kazanjian: *Given your upbringing, was your plan all along to get into the investment business?*

Thompson: Not at first. I was in engineering school. I really liked math and science a lot, better than English and history. So I went into engineering largely because you didn't need many credits in humanities courses to graduate. For me, studying calculus, physics, and thermodynamics was much easier than writing a paper on why I liked a certain book. But when I got to school, I found I didn't like the actual practice of engineering. It just wasn't that interesting to me. After practicing engineering for a while, I realized I liked the investment business a lot better than the science side of the world.

Kazanjian: *Did you start at your dad's firm right away?*

Thompson: I did, but it's kind of an interesting story. I was working for an engineering consulting firm in Chicago, which helped companies improve their quality control systems. We'd go into a company, consult for three weeks, write a report, and then move on to the next one. It wasn't very satisfying. For one thing, we talked and showed them what could be done, and then we were gone and didn't get to see the end results of our recommendations. It was also a one-shot deal. You'd put in all this effort, and once the work was done, it was over. I was really worried about this non-recurring revenue aspect of the business. After two years on the job, my father wanted some help in the analytical department of the firm. He called and asked if I'd be interested in starting at the entry level doing some research on technology and other types of companies. Since we had done consulting for some technology companies, it was a good fit. That was in 1993 and I've been here ever since.

Kazanjian: *How large was the firm when you began?*

Thompson: We were running about $250 million.

Kazanjian: *Now the fund alone has almost $1.4 billion, compared to $2.2 billion for the firm overall. You've certainly come a long way. When did you take over management of Thompson Plumb Growth?*

Thompson: I began working on it in 1994, and became a portfolio manager in 1996.

Kazanjian: *Did you learn your overall investment process from your dad?*

Thompson: Yes, I did. I think I refined his approach a little bit, but the overall process is the same.

Kazanjian: *Does he still work with you on the fund?*

Thompson: From a big picture perspective he does, but I make most of the day-to-day decisions. He runs mostly individual accounts at the firm.

Kazanjian: *Let's talk about your investment process.*

Thompson: Our process is part technical and part qualitative. First of all, we're looking for companies that generate free cash flow. We don't want to be invested in companies when they're in the huge investment phase. We prefer to buy them in what I'd call the harvesting phase.

Kazanjian: *What kind of free cash flow are you looking for?*

Thompson: We mostly want to see that the company creates more cash than it consumes. Some make more than others. The bottom line is that we don't want companies borrowing $5 billion a year to build fiber optic networks around the world and laying cable across the Pacific Ocean hoping that someday people will use it. We also like companies with an average return on equity of 15 percent or better over time. The higher, the better.

Kazanjian: *How do you find those companies?*

Thompson: We do some screening, but after being in the business a while, you start to just know them. I know that companies like Abbott Labs, Automatic Data Processing, Intel, and Microsoft all have huge ROEs without even looking at a screen.

Kazanjian: *Those are all big-cap stocks. Do you focus on larger companies?*

Thompson: That's our preference, but not always. At certain times, especially in the late 1990s, big-caps were not the best place to be.

Kazanjian: *I've seen you describe your approach as being "flexible." What do you mean by that?*

Thompson: We can go anywhere within the Russell 1000 index, which means basically any company with a market capitalization of more than $1 or $2 billion. But we're not entirely constrained. We can buy a large-cap growth company on the same day we're buying a mid-cap value company. We're frankly not even watching what category stocks are in when we're buying them.

Kazanjian: *How does your discipline change when you're buying what would be perceived as a pure growth stock versus a value stock?*

Thompson: It doesn't. That is a very important point. Charlie Munger (Warren Buffett's business partner) has gone off in detail about this. The only difference between a value stock and a growth stock, theoretically, is that the growth stock is growing faster. So you're discounting a faster rate of growth for the earnings. This is merely a mathematical formula—the present value of the future free cash flows. If the future free cash flows aren't growing very fast, you pay a lower price. If they're growing fast, you pay a higher price. Those very strict disciplines that say, "I'm only going to pay X times earnings," or "I'm only going to buy at a huge discount" are creating a moral hazard. They'll always wind up with a portfolio of poor-quality companies. On the growth side of the world, they look for companies growing fast, with high returns and great prospects for the future. The problem with that style of investing is that often these companies can slow down and decelerate, and you can lose a huge amount of money in the process.

What we're trying to do is stay in the middle of the two extremes. We don't want some company in decline that we buy on the notion that it's cheap enough that we'll be okay. We want companies growing at a decent rate—at least the same as the economy or better over time, which is about 7 percent on a nominal basis—and we try to buy them at very reasonable multiples.

Kazanjian: *On top of that, you want the company to be generating free cash flow and to have an ROE of 15 percent or higher?*

Thompson: It's not a requirement of every single stock, but 90 percent or more of the companies in our portfolio would fit into that categorization.

Kazanjian: *What other criteria do you look for?*

Thompson: There are four other variables. We look for the price-to-earnings multiple to be significantly under its long-term average, meaning 10 years or more. We also want to see the price-to-sales ratio below its long-term average. And we want the Standard & Poor's quality rating of the company, which is similar to the credit rating, to be at least B+ or better.

Kazanjian: *These sound like quantitative variables. Do you get them by running a computer screen?*

Thompson: No, we normally do it manually. Screens have some great points, but they can kick out good companies or give you names with numbers that are artificially high and unsustainable. We prefer doing it the other way, meaning watching the news and price action every day, spotting good companies that are down in price, and then doing work to see why that's the case. We do a lot of our work just by watching stock prices and looking at the new low list.

Kazanjian: *You're starting to sound like a value manager.*

Thompson: Right, but we buy companies most value managers won't. While we're sort of using a value methodology, we want better-quality companies. Price is just a trigger to get us interested. If you look at Coke, Microsoft, of Pfizer, very few so-called value managers would own those stocks. Those are all companies we either own now or have owned in the past. We started buying Coke in mid-2004 after the company became guarded about earnings over the next few quarters and the stock dropped from $50 to $43.

Kazanjian: *How many holdings do you have in the portfolio at any given time?*

Thompson: About 60, but 80 percent of the money is concentrated in the top 20 holdings.

Kazanjian: *In looking through your current list of holdings, they all seem to be household names, such as Fannie Mae, Microsoft, Pfizer, Johnson & Johnson, Office Depot, and General Electric.*

Thompson: They are now, but in the past we've owned smaller, more obscure names. Everything being equal, if Company A grew its earnings at 10 percent a year, sells at 15 times earnings, with a 15 percent ROE and $200 billion market cap, while Company B has all those same statistics with a $4 billion market cap, I'd prefer Company A.

Kazanjian: *You've discussed some of the quantitative factors. What do you look at from a qualitative perspective? Do you meet with management?*

Thompson: We see them occasionally, but it's not a requirement. The numbers are the score of the game. You can go sit down with a fellow who seems perfectly pleasant and honest, he can say the right things, yet make poor decisions. I think management is a very difficult thing to determine the quality of ahead of time unless you're talking about somebody who has been in that position for many years with a proven track record. Most companies don't have CEOs that have been there a long time with great records. If they do, they're quite old, and that in itself becomes a risk. Management is a variable. It's not a constant.

Kazanjian: *So while you're not a pure "quant," it sounds like the numbers are the most important variable you look at when making investment decisions.*

Thompson: They are. But we look at other forces, such as barriers to entering the business. We want to know the suppliers and how powerful they are relative to the company. How does the company stack up versus its competition in terms of market share? We look at a bunch of data points like this—for example, Coke versus Pepsi. Pepsi is doing better right now and we own both stocks. But if you think about it, Coke has double the worldwide market share of Pepsi. It can advertise 50 percent more than Pepsi worldwide and still have a lower cost per can of soda for advertising. In the long run the ability to outadvertise is an enormous barrier to entry for Coke.

Kazanjian: *And you want to buy these companies at a PE significantly lower than their long-term average?*

Thompson: Exactly. All companies have stock price charts that go up and down over time. No company goes up every day. There are definitely moods and differences of opinions, varying earnings outlooks, and so on that drive stocks up and down in the short run. Now, if you bought high-ROE, market-leading, growth companies and held them forever, in my opinion, you'd do as well or better than the S&P 500, even if you bought them somewhat poorly. But if you buy them at a low point, you'll do even better. Having said that, I think investing is like flying an airplane. Most of the time you can fly it without instruments and do just fine. But at certain points in time, when you're in the clouds and it's raining and you don't know which way you're going, you need to be able to read the instruments and understand where you are and what you're doing. It's similar with investing. If you don't understand PE multiples and cash flows, and if you don't understand that PEs go up and down, I don't see how you can do a great job in the long term. That doesn't mean you can't buy Starbucks because you love their coffee and make a lot of money in it. But over a long period, I'm not sure just buying and holding is the best approach because any stock can become overvalued.

Kazanjian: *Unless you buy when the prices are at their lows, of course. Even then, presumably there's a reason these stocks are trading at lower multiples.*

Thompson: It's our job to figure out whether the reason is a significant long-term problem or just a shorter-term issue. There are companies with long-term problems that might not recover. Kodak is one, in my opinion. There is no way it is going to replace this multibillion-dollar-a-year profit stream of film with digital cameras. Sony, Canon, Nikon, and Pentex are going after the digital camera in a significant way and film is going away. If that's the case, we just don't want to have anything to do with a company like Kodak. If the stock fell down to three or four times earnings, maybe we'd consider it. But it's very hard to make money in a declining business.

Kazanjian: *Once you buy a stock, how patient are you willing to be for it to work out?*

Thompson: I'm probably too patient sometimes. We've owned Merck the entire time I've been here. That one has clearly been an underperformer.

Kazanjian: *Say a stock goes down considerably. At what point do you admit you've made a mistake and get out?*

Thompson: We rarely sell when a stock is going down. We will, however, sell when we know we've made a mistake. It really comes down to the fundamentals. Is it a good long-term company or not? If it remains a good long-term investment, we'll stick with it no matter how low the price goes. In theory, if the value is x, you buy it at $.7x$, and it then drops to $.6x$, you should like it better, right?

Kazanjian: *Presumably, although you could have also made a mistake.*

Thompson: And we have done that. One was Qwest Communications. The company's phone lines were worth a certain amount, which you could calculate. But the price of phone lines dropped, and so did the value of the company's assets. We paid on average $9 a share for the stock and wound up selling out at around $5. We made a mistake in valuing these phone lines and, quite frankly, buying a company with such poor-quality ratings. It helped to define our strategy a bit better. We made multiple mistakes with this stock. It had a low credit rating, too much debt, a declining business, and instead of paying a multiple of free cash flow or earnings, we paid a percentage of private asset value, which proved to be wrong. It's when we stray too far away from our discipline, as we did with Qwest, that some of our most painful mistakes are made.

Kazanjian: *When you stick with the rules and a stock works out, what makes you sell?*

Thompson: We sell for a number of reasons. Number one is if the price rises significantly above its long-term PE average. The more typical reason we sell is if we find a better investment with a potentially better risk-adjusted return. We assign an opportunity cost to every stock. Let's use Coke and Pepsi because they're easy examples. If you think Coke could trade at $60 based on its average PE multiple, and it's $45 today, you could make 33 percent on your investment, which is a great return. If Pepsi was selling at a similar valuation, and you thought you could earn 33 percent on Pepsi in a year or two, you'd hold both. However, let's say there's some potato scare, Frito-Lay has to recall a ton of chips, and the price of Pepsi drops 30 percent. All of a sudden Pepsi stock has an appreciation potential of 60 percent, while Coke is still around 30. In this case, assuming our outlook for Pepsi remained positive, we would sell some Coke and buy Pepsi. Let's say Pepsi recovered and drastically outperformed Coke. Then we may sell some Pepsi and buy Coke. We're constantly assigning opportunity costs to each of these stocks relative to each other within the portfolio. We also do this between sectors. For example, when financials are very cheap relative to technology stocks, we may have very little tech and a ton of financials and vice versa.

Kazanjian: *Carrying on this thought, if you thought financials were more attractive, would you purposely overweight them?*

Thompson: It's really all done from a bottom-up perspective. It's more a function that you find a lot of attractive financials and wake up one morning to see that you're 50 percent overweight in financials.

Kazanjian: *Do you remain fully invested in stocks at all times?*

Thompson: For the most part. We rarely have a material amount of cash.

Kazanjian: *How do factors such as the overall economy and the threat of terrorism fit into your decision-making process?*

Thompson: We don't pay much attention to the economy. The problem with terrorism is that it's going to be with us forever to one degree or another. If you say, "I'm scared of terrorism," why would that change a year from now or two years from now or five years from now? In essence you'd be out of the market forever.

Kazanjian: *Your performance in 1999 was weak compared to the competition and the S&P 500 (Thompson Plumb Growth was up 6.4 percent versus 21 percent for the S&P 500). That caused some significant outflows from the fund. What happened back then?*

Thompson: We owned financials and relatively boring companies that weren't interesting to the market in general. Ironically, they were being sold by managers to fund purchases of tech and Internet companies. The crazy part was that it created a huge opportunity for us to take advantage of, allowing us to really outperform in the following years. I'm not sure we'll ever see a period of time again where it's possible to beat the market by 30 percent a year with a diversified portfolio like we did. But I won't kid you. It was a difficult time. Many of our customers were extremely frustrated. They were plagued by the cocktail-party syndrome, where people would run around, talk to all their friends, and hear about how much money they were making in some Internet stock or fund. We, on the other hand, were sitting around with stocks like Wells Fargo and AutoZone, which were going down.

Kazanjian: *Did you own any technology stocks back then?*

Thompson: I think around 12 percent, compared to 35 percent for the overall market. I would have liked to own zero technology, but politically inside the firm it wasn't possible. Wall Street was funneling all this money into areas with unsustainable growth and fundamentals.

Kazanjian: *Looking back, do you believe you made the right decision, or do you wish you had owned more tech?*

Thompson: Oh, we made the right decision. In retrospect, we should have sold everything in the tech sector.

Kazanjian: *While 1999 was difficult, 2002 was the first losing year in the history of your firm, even though you still weren't down quite as much as the S&P 500 (20.4 percent versus 22.7 percent for the S&P). What happened?*

Thompson: It was really a function of the breadth of the decline. There was no place to hide. The optimal strategy there would have been to have 30 percent cash but, again, we don't do that. We also had a couple of mistakes like Qwest and Conseco, which didn't help. And we owned America Online and Tyco, which were very volatile that year.

Kazanjian: *What lessons did you learn from that experience?*

Thompson: I think the key thing is to stick with higher credit rating companies. If you go into a bad stock market with a low-quality company, your bankruptcy risk is high and the market slaughters your stock. A risk–mitigating strategy is to stay with strong balance sheet companies. Also, strong balance sheet companies can take advantage of the weakness by buying the assets of companies in trouble.

Kazanjian: *Does that also mean paying up for quality, since lower-quality companies are probably a bit cheaper?*

Thompson: That's the whole point that I made earlier between growth and value. Most value managers are loathe to do that.

Kazanjian: *What's interesting is that this approach has allowed your fund to perform well in both growth and value markets, although because of your more cautious approach, you tend to have more market-like returns when aggressive growth is in fashion. Does this also reflect your cautious approach? In other words, I understand that not losing money is one of your primary goals.*

Thompson: Yes. Part of that is because in our business, we manage the entire net worth of most of our customers. We must have this principal–preservation mindset. Any stock can lose 10, 20, or 25 percent with random bad news. The permanent losses come when you lose 50 percent or more of your money.

Kazanjian: *What's the biggest lesson you learned from the most recent bear market?*

Thompson: How crazy people can act as a group in buying stocks and pushing multiples up way past expectations. Probably the converse will be true at some point, where stocks fall for no good reason and the PE gets pushed way down. Markets travel farther in both directions than any rational person would think. There's this quote that says, "You have to be fearful when others are greedy and greedy when others are fearful." The time to be scared is when everybody's making money hand over fist in the markets. You shouldn't be scared when the markets are going down. I can't tell you how many times people called me early in 2004 to say, "The market sure did great last year. Do you think it's time to put my money back in?" I was thinking, "Where were you 30 percent ago?"

Kazanjian: *I suppose it's human nature. We get excited when the market goes up and don't want to miss the ride.*

Thompson: But you have to fight your own human nature.

Given that Thompson works out of Madison, Wisconsin, I asked whether he felt out of touch with the rest of Wall Street. "Not at all," he responded. He actually believes the distance is an advantage, and boasts that he doesn't have any friends in the business, preventing shoptalk from coming into regular socializing. "It keeps people from second-guessing our decisions," he says. Thompson adds that, in some ways, he has even better access to analysts and management teams in Madison because when they come through town, they usually have an open schedule and plenty of time to meet because of the small number of investment managers in town, especially relative to New York.

PART TWO

The VALUE MASTERS

ROBERT LYON

Institutional Capital

Coming from a family of lawyers, Rob Lyon once thought he, too, would follow down this same judicial path. But after figuring out what attorneys really do, he opted for a career in business instead. It wasn't much of a stretch for Lyon to use his financial smarts in the investment field. After all, he bought his first stock at the age of 12, and spent his childhood reading the *Wall Street Journal*.

After college, where he majored in business, Lyon started working in a bank trust department and was elevated to a much higher position while still in his mid-twenties. A chance meeting with William Maloney, founder of Institutional Capital (ICAP), turned into a job interview that landed

Lyon a spot analyzing stocks at this Chicago-based classic value firm. Maloney started ICAP in 1970, after spending several years managing the Sears profit-sharing fund. Maloney was an extremely conservative investor by nature whose mantra was, "If you preserve your capital, the rest will follow."

For a time, Lyon went to work for Fred Alger, one of the famous go-go investment managers of the 1980s, before returning to ICAP as director of research in 1988. Lyon eventually led a buyout of the firm from Maloney, and is now ICAP's president and chief investment officer. The firm manages both institutional accounts and several mutual funds, including the top-rated ICAP Select Equity, using the same general approach employed by the firm for more than three decades.

In addition to investing in large U.S. companies, the 54-year-old manager is a big fan of European equities, which he feels are often cheaper and come with the promise of greater future profit.

Kazanjian: *I understand you had your first exposure to stocks at very young age.*

Lyon: I first got interested in the market around 1961, largely as result of getting some shares of stock for Christmas from a relative.

Kazanjian: *Do you remember what company you got?*

Lyon: I do. It was Pep Boys—Manny, Moe, and Jack. I grew up in a little town called Greencastle, Indiana, where DePauw University is located. My grandfather was a lawyer and I used to spend a lot of time with him when I was a kid. This may sound strange, but on Sunday mornings I would watch *Face the Nation* and *Meet the Press* with him. He also got me to read *US News and World Report* and the *Wall Street Journal*. Somehow I ran across a copy of *Reminiscences of a Stock Operator*, the Jesse Livermore story, when I was in junior high school. I thought it was fascinating how the markets operated. When I was 12, my grandfather set up a brokerage account for me and let me buy stocks that were on the S&P approved list. I got interested in RCA when color TV was just starting, and Brunswick, the bowling company, as they were automating the lanes.

Kazanjian: *Did that fascination with the stock market stay with you as you entered high school and then college?*

Lyon: It did, although since both of my grandfathers were lawyers, I entered Northwestern as a political science major. Not long after that I shifted to economics. I thought about going to either law school or business school and applied to both. Ultimately I decided on Wharton because of its expertise in finance. My grandfathers were both small-town Indiana lawyers. Once I found out what junior Wall Street lawyers did, it didn't seem that exciting. You basically just sat around and ground out prospectuses. I decided business school would be better for me.

Between years in business school, I got an internship at First Chicago, working in the portfolio management area of the trust department. That was exactly what I had secretly been hankering to do all along. I thought that was where all the action was. Back then, First Chicago was about the fifth or sixth largest bank in the United States, and the trust department was commensurate in size. The mutual fund and boutique money management industries were very small, and there was essentially no hedge fund industry.

Kazanjian: *What did you do after graduating from Wharton?*

Lyon: After the summer internship at First Chicago, they invited me back to work there. They were in an arms race with Citigroup to hire MBAs from top universities. The people in human resources asked what area I'd like to get into, and I said I wanted to go back to the trust department. They frowned, and told me the trust department was essentially the backwater of the bank. They explained that the bank was all about multinational lending, and said I could go from the bank to the trust department, but never from the trust department to the bank. I told them I wanted to be in the trust department and thought I'd be good at it. About a half dozen of the 200 MBAs they hired that year signed up for the trust department. I was only there about two years, but it was a great two years. I started off as assistant to the chief portfolio manager for institutional accounts in May 1974. I was his gofer.

Kazanjian: *That wasn't a great time to enter the stock market.*

Lyon: Tell me about it. The market that first year was terrible. The Dow was a little over 900 when I started. Nixon resigned in August, interest rates were going up to the highest levels since the Civil War, and the economy was going down a rat hole. Alan Greenspan was chairman of the Council of Economic Advisors. They had these WIN buttons, which stood for Whip Inflation Now. I'd only been at the job for about six months and the market was already down by a third. It didn't significantly climb above where I started for eight years.

The following year I got a great break. An older fellow at First Chicago, who was a full vice president within the trust department, had become the department's chief strategist and economist. He left to take a job in Boston. Because of all the real estate problems in the early 1970s, banks were taking big chargeoffs and had on both a hiring freeze and salary cap. When the other fellow left, instead of hiring someone who was really qualified to do the job, they promoted me. One of the great things about getting this spot involved exposure to some of the great Wall Street minds. My predecessor and the senior investment committee had in place relationships with some of the premier economists of the time, including Peter Bernstein, Gary Shilling, and Sam Nakagama. I got to sit in on these sessions as they cycled through every few months. In addition, there was a routine of visiting with Townsend-Greenspan in New York, one of the key Washington, D.C. groups that consulted on issues that affected the investment arena. I was able to make those trips and then report back to the senior committee with a summary of their thoughts. In addition, I met Ed Hyman (currently head of the ISI group), who was really just starting an econometric forecasting service for CJ Lawrence, and was able to add him to the list. I also had to generate detailed GDP and inflation forecasts and writeups that went out to the correspondent banks. Since we were still in "pre-PC" days, these big spreadsheets were done by specialized typists armed with a lot of white-out. That was a nightmare. Given that I was still only 25 or 26 when I had this opportunity, it allowed me to see more of the big picture at an early age.

Shortly thereafter, at a lunch for an investment strategist, I met Bill Maloney, who was the head of ICAP. He interviewed me while we had lunch. I got his card and called him the next day. He invited me over to talk and it led to an interview that lasted for several months. Part of the process involved going to Cambridge, Massachusetts, to meet with Dr. Charles McArthur. In Adam Smith's original *The Money Game*, written back in late 1960s, there's a whole chapter on Dr. McArthur. He was a former psychologist affiliated with Harvard Business School who came up with a career counseling technique that included a perfect paradigm of what it takes to become portfolio manager. I did well on his test and that carried a lot of weight with Maloney in terms of getting a job with him.

Maloney had managed the Sears profit-sharing plan during the 1960s. He left at the start of 1970 to open his own boutique business, Institutional Capital (ICAP), and built up a small and extremely loyal clientele in the

1970s. He was very conservative and escaped almost all the damage from the 1972–74 bear market. He was a pretty tough guy but a great mentor for all of those who worked for him. He was always encouraging us to not lose money, and to buy good risk-reward situations. He didn't care what industry or sector it was in. All he wanted were really washed-out stocks with a lot of upside, and he generally wanted to buy them when there was something different going on that would cause the price to rise. Importantly, he also wanted to know what the "climate" was, or where you were in the macro environment.

Kazanjian: *What was your original job at ICAP?*

Lyon: I was an analyst. An analyst to him was somebody who understood the big moving pieces, not necessarily one who knew how to disassemble a balance sheet. He wanted analysts who understood what was and wasn't cheap and could find stocks with good risk-reward characteristics.

When I first showed up for work, he brought me a stack of all the *Bank Credit Analyst*s that had come out over the last several years. This publication was very macro-oriented and global, in terms of talking about the direction of the dollar and gold, and so on. He wanted me to work on building a model for predicting the direction of the stock market based on a variety of cyclical trends. Of course, you can always find a system that works well historically, but then breaks down in the future. I'd also travel with Bill to New York to meet individually with analysts who had good stock ideas. He would line up a series of interviews at a couple of the big firms. My job was to sit there with a big yellow pad, keep my mouth shut, and take notes. We would then review those notes on the plane on the way home.

Kazanjian: *You went from ICAP to Alger, which is much more of a growth shop. Tell me about that transition.*

Lyon: In 1980 I met my wife, Donna, who was originally from New York. I thought it would be great to see how I could do in the big city. I was ready for a change. Fred Alger was having a terrific run in the market and getting an institutional following. He started to build his own research staff internally and partnered with Monica Smith, who had been an executive recruiter at International Paper. She's still in business today with her company called Analyst Resources. The concept was to scour the country interviewing analysts outside New York City who were really "stock-oriented" and willing to relocate to New York. She got in touch with me. Her style was to tape and transcribe the interviews. She gave the tapes to Fred Alger and his brother David, who was director of research. They would sift through and find people they thought were interesting and invite them to New York. Only a small handful passed muster with Fred and David. It was pretty competitive getting a job there.

They invited me to come for an interview. By that time, they had hired around 10 people and were looking for a couple more. The interview was like an early version of *The Apprentice*. After our talk, they asked me to come back to present a stock story to the entire investment team. Based on that, they'd decide whether to make me an offer. I told Fred and David I was ready to do my story right then. I had been working on Holiday Inn, which had just gone into the casino business by buying Harrah's. It was an interesting stock and I thought I knew it pretty well. They pointed out it wasn't the way they normally did things, but told me to go away for two hours, pull together my thoughts, and be back in the conference room at noon. I went to Schrafft's, an ice cream parlor, and put my notes together.

I came back and had barely opened my mouth before one of the analysts was all over me. Then David was all over me. They all knew a lot more about gaming than I did. Fred delivered the coup de grace by asking if I'd read the last issue of *Rouge et Noir*, some esoteric gaming periodical I had never even heard of before. I couldn't even cuff that answer. I kind of went down in flames on this stock. Fred said to wait outside for a minute, though the jury didn't take that long. He came out and said, "We didn't buy your story, but it's not the way we normally do things and we thought you had a lot of chutzpah to try to do this off the cuff. We think you might have more to offer, so if you want to come back and try again, that's okay with us."

I went back to Chicago and tried to come up with a stock interesting enough that they'd like it, but obscure enough that they wouldn't know it as well. I settled on Taft Broadcasting, controlled by the Taft family of Ohio. They were in the TV business and also owned Hanna-Barbera, creator of Yogi Bear and lots of other cartoons. They also owned a theme park operation that was second only to Disney. I had already done a lot of work on the stock. I put together a big 40-page report and 40-page appendix, and made sure I had read *Broadcasting*, *Variety*, and all the major industry periodicals. I wasn't going to fall into the same hole again. I even went to Cincinnati and met with Dudley Taft, who was the company's chairman at the time.

Kazanjian: *How did the folks at Alger like your second presentation?*

Lyon: Well, they didn't buy the stock, but they thought I did a thorough job with the presentation. They hired me and I went to work a couple of weeks later. I started on a Monday and it turned out that one of the key analysts there had left on the previous Friday. This was in the summer of 1981. I inherited a lot of the stocks the other analyst had already bought in the portfolio, including Warner Communications, Apple, and Toys R Us, which were in vogue at the time. I added coverage in conglomerates, media, pollution control, and some financials.

Kazanjian: *But you had come from a value background. These were clearly growth stocks. Wasn't that kind of a strange transition, especially given the low-risk mantra Maloney had drilled into you?*

Lyon: Fred wanted companies with rapid earnings growth, but he felt there were three ways to get this: rapid volume growth, rapid price growth, or rapid earnings growth coming from a low base; in other words, a turnaround situation. In 1980 the entire stock market was selling for around nine times earnings and one time book value, so to a certain extent everything was a value. The point was at Alger, at that time, you didn't have to buy a pure growth company. You just had to buy companies where earnings were growing at a well-above-average rate.

Kazanjian: *So you didn't feel out of place?*

Lyon: I never felt out of place. I had several conglomerates to play with, as well as media stocks. The first stock I recommended in 1981 was The Washington Post Company. I recommended it because it had just become the only game in town after Time, Inc. closed up the other competitive daily in Washington, D.C. The *Washington Post* became a monopoly newspaper and I knew that was good. At $25, it traded for about 10 times earnings back then. It did very well during the entire seven years I was at Alger.

Kazanjian: *What made you leave Alger to return to ICAP?*

Lyon: It was a combination of things. By 1988 our family had grown to five kids. Although my career at Alger was going well, and I was head of one of their two investment teams, I was from the Midwest and we decided we wanted to raise our children back in the Midwest. I was also kind of traumatized by the stock market crash of 1987. I mistakenly thought it was going to take a lot of juice out of the investment business and that I might be better off at a more value-oriented shop. When I came back to

ICAP in 1988, it was like a homecoming. While a few people had come and gone, it was pretty much exactly the same group of people. It was Bill Maloney, Gary Maurer, Russ Walter, and Don Neimann, plus four or five professional analysts and traders. Maloney had pretty much sidestepped the whole crash of 1987 by having nearly 50 percent in cash on the day of the crash. He earned a tremendous loyalty from his clients as a result of that. By then it was a $1 billion firm. I came back to work with the title of director of research.

Kazanjian: *A short time later, you actually led a buyout of the firm from Maloney, right?*

Lyon: That's correct. It took about a year (1991) to get everything in place. We had to get financing from two banks, and it was a very difficult lending environment due to the savings and loan and junk bond fiascos.

Kazanjian: *How do you describe yourself as investor?*

Lyon: I'd say we are relative value investors. There are also certain things we're not. We never buy momentum-oriented stocks. We don't buy any pure buy-and-hold growth stocks. But we will buy a growth stock that has fallen on hard times, and we will clearly buy classic value stocks. When I was at Wharton I did research showing you could beat the market by buying underfollowed securities. I've always believed there are many pockets of inefficiency in the market. These inefficiencies can even be found in really big companies that are not well followed. Sometimes they are spinoffs of even larger companies; other times they are complex multi-industry companies that fall through the cracks, or those with some pretty serious baggage. But, for whatever reason, they get less attention.

Kazanjian: *Do you strictly follow and invest in large-cap stocks?*

Lyon: Yes. Our universe is about 450 companies, which is not huge. We'll go down to market caps as low as $2 to $3 billion. So large and mid-cap.

Kazanjian: *What is this 450 stock universe comprised of?*

Lyon: Generally speaking it's the 400 largest stocks in the S&P 500, and the 50 or so largest non-U.S. multinationals that compete with major U.S. companies—such as Daimler Chrysler, Glaxo, or Royal Dutch. We've done very well with these big European companies and have used them widely in our portfolios since the early 1990s.

Kazanjian: *In fact you have a fund that invests exclusively in European stocks. Why do you like equities in that region so much?*

Lyon: We think Europe is less efficiently priced than the United States. The analyst community is smaller and the market isn't picked over as widely. We also thought the whole introduction of the euro and the integration of eastern Europe into western Europe would be a bigger deal than it turned out to be, and felt that the people there would develop a bigger habit for mutual funds and equity investing. We still think European stocks are less well analyzed, though we've been pretty disappointed in the economic progress there.

Kazanjian: *Does that mean you're less excited about Europe today than when you started the fund?*

Lyon: No. In fact we might even be more excited on a relative value basis for two reasons. One, we can go down the line and find European multinationals that are fully the equivalent in terms of size, scope, balance sheets, and growth prospects compared to their U.S. counterparts, yet sell for a lower multiple. They may even have just as much business in the United States as in Europe. Take Diageo, the U.K. spirits company. It has more U.S. business than Coca-Cola as a percentage of sales. Nestlé is a better business than General Mills and it's cheaper. You go down the list and we can find example after example where we are able to buy the same amount of growth for a lower multiple and probably a better balance sheet. You also don't have options problems, because stock options aren't big in Europe, and you generally have fewer pension issues and other baggage.

Kazanjian: *What percentage of your domestic portfolios do you keep in Europe?*

Lyon: It's about 10 percent of our core portfolio and 15 to 20 percent of the more concentrated Select Equity Fund. But it's been as high as 20 percent of our core portfolio. Our European fund is obviously 100 percent in that region.

Kazanjian: *Are there any other countries you invest in, or do you stay exclusively with Europe?*

Lyon: Except for Canada and Australia, we don't go beyond Europe. We have not gone into Asia or any of the emerging markets. We feel that our traditional skill set works just as well in Europe. We've always felt that in Europe you are more or less speaking the same language, with similar accounting, and more or less the same time zone. And you have more or less similar securities laws, which isn't always the case in other parts of the world.

Kazanjian: *What about currency fluctuations? Does that figure into your thinking?*

Lyon: Our view is that the impact of moderate currency moves is frequently offsetting. Most of the companies we own over there have substantial U.S. earnings such that if the dollar is going up or down, it may be largely neutralized. In other words, if the euro is going down, U.S. earnings get translated into more euros, so the amount of earnings per share goes up, and it balances out. In addition, if the euro declines, it may lead to more export growth, and so on. We don't hedge. We just don't think it's worth the extra expense.

Kazanjian: *So you start with this list of 450 U.S. and European stocks. How do you narrow those names down to the ones you actually want to buy?*

Lyon: We put the names through two quantitative screens. The first screen looks for relative value by putting a price target on every stock. This price target is computed by taking the market (S&P 500) multiple, multiplied by our relative PE target, times our estimate of earnings per share. You compare that number to where the stock is right now. Anything with a 15 percent potential upside from where it is today makes it through the first filter.

Kazanjian: *Can you expand a bit on how you come up with the relative value for a stock?*

Lyon: It really comes down to our view of the relative PE. Let's say the market PE is 16. We look at five different elements to come up with what we think is the appropriate relationship relative to the market for that specific company. The first thing we look at is the historical relationship over the last 5 to 10 years. Let's say a company has historically averaged about 80 percent of the stock market's PE. We'll take that 80 percent as a baseline and then qualitatively go though four other factors. The first is whether the industry the company operates in is accelerating or decelerating. At the margin is it doing better or worse? We'll count that either for or against the relative value. We then look at the company itself. Is it gaining or losing market share within its industry? This would add or subtract our view of the appropriate relative PE as well. We then look at the company's balance sheet, free cash, and other financial characteristics. We tend to adjust the relative PE up or down depending on strength in that dimension. Finally we look at the track record of management in terms of creating shareholder value.

Hypothetically, let's say we started with an 80 percent relative PE for a specific company and all of these other variables looked good. We might conclude that even though the stock used to sell at an 80 percent relative PE, it should now sell at a PE of 90 or 95 percent of the stock market and we would then multiply that number by our earnings estimate to get the potential upside.

Kazanjian: *It sounds like this model is actually part quantitative and part qualitative.*

Lyon: There's definitely some artistry to figuring the appropriate relationship between a stock and the market, and that is a key part of security analysis.

Kazanjian: *Looking for 15 percent upside seems to be a relatively modest expectation.*

Lyon: Yes, but again that's the minimum. And remember it's *relative*. You assume that the market normally has 10 percent upside, so if you add another 15 percent to that, the expectation is much higher. We're looking for 15 percent plus whatever you want to assume for stock market appreciation.

Kazanjian: *What's the other quantitative screen you put the stocks through?*

Lyon: We next screen all 450 stocks looking at the trend of First Call earnings estimate revisions. We're looking at the one-month change in these revisions. We then look at the five-year record for that company. We compare the change to how volatile the company revisions have been in the past. For instance, if Johnson & Johnson's earnings are drifting by a penny or two, that may be more important than General Motors' earnings vacillating by 50 cents because GM always vacillates by 50 cents. But J&J is so predictable that one or two pennies either way is a big deal. We then put all of the companies into deciles from best to worst.

We're not necessarily looking for positive trends, but rather trying to avoid major negative trends. We're trying to screen out companies where earnings are in a freefall on the cockroach theory that if you've seen one, there will be more. Of course, we'd rather have positive than negative revisions. Ultimately we're really trying to find the intersection, or sweet spot, where you've got more than 15 percent relative upside and revisions that are not extremely negative. Usually the combined screens will give us 50 to 75 names that meet this criteria. Our analysts then take this list and try to identify companies with powerful catalysts—like a new management, new products, strong pricing conditions—which could be the feature that unlocks this value. For example, a drug company may have a new product that will cause the stock to go up the requisite amount we require. Our analysts put together about a 15-page packet of information on each company along with a lot of data to document that catalyst. They make a presentation to our senior committee. We are trying to decide if the catalyst is truly in a new stage of understanding, or it is something that's well known.

Kazanjian: *A lot of people talk about looking for a catalyst, but how do you really find it?*

Lyon: It comes down to really identifying what a fairly powerful, but largely recognized company is. One of my favorite types of catalysts is a large, old company with a lot of great assets that has been run to the ground by previous management, and has now brought aboard a new person who's already successfully turned something else around. Those characteristics generally have a good risk-reward dynamic, and have worked well for me throughout my career.

Kazanjian: *If a company doesn't have an identifiable catalyst, is it automatically excluded?*

Lyon: Yes. It must have a meaningful catalyst for us to buy it.

Kazanjian: *Once you've found the catalyst, what else do you look at before deciding whether to buy the stock?*

Lyon: Corporate governance. Obviously we've already checked out the accounting and balance sheet. But we definitely want shareholder-friendly companies.

Kazanjian: *Perhaps you can give us an example of a stock you found to demonstrate this process in motion.*

Lyon: Philips Electronics in the Netherlands is a classic example of a large-cap turnaround. We bought the stock in the fall of 1993. At that time, Philips owned 85 percent of Polygram, which was one of the largest record companies in the world. That 85 percent was worth more than the whole price of Philips stock, so you got the rest of company for free. Philips was a huge industrial conglomerate that you were just being given. The company had been going nowhere for years. It brought in a new manager in the mid-1990s named Cor Boonstra who had worked at Sara Lee in the States. It was the first time a real outsider had come in to lead Philips. He began disassembling the company and the stock had a nice run after that. It was dramatically out of favor and had a really bad reputation when we bought it.

Kazanjian: *Do you still own it today?*

Lyon: We do. They've done something similar to what Jack Welch did with GE in the 1980s, in terms of simplification and focus.

Kazanjian: *As you're putting your portfolio together, do you pay attention to the market and the economy?*

Lyon: We have a monthly event called the ICAP macro overview. This goes back to the time when I first came here and Maloney slapped down all the *Bank Credit Analysts* in front of me. It's part of our culture. A lot of institutional investors disavow any market forecast and say they just buy stocks on a bottom-up basis. They tell investors they're economically agnostic. I think that's disingenuous. Are you going to buy American Airlines or General Motors if you think the price of oil is going up and the economy is going down? No matter how big a turnaround you forecast you're not going to buy into what you foresee as a very negative economic scenario. Implicit in all of this is that everyone has some type of overview.

We have our own proprietary economic checklist, our own analysis of earnings trends, and our own view as to what parts of the market are most likely to do well. It's kind of like watching a pilot. He sits there with a clipboard to check off all the key factors before taking off. It's basic common sense that if you're going to buy a retailer, you want to know what's going on with the economy, debt levels, and those sorts of things.

Kazanjian: *By the same token, does this macro forecast lead you to overweight certain industries, and therefore specifically to go out looking for companies in those industries?*

Lyon: Yes. In fact, currently we have a very large overweight in agriculture. It's an industry that really has no stock market weight. Most investors just ignore it. We own the two biggest plays—John Deere and Archer Daniels, Midland.

Kazanjian: *What led you to agriculture?*

Lyon: It's supply and demand. Demand for high-protein diets coming out of Asia is growing. There's a certain core level of income, and once you get past that, the desire to have luxuries, including meat, goes up. Every day in China, India, and Vietnam, thousands of people are crossing that threshold and all of a sudden they want, and need, more protein. Many of these countries have only a limited amount of arable land. In addition, all of the key drivers for U.S. farmers are positive. Demand is strong, inventory is low, cash flow and land prices are up, and debt is down.

Kazanjian: *Did John Deere and Archer Daniels Midland show up on your list anyway?*

Lyon: Yes, but the macro view added to their attractiveness. Sometimes we have what we call a thematic catalyst, which in this case is that the growth of high-protein diets in Asia is good for U.S. agriculture.

Kazanjian: *What makes you sell a stock?*

Lyon: We've had the same common-sense rules for 34 years. We set very specific price targets based on our relative PEs. When a stock gets to within 5 percent of the target, we will start to sell the stock unless the analyst can document a case that the target should be raised. The only way a target is raised is if the earnings estimate is higher or our relative PE should be bumped up. The relative PE can be boosted only if one of the other elements I referred to earlier has improved. You want to sell on strength, so when a stock reaches its target, you should be disciplined about selling. Second, if a catalyst isn't working, we'll sell the stock. We buy stocks for very specific reasons and if they don't work, we get out. The third reason to sell a stock is that in our core portfolio we'll only own up to 45 stocks. So if we are full and we approve a new idea, we've got to sell one to make room.

Kazanjian: *You have a couple of stocks in the portfolio that wouldn't normally be associated with a value investor, namely Microsoft and General Electric. Are they there because of the so-called relative value?*

Lyon: Yes, they are. We bought Microsoft in the spring of 2004 when the European commission was all over them. We knew they were under a lot of pressure to unleash some of their cash horde, which had reached $60 to $70 billion. We thought one of the catalysts would be Bill Gates sharing some of this money with his shareholders. We started buying the stock at around $23 to $24 a share when it had $5 a share in cash. At the time it was selling at about the same multiple as the market net of the cash. Even if Microsoft didn't grow more than 10 percent a year, that's faster than the market and the quality of those earnings is more predictable. You can't get more predictable than a virtual monopoly.

Kazanjian: *What's your outlook for the market over the next few years?*

Lyon: We're starting with a market multiple in the United States that's somewhat higher than average. Interest rates are below where they should be and profit margins are high, so 1990s-type returns are impossible. I think you're probably looking at a market return similar to the rate of growth in earnings.

As for market styles, Lyon believes value and growth are pretty much in equilibrium at present. Still, he feels that over longer time periods, value will do better because the style prevents you from owning too many losers. "The problem with growth stocks is the survival factor," he says. "I call them the trap doors, where you can lose 30, 40, 50, 99 percent." Lyon says his research shows growth outperforms value by about 1 percent annually over long stretches of time. "It's not because value stocks go up so much, it's because growth stocks have these periodic trap doors," he adds.

Lyon also notes that small-caps seem rather expensive to him right now, so he recommends overweighting large-caps in a diversified portfolio.

ANDY PILARA

RS Investments

Like most young boys, Andy Pilara once dreamed of becoming a professional baseball player. In fact, his love of sports is what originally sparked his interest in stocks. As a youth, he'd devour the sports pages of his hometown newspaper, the *San Francisco Chronicle*. Back then, the stock tables were part of the sports section, and all those funny-looking numbers fascinated him. Before long, Pilara found himself taking an investment class and developing a friendship with the instructor that eventually would pave the way to his future in the business.

After almost two decades of running his own value-oriented one-man boutique, Pilara joined RS Investments in 1993. While the firm has long been known as a growth-oriented shop, Pilara has made a strong name for himself as head of the RS Investments value group. Pilara, 63, runs three funds, all of which have been top performers in their respective categories, including the RS Partners, Global Natural Resources, and Value (formerly known as Contrarian) funds.

In describing his strategy, Pilara says he's a low-expectation investor who focuses on bottom-up analysis and cash flows. He follows small- and mid-cap stocks and has found some of his biggest winners over the years in some rather unusual places.

Kazanjian: *Is it true that a friend took you to an investment course when you were in junior high school?*

Pilara: It is. When I was 12 or 13, the mother of the catcher of my baseball team brought me to an investment class taught by Claude Rosenberg, who was the head of research at the time for J. Barth and Company. I really enjoyed it. In the summer, I would go down and walk along Montgomery Street in San Francisco, sit inside the brokerage houses, and learn as much as I could about this fascinating thing called the stock market. I made an investment a year or two later in a company called Yuba Consolidated. The stock went from $4 to $16 and I got hooked. My dad was a printer for 40-some years and I watched him sweat and toil with his hands. As I made four times my money in Yuba, I saw that you could make money investing without using your hands. During the class, I told Rosenberg I'd like to work for him someday. We kept in contact, and when I graduated from St. Mary's College, I called him and said I'd like to work for him, but had other things I needed to learn. Instead, I took a job with the Federal Reserve Bank of San Francisco.

Kazanjian: *What did you do there?*

Pilara: I was a bank examiner. That job lasted about 13 months. I then went back to Rosenberg and said I'd like to work for him. He hired me to be a runner in the research department. It was a great experience. It was my first exposure to my most important lesson: the value of grassroots research. Getting out there and seeing companies, walking through the stores and factories, talking to customers, vendors, and competitors. After working in the research department at J. Barth and Company, I became the first candidate for the firm's registered rep program in training to become a retail salesman. I spent three years doing the things salespeople do. I then moved into an institutional sales position. J. Barth and Company specialized in West Coast research. As institutional salespeople, we sold this research to investment management firms throughout the country. Among my accounts at the time were Capital Research (managers of the American Funds) and several hedge funds in New York. That job was really my MBA. I probably spent more time asking these managers questions than I did servicing the accounts. It was especially insightful to be exposed to the Capital Research process. One of my New York accounts was Steinhart, Fine and Berkowitz. Michael Steinhart was the guru of trading, and I learned a lot just watching him at work. I also learned a great deal about research from Jerry Fine.

At that time I knew I wanted to manage money. I started to get involved in trading and research at J. Barth and Company. I would try to go on research visits with our analysts. Salespeople don't do that any more. I also would sit on the trading desk.

Kazanjian: *When did you make the move from selling to managing money?*

Pilara: In 1974 I created a value investment management boutique called Pilara Associates. It was a one-man shop. Part of my education was picking up accounting books that I knew some of the Harvard MBAs used when they were in school. I educated myself in accounting and read some of the popular investment books of that era, including Phil Fisher's *Common Stocks and Uncommon Profits*. I would make notes about how Fisher approached analyzing a company and work that into my own template. When I went out to visit a company, I had one sheet for all my production questions, one sheet for all my marketing questions, and one for all my financial questions. It helped me to organize and pattern myself after a very successful investor.

Kazanjian: *When you started your own shop, why did you decide to focus on the value style and study value managers? Was it deliberate?*

Pilara: I kind of grew up in the business in the era of companies like Ampex and Memorex. When times were good, you made a lot of money. When times were bad, you lost a lot. That didn't fit my personality well. I'm a poor loser. I found the pain of losing far outweighed the pleasure of the gain, and became a value investor very quickly after some losing experiences. I really became a value investor two or three years before starting my own operation. I was a security analyst in the mold of Ben Graham, doing deep book-value work. It worked well, and 1974 was a great time to be a value investor and small-cap stock picker.

Kazanjian: *So you originally were led to the value style because of your desire to lower the risk of investing in stocks?*

Pilara: Yes. Emotionally I was trying to remove that pain of loss. As I say to my analysts, tell me about your serious money ideas. Tell me where we can invest big money. Don't tell me the latest fancy stocks. That's not what we're about. I really invested in plain-vanilla companies.

Kazanjian: *Have you always been value-oriented in life as well, like many of the other value managers I've interviewed over the years, including several of those in this book?*

Pilara: I'd say so. I grew up in an Italian-Catholic household that was both economically and religiously conservative. Marrying that background with my growth stock investing experiences made the transition to value easy.

I also made a transition in my "value process" from deep value to a focus on cash flow returns. At a point, I looked at my portfolios and while they were doing well, I asked myself if there was a common denominator to my losers. The stocks were cheap for a reason: They were poor businesses. I then started to investigate how I could improve my process. I still spend a lot of time on process. I went to Northwestern University, which in those days had something called Merger Week at the business school. It focused on cash flow return and how to create shareholder value. This really turned my head. I realized I could look at and evaluate businesses with this tool, using a discounted cash flow methodology. I moved from a process driven by PE and book value to a cash flow return methodology designed to improve results by avoiding poor businesses.

Kazanjian: *What made you leave your own firm to join RS Investments?*

Pilara: I met Paul Stephens in the early 1970s. He was one of the principals at Robertson Stephens, an investment banking firm that also had a money management arm. He was building a very successful money management business and I really liked the people at the firm. I talked to Paul in 1993 about joining the firm, and ultimately did in September 1993.

Kazanjian: *You must have been a bit like a fish out of water, because Robertson Stephens was very much a growth shop at that time.*

Pilara: Yes, and it still is. What interested me is Paul ran what was called the Contrarian Fund. Paul has always been a growth stock investor, but he has valuation disciplines and I felt comfortable bringing him my ideas. In 1995, I started the Partners Fund, which is our small-cap value product. A year later I launched the Natural Resources Fund. And in 1999 I became portfolio manager of the Contrarian Fund.

Kazanjian: *Why did you start a natural resources fund?*

Pilara: I've always been drawn to the natural resources area because I like putting my hands on a product. Unlike a technology company or retailer, once you have your mine in the ground, all you have to worry about is being a low-cost producer. This area of the market lends itself to financial analysis. You can easily run discounted cash flow models with different commodity price assumptions. The natural resources sector has become a good diversifier to technology. Natural resources stocks are negatively covariant to technology stocks and this makes them a good addition to one's portfolio. Plus, I think we're in a new area for commodities. Natural resources look like an even more attractive asset class today than when we started the fund.

Kazanjian: *Why?*

Pilara: I think if I were to ask a company one question, it would be how much capacity have you built in the last three years and how much do you plan to build in the next three years? Had investors asked that question in technology a few years ago, they would have saved themselves a lot of pain. There's been very little capacity added in most major commodities in the last three years. Commodity prices are primarily driven by supply, not by demand. We have major structural events going on, in which the two largest populations in the world—China and India—are moving toward a more middle-class society. When you move toward middle class, your consumption of basic materials increases dramatically. Commodities are the basic building blocks of a middle-class economy. I've not seen resource companies generating as much free cash flow as they are today. When I visited all the paper companies in Canada four or five years ago, I started hearing talk about return on investment rather than the next big paper machine they were going to build. All of a sudden the energy companies are starting to talk about return on investment and so are the mining companies. The mindset and fundamentals of the resource business have changed. These companies are now terrific cash flow generators. Some of them realize they can get good stock performance if they can get their rates of return above their cost of capital.

Kazanjian: *The natural resources group has done well in recent years. Is the sector still fertile ground for value investors?*

Pilara: Yes, assuming you pick and choose your spots. We think that the resources sector has favorable supply/demand fundamentals for the next three to five years. China will certainly be a major factor on the demand side. Keep in mind that commodity stocks will always be more cyclical than the general stock market.

Kazanjian: *Because of your affinity for this sector, do you keep large weightings in natural resources in all of the funds you manage?*

Pilara: No, we are generalists. We do not have an affinity for any particular sector. We don't make big sector bets in the Partners and Contrarian funds. We try to have a diversified portfolio where we can get appropriate negative covariance. That negative covariance is sometimes presented by the natural resources investments. But it's strictly a bottom-up process with an affinity for good business models available at a cheap price.

Kazanjian: *You look for stocks with market capitalizations from $100 million to around $16 billion. That's a pretty wide universe to choose from. How do you find your investment ideas?*

Pilara: We try to work with a focused list of 150 to 200 companies. This includes the 50 to 70 stocks in our typical portfolio. Our ideas come from various sources. Grassroots research generates ideas. We like to turn over as many rocks as possible. These company meetings also generate candidates for our portfolio.

Over the last 30 years I've had contact with a number of good companies and executives that I want us to always follow. I call this our farm team. It wasn't created from a screen, but from my experiences observing these executives allocate capital.

In addition, because the market today is so short-term oriented, when companies miss earnings in one quarter it creates opportunities for us. I look for companies with good business models experiencing short-term problems. We take a three-year view, so we think of ourselves more as business analysts than stock market analysts. Nobody analyzing a business would get too concerned about one bum quarter.

Kazanjian: *What's more of the company-specific analysis you do when deciding whether to buy a stock?*

Pilara: Above all, what we're doing is trying to assess the business model. It's all about unit economics and returns on capital. If we're looking at a retail concept, we'll go look at the store model. How much capital does it take to open one store? If the company is leasing this store, we will capitalize the lease. Then we'll look at the store model in terms of cash flow returns. If it looks like a company has an ability to earn above the cost of capital, we'll do additional due diligence. This includes looking at 10-Q's and 10-K's. We also look at the annual meeting proxy letter. This tells you how management is compensated. We always pay attention to the difference in pay between the CEO and the executive vice president or the CFO, whoever is next in line. If the CEO is making $1,000,000 and the executive VP is making $250,000 a year, you're wasting your time talking to anybody but the CEO.

We read annual reports backwards. The first thing that's usually inside the back cover is the board of directors. All of this has become much more important in our post-Enron world. We want to read the footnotes. It's sort of like being a detective. The best compliment I received was when a CEO said to me, "I feel like I'm talking to Detective Columbo." Columbo asked the apparently inane questions, but at the end of the day he solved the murder. That's what we're trying to do: ask simple questions that will lead us to an understanding of the business.

The first financial statement you come to by reading the annual report backwards is the flow of funds statement. I want to marry that with the balance sheet. Residually we look at the profit and loss (P and L) statement, because earnings result from capital deployment. That's why it's foolish to concentrate on quarterly earnings. The quarterly outcome has been decided a year or two before by the capital deployed to drive those earnings. When we visit with a company, we spend most of the time on our first visit discussing capital deployment.

One of the other ways we'll make a judgment about whether we want to continue with the analysis is by looking at the company's enterprise value and capital account. I define the capital account of a company as the total assets less non–interest-bearing current liabilities minus cash. We also look at it on a gross basis. By that I mean we add back the accumulated depreciation on the property account. What I'm really trying to do is see what we are paying versus the company's imbedded capital. The other things we'll take a look at are EBITDA (earnings before interest, taxes, depreciation, and amortization) and estimated free cash flow.

Kazanjian: *It sounds like a fairly complicated process, especially for those without an accounting background.*

Pilara: It's really not. It's not high math. What's noticeable is there's not a focus on the income statement. If I look at one thing on the P and L it is gross margins. We want to know whether this is a commodity business, or one in which the company has a proprietary advantage. If somebody tells me he's got a proprietary product and I see gross margins of 17 percent, he's fooling himself. As far as we're concerned, a proprietary product has growth margins north of 30 percent. But the key point for us is cash flow returns.

Kazanjian: *You do all of this research before talking to management. Is having a discussion with company executives required before you'll buy the stock?*

Pilara: Yes, and we can't do a management visit without doing our homework first because we want to be prepared.

Kazanjian: *Perhaps it would help if you gave us an example of a company you bought and the analysis that led you to this decision.*

Pilara: Several years back we bought a company called Fresh Del Monte. It's a fresh produce company that sells Del Monte bananas and pineapples. I first met the company when it went public. Management came into our offices. I liked the fundamentals of the business, and I admired the way they managed their capital allocation process. This was all confirmed when I went down to see the company shortly after the IPO. I sat down with the chief operating officer and asked him about the capital allocation process. He had a stack of papers on his desk and pulled out a paper with numbers on the acquisition of a motorcycle. He had the capital they spent and the rationale for spending it. I was impressed. Also, this was a company with new management and I saw there would soon be a material improvement in the balance sheet. They were using free cash flow to pay off debt. The returns on capital were above the costs of capital and it met our criteria at that time on our cash flow model.

Kazanjian: *What happened to the stock?*

Pilara: Subsequent to the IPO it eventually went down to $4 a share.

Kazanjian: *Did you buy in at the IPO?*

Pilara: We made an investment on the IPO. The stock price declined after the company went public.

Kazanjian: *Were you buying more as the stock went down?*

Pilara: We purchased more as the stock declined and substantially increased our position when shares were trading below $6. It was obvious that banana pricing was deteriorating, but while this part of the business had the largest revenues, it made the smallest contribution to cash flows. All the while, the higher gross margin pineapple business continued to improve. At $4 a share the company had a market cap of $200 million and an enterprise value of approximately $500 million, with cash flows in the $150–$200 million range. At that level, I figured I was buying a good brand name for a cash flow multiple under 3. Within the next three years, the company's earnings per share were almost as much as the lowest price I bought the stock at. It went from $400 million in debt to zero in two and a half years. The stock went from $4 to $28.

Kazanjian: *When did you sell out?*

Pilara: I sold the stock in the $20s. Our target price was reduced after fundamentals in the pineapple business changed and it became a more competitive business.

Kazanjian: *Do you have specific rules for when you sell a stock?*

Pilara: We have a couple of sell disciplines. If a stock reaches our warranted value and there's been no change in the fundamentals, we sell. If the returns of the business start to deteriorate, we make a call to management. We may or may not sell, but it raises a red flag. If returns are deteriorating and we become uncomfortable, as at Fresh Del Monte, we sell. If the company makes a large capital acquisition, we discuss it with management. If we don't believe it's creating value, we will sell.

Kazanjian: *Fresh Del Monte turned out okay for you, but my guess is the average investor wouldn't have held on as the stock went from $16 to $4. They probably would have sold out sooner, to keep a cap on losses. Weren't you tempted to get out?*

Pilara: This was an unusual example. I would say that 90 percent of the time if a stock goes down 15 percent and the fundamentals haven't changed, we'll add to our position. I think the reason for our good performance is not because we've had a lot of home runs, but rather because we haven't had a lot of big losers in the portfolio.

Kazanjian: *Does that mean that if the price drops 15 percent and something has changed for the worse you'll get out?*

Pilara: If the fundamentals have changed, we get out. Part of our philosophy here is that we're low-expectation investors. I tell my guys, "If you fall out of a window, fall out the basement window. Don't fall out the top-floor window." Most times we go into stocks with low expectations. We're all about losing less, not making more. For the most part, when one of our companies misses its earnings, nobody cares because it's not a high-expectation stock.

Kazanjian: *True, although you mentioned that most of the names you buy are having some short-term problems. I suppose there's an investment risk that these problems will get even worse.*

Pilara: No. Most of our companies do not have short-term problems. Occasionally we look at companies going through some short-term problem, but we're trying to buy after the short-term problem has been worked out. We're not playing turnarounds. We still want a company with a good business model.

Kazanjian: *One of your huge home runs over the last few years was China Yuchai. What led you to that unusual company?*

Pilara: When I took over the Contrarian Fund in 1999, China Yuchai was in the portfolio. This was the second largest diesel motor company in China. Unit volumes were increasing at a dramatic rate. The fundamentals looked very good, and the stock was under $2. Within 18 months, the company would almost earn our inherited cost basis. Yuchai was a "10-bagger." Home runs like that don't come along that often. I certainly don't expect them. I'm just trying to hit singles and doubles without striking out along the way.

Kazanjian: *Do you pay any attention to PE ratios at all?*

Pilara: Sure, we look at the PE, but we don't think it's robust enough to give us the information we need as a primary assessment of whether this is a business we want to own. The reason is that when you look at the price-to-earnings, you don't solve for how much capital it took to generate the earnings, which is really important. Nor will it tell us about free cash flow.

Kazanjian: *Given that, let's say you're looking at a company selling at what you deem to be 50 percent below what it's worth, yet it has a PE of 30 or 40. Would you still buy the stock?*

Pilara: That really doesn't happen very often. But there are instances where a company is currently losing money, there is no PE, and it is selling below its business value.

Kazanjian: *How diversified do you keep your portfolios, in terms of the number of holdings?*

Pilara: In the small-cap portfolio, we own around 60 names, and approximately 50 names in the mid-cap portfolio. Our core position is 2 to 4 percent at cost.

Kazanjian: *When looking at the mistakes you've made over the years when it comes to picking stocks, do the losers tend to have any common themes?*

Pilara: The common theme is that we made a mistake in evaluating the business model and its sustainability. Sometimes you make people mistakes, but more often it's not properly assessing the business model.

Kazanjian: *Carrying that further, what would you say is the biggest mistake individual investors make?*

Pilara: Not understanding the business and unreal return expectations.

Kazanjian: *What are some realistic expectations over the next 5 to 10 years, in your opinion?*

Pilara: Less than a 10 percent annualized total return from the market. I say that because when you look back at market history, a significant part of total returns have come from the dividend yield. Dividend yields today are only 1.7 percent. If you look at the last 20 years, you had a period of declining interest rates and declining inflation. It's been the best of times for stocks. I do not expect interest rates and inflation to exert such a positive influence on equities in the next few years. I believe we're in a low return environment for most asset classes.

While Pilara still loves sports, and emphasizes that just about everyone else on his investment team does as well, golf is about the only game he actively plays these days. In his spare time, Pilara collects photography, especially post–World War I social documentary photographs, but maintains his real passion in life is the investment business. "I'm one of those guys who says, 'Thank God it's Monday,'" he adds.

RICHARD PZENA

Pzena Investment Management

Rich Pzena is always on the prowl for solid companies with temporary troubles. That way he can pick up shares at bargain-basement prices as they're being thrown out by the rest of Wall Street. Granted, it's not easy finding companies like this. When stocks get cheap, it's usually for a good reason. So Pzena and his team have to dig deep to figure out whether the current problems are fixable or permanent, and they must constantly reassess their evaluations.

While Pzena studied investing while earning his MBA at Wharton, and even wrote a thesis exploring the theories put forth by value investing leg-

ends Benjamin Graham and David Dodd, he originally started out working in the oil industry. A headhunter soon convinced him he could make a
lot more money as an oil industry analyst on Wall Street, and he has been
involved in the investment industry ever since.

After holding a number of senior-level industry jobs, including director
of research for Sanford Bernstein, Pzena gave in to his entrepreneurial
yearnings and started Pzena Investment Management in 1995. In addition
to managing money for a number of large pension and institutional
clients, the 45-year-old investor and his team also run the top-rated John
Hancock Classic Value Fund.

A classic contrarian, his ideal company sells for a low price relative to
normalized earnings, is run by a management team armed with a sound
recovery plan, has a good business model, and is cheap enough that the
share price offers significant downside protection.

Kazanjian: *How did you first get interested in investing?*

Pzena: My father was very interested in the stock market as a hobby. He
was an engineer and always wanted to make his million dollars in the
stock market.

Kazanjian: *Did he accomplish that goal?*

Pzena: Twice, but he lost it both times. He made it prior to the 1987 crash
and then lost a lot. And he made it again in the late 1990s, though he held
on too long.

Kazanjian: *He should have just let you manage his money.*

Pzena: He really should have.

Kazanjian: *Is your father a value investor also?*

Pzena: He used to be until the Internet bubble. He got this idea that fuel
cells were the way of the future. He tied up all his money in fuel cell, alternative energy cars. Now he's starting over again.

Kazanjian: *As a student at Wharton, did you plan to get into the investment
business?*

Pzena: I had more of an entrepreneurial orientation. It's funny how you
figure things out over time. I had an uncle who was accountant. He did a
lot of work with small businesses and I was really intrigued by that. I
wound up majoring in accounting, all the way up to my last course in au-

diting. A partner in an accounting firm taught the class. When I started to figure out what you did as an accountant, I said, "Forget it! This isn't for me." They have a program at Wharton where you can enter graduate school for your MBA before getting a bachelor's degree. They effectively let you double count your last year. I switched my major to finance and got very interested in the stock market. For my master's thesis, I teamed up with two people and did a paper revisiting Graham and Dodd. (Benjamin Graham and David Dodd are considered to be the fathers of value investing.) Our research was published in the *Journal of Portfolio Management* back in 1981.

Kazanjian: *What did your research conclude?*

Pzena: That their method of investing was alive and well, although it was a bit tough to test because you couldn't run computer screens. We just went through stock books looking for companies selling below the value of their working capital, and the method worked great.

Kazanjian: *By that point, were you determined to be a value investor, or was this paper just testing the waters for you?*

Pzena: I think value investing is sort of innate. It's not something you learn. You're either a bargain hunter or you're an optimist. The bargain hunters are the ones where it's ingrained in you from the first day you're born because your mother's taking you to buy clothes only when they're on sale. I still have that orientation in all aspects of my life. The people who are trying to find the next Microsoft are a totally different breed.

Kazanjian: *Does the Graham and Dodd method still work today?*

Pzena: Something similar works. The problem is there's almost nothing selling below net working capital right now. Graham's original book said if you can buy these stocks at less than what you could liquidate the business for, and it's earning a profit, that discrepancy doesn't make any sense and you should just buy it. In 1980 the Dow was 800, so you could still find stocks like that. Today you have to modify it a bit or you would find absolutely nothing to invest in because of where the market is.

Kazanjian: *I want to pick up on something you said about value being a way of life. I couldn't agree with you more that those with more of a value orientation should follow a value strategy when choosing individual stocks. In all my years of interviewing managers and writing about the markets, I've found that following a discipline and sticking with it is really the key to long-term success. But for those* *value-oriented folks investing exclusively through mutual funds, does it make sense for them to put all of their money in value funds, or should they also seek out good growth managers for proper diversification?*

Pzena: It's an age-old question that's very tough to answer. It would be hard to advise somebody that my way of doing it is the only right way. I know that's not true. On the other hand, I know growth stock investing is very hard. With value investing, the odds are with you arithmetically. Unless you really screw it up, you should do okay. With growth stock investing, you must be able to uncover good companies that are going to do even better than everybody already thinks. I don't put any of my money in growth stocks, but I never advise other people to do that. There are good growth managers. I especially think that momentum investing is a sensible strategy because it works. There's enough data to show that if a stock is going up based on whatever momentum you're looking at, be it earnings or price, it will continue to do well until it reaches some point. If you can ride that and do it well, you can make money.

Kazanjian: *The key is sticking with your own discipline or giving your money to managers who do the same.*

Pzena: That's right. Over the course of my life I've had people show me venture capital investments that sounded so great. I've been tempted a couple times and not once have I made money on those.

Kazanjian: *What did you do after getting your MBA?*

Pzena: I went to work in the oil industry for a few years at Amoco. I originally started in the treasurer's office doing financing work. It was pretty fascinating. Oil was the largest segment of the S&P 500 then, at over 30 percent. The industry view was that oil prices were going to $200 a barrel.

Kazanjian: *When did you make the transition into the investment business?*

Pzena: After about six years at Amoco, I got a call from a headhunter who asked whether I wanted to be an oil analyst. I couldn't see why anyone would want to do that. I read the Wall Street research published on Amoco and felt they really didn't do anything other than copy what was in the annual report and give a one-year forecast. I certainly never thought of it as being a high-level career. Then the recruiter told me I could make a lot of money doing that and convinced me to meet the guy at Sanford Bernstein who later became my boss. I really hit it off with him. While at Amoco, I was investing on my own and had started an investment club, so I definitely had an interest in investing. I went over to Bernstein in January 1986 where I followed the oil industry and wrote reports on big oil stocks.

Kazanjian: *Where did you go from there?*

Pzena: I never liked the sell-side of the business. After a couple of years, I was anxious to move over to the money management side. I started making lots of noise, and they finally gave me the job of starting up their small-cap product. Bernstein is purely a value shop, so it was a perfect fit. I think that's why I hit it off so well during my initial interview. Before long, there was a big shakeup in the research department, and the firm asked me to take over as research director for all of the domestic equity portfolios. A couple of years later, Zalman Bernstein retired and they asked me to become director of U.S. equity investments. That meant overseeing both the investment and research side. I was also helping to manage a $20 billion portfolio of large-cap value stocks.

Kazanjian: *That's quite a responsibility for such a young guy.*

Pzena: Yes, I was still in my early 30s. I held this job for five years, and decided to go out on my own at the end of 1995.

Kazanjian: *Why leave such a lucrative job?*

Pzena: Two reasons really. One is that I heard from my father all his life about how he wanted to start his own business, but never did, and it was a personal dream of mine. Second, Bernstein was after me to take a global investment job, and at 37 I started to wonder whether I wanted to be committed there forever. I decided it was the right time in my life to go out on my own, and if it didn't work, I'd go back and get a job. As it turned out, it worked great. The first two years we did really well, in terms of performance, but 1998 and 1999 were probably the worst years of my life. The Internet bubble was in full force and everything was going through the roof except what we were investing in.

Kazanjian: *Did you have a hard time building assets?*

Pzena: It went faster than I expected. The hardest part was finding competent staff. We had $100 million by the end of the first year, $400 million by the end of the second year. We had a good first year and were up 30 percent, which helped.

Kazanjian: *As a value investor, what types of things do you pay attention to from a macro perspective? Oil prices? The level of stock market? The economy?*

Pzena: None of those. It's really more mundane than that. It's really just looking at businesses and seeing if you can get them at a good price. When you start predicting where the economy or oil prices or interest rates will go, it's not the same as buying a stock worth $100 for $50. While we tend to buy businesses when they're depressed, one might look and say we're forecasting that the business will be better in the future. Yes, we are doing that. But we're forecasting this based on years and years of historically demonstrated success, not on what's happening in the world today. I do, however, sometimes react to situations. The most recent example I can cite is air travel. People stopped flying in airplanes after we had a global economic slowdown because of terrorism, SARS, and corporate travel budgets that were put under pressure. The airlines have big fixed costs. One of the first things they do to deal with that is cancel orders for new planes. When the delivery of airplanes plummeted, Boeing's stock collapsed. We felt this was a spectacular opportunity to buy a business where the future earnings would rise once the level of demand returned to normal. When you count the airplanes that have to be replaced because they wear out over time, and couple that with the normal growth in air traffic, you can do the arithmetic to see what Boeing would earn if it was delivering aircraft at a normal level of demand. Were we predicting the economy? I guess we were predicting that things would rebound to where they've been over long periods of time. But what we really spend time on is looking for areas where the present reality deviates dramatically from long-term trends. Then we ask ourselves whether something has permanently changed or whether this is just a temporary condition.

Kazanjian: *Do you find these companies using computer screening?*

Pzena: We use a computer model that simulates what I just articulated. The model looks at the long history of Boeing, for example, and says if things keep going at the same rate of growth and margin structure this business had over long periods of time, how much money should the company earn? The model merely ranks the current price you pay for shares relative to this naïve extrapolation of history. Boeing historically grew 8 percent a year and produced 8 percent margins. Extrapolating that into the future you would see that Boeing should earn $5 a share. If the stock is selling in the $20s, it's waving its hands saying, "Look at me. I'm a potentially cheap stock." With this list in hand, we apply additional research to the stocks trying to answer three simple questions. Are the problems temporary or permanent? Is the business itself any good? And should it earn more money than it's currently earning?

Kazanjian: *Can you expand on the specific financial variables you are screening for?*

Pzena: We're ranking stocks on current price compared to what we call normal earnings power, or a simple extrapolation of their historic trends into the future. It's not simplistic, in that we're not looking at PEs, price-to-book, price-to-sales, or price-to-cash flow. We're looking at price-to-implied earnings given the history of the company. If the company has historically grown at 10 percent a year, we'll assume it keeps growing at 10 percent a year in the model. If it's producing 4 percent margins, we'll assume it keeps producing 4 percent margins. It's complex to implement, but the concept is very simple.

Kazanjian: *Can you give us another example of a stock you found through this process?*

Pzena: One we're looking at right now is Hewlett-Packard. HP was in the news in the summer of 2004 after missing its earnings, and the stock got killed. It recently showed up in our computer screening. HP has grown its revenues 10.6 percent per year over the last 10 years. Its margins have averaged 8.1 percent over the last 10 years, and 4½ percent over the last three years. We use an average weighting of the two to come up with a naïve margin projection. Our naïve margin projection in this case is 6.7 percent. So, if this company continued to grow at 10 percent a year, and produced 6.7 percent margins, five years from now it would earn $2.40 a share. The current price of the stock, as we're talking today, is $16.50. Divided by $2.40, that means it's trading at 6.9 times its normal earnings power. Out of the 500-stock large-cap universe I'm looking at, that ranks HP as 19, meaning it's the 19th cheapest stock.

Kazanjian: *Cheap because it's selling for 6.9 times your estimated earnings power?*

Pzena: Yes. The average stock today sells for 13 times normal earnings, so it's quite inexpensive.

Kazanjian: *In essence, you are looking at what the future PE of the company will look like.*

Pzena: That's right. We're ranking it on what its earnings should be five years out as a first pass.

Kazanjian: *Once you find an idea that looks good on a valuation basis, what comes next?*

Pzena: Next we do a sanity check in a two-week research project. We read everything we can find about the company, including their own propaganda and what analysts are writing, to see what's going wrong. In the case of HP, the issues are competition from Dell and the merger with Compaq. The company missed earnings in its large enterprise systems group, so we'll see what's going on there. From our perspective, when you really dig into HP, you see it has a spectacular printer business with very high profit margins from the ink and laser cartridges. The computer business is pretty hard to figure out. The investment question in HP's case becomes how sustainable the printer franchise is, and whether the computer franchise is just underperforming right now or whether it's a permanent mess. An analyst will look into this and come back with an answer. In this case, the analyst and I both think that HP is interesting. It has the second largest global technology franchise in the world. IBM can't possibly be the only player making money on a broad range of products. But there's still a lot to figure out, in terms of whether HP's servers are competitive with Dell's, and whether the problems in other divisions are temporary or permanent. HP is a good example because the reality is, you don't know what's going to happen in the future. What we can do is see there really is a franchise here. If all goes well, it should earn $2.50 a share. The downside case is probably what the stock is currently trading for. That means the upside case is significantly better.

Kazanjian: *How do you determine what the right price to pay is?*

Pzena: It's pretty straightforward. When bargains galore exist, you can build portfolio trading at around 6 times normal earnings power. When there aren't a whole lot of bargains around, you pay 9 to 10 times normal earnings power. We view anything below 8 times normal earnings in the present environment as being particularly cheap. Again, that's normalized earnings looking out five years. We're trying to buy companies at half of our objective price. Going back to HP, if I take $2.50 a share times 13, or the normalized earnings power, I get $32.50 as fair value for HP. If I can buy it for around $16, this means it's selling for about half of our objective.

Kazanjian: *How many stocks do you keep in the portfolio altogether?*

Pzena: Around 30 to 40. We're pretty concentrated.

Kazanjian: *Given this concentration, if you find a new idea you like, will you sell another stock you currently own to make room for it?*

Pzena: When you look at a portfolio, some of the things will be as cheap as what you're buying today, and others will have worked out fine. If we want to buy something new and don't have cash in the portfolio, we'll sell whatever stock is closest to fair value. Alternatively, we'll sell stocks that reach fair value and sit on the cash if we don't have something else ready to buy.

Kazanjian: *Do you always sell a stock once it reaches fair value?*

Pzena: Always. There are no exceptions.

Kazanjian: *But who's to say the stock won't keep going higher?*

Pzena: It could, but when you're paying above fair value for a stock, you have to consider whether holding cash is better. You could play the momentum game, and come up with all sorts of great reasons why you should continue to hold it. But I think you do that at your own peril. Once a stock reaches fair value, if anything goes wrong, and things always go wrong, you don't have a favorable risk-reward trade-off.

Kazanjian: *What you just said assumes the stock has worked out for you. What about when either the story doesn't play out, or the stock keeps going down? At what point will you get rid of it?*

Pzena: I believe that having rules about selling, like selling if the stock drops 20 percent, makes absolutely no sense. If something I own goes down, I want to be able to go look at it again completely from scratch and see whether I got it wrong, putting emotions aside. Were my earnings estimates out to lunch and did I just blow it? If so, I'll sell. If instead I conclude the market is crazy, there's nothing wrong with this company, and it has the same earnings power as I previously thought, that means it's now even cheaper, and we want to buy more. Sometimes it's in between. It's not quite as good as we originally thought, but now the price is lower, so we'll hold. We're remaking the same investment decision over again. It just so happens we already own the stock.

Kazanjian: *What's an example of a stock that just didn't work out, where you concluded your original thesis was wrong?*

Pzena: A few years ago we bought RR Donnelley, the printing press company. They print magazines and catalogs, but the gem was in printing IPO prospectuses. The company has a great history. It had higher margins, lower costs, and a higher return on capital than any competitor. We bought the stock in 2001, when the IPO boom went bust and the economic downturn caused advertising pages in magazines to shrink. We visited with the company, listened to their strategy, and it totally appealed to us. These were the most frugal people you can imagine. They derided competitors for wasting money on fancy new printing presses. It all sounded great. Around nine months later, Donnelley announced a massive capital spending program to upgrade all their printing presses to state-of-the-art technology. We were pretty shocked, given what they had said to us. We went back, talked to them, and concluded that we really blew it. They were milking their business and underinvesting in it. We concluded it didn't have the $3.50 of earnings power we originally projected when buying the stock for $28, but rather around $1.75. We didn't lose a whole lot of money because we bought it at a low enough price.

Probably the worst investment of my life was buying Fruit of the Loom in the late 1990s. It was a great business, selling men's and boys' underwear in Wal-Mart and Kmart. It also had a commodity fleece and T-shirt business, which didn't have as great characteristics and we felt it was susceptible to the weather. There was a warm winter and Fruit of the Loom had excess fleece inventory that had to be marked down. It shut down factories, and that caused a disaster in earnings. The stock went from something like $45 to $14. We thought it had $3 of normal earnings power. Buying that franchise for $14 was a spectacular bargain, we thought. We bought the stock. What happened? While Fruit of the Loom was shutting down facilities, it completely rejiggered its manufacturing logistics—moving equipment between plants, doing all kinds of stuff to take more cost out. The company blew it. When it went to restart factories for the T-shirt season, using the same equipment that makes sweatshirts and T-shirts, it was eight weeks behind on its promised deliveries to Wal-Mart. The company went out on the commodity market to try and buy cotton fabric and, as the biggest spinner of cotton in America, totally screwed up the market. It had quality and logistics problems, and blew its manufacturing budget by something like $200 million. The banks pulled the plug. We figured it out before Fruit of the Loom went bankrupt, but still lost about 75 percent of our original money.

Kazanjian: *I think Warren Buffett owns that company now.*

Pzena: Yes, he bought it out of bankruptcy for a much lower price.

Kazanjian: *What percentage of your ideas don't work out?*

Pzena: About 40 percent. But "don't work out" typically means you don't lose a lot of money. The percentage of times you lose a lot of money doing what we're doing is very rare. The ones that don't work out just sort of stagnate.

Kazanjian: *When you take a new position, do you buy it all at once, or do you start nibbling and add to your holding over time?*

Pzena: It depends on three factors. One, how cheap is it? That's really the most important. If something is selling for 5 times its normal earnings power, we'll take a bigger position than something that's 8 times normal earnings power. Second, how much industry confirmation is there? If the whole industry is cheap, we'll be more inclined to take a bigger position than if it's just one cheap stock. Third, how certain are we of the outcome? That's a function of how much we know and how predictable the results are.

Kazanjian: *Is there a maximum percentage of the portfolio you'll put in any one company?*

Pzena: We'll put up to 5 percent of the portfolio at the time of purchase in one holding, and will let it ride up to 7.5 percent. We have a pretty broad sector constraint, but won't put more than 25 percent of the portfolio in any one sector.

Kazanjian: *Would you classify most of the companies you buy as turnarounds?*

Pzena: Almost all of them could be described that way, whether it's the fault of the industry, management, or just the economy.

Kazanjian: *When the turnaround plan doesn't work out, what's usually to blame?*

Pzena: It's normally not management messing up. Going back to Boeing, the problem was that nobody was buying airplanes. Management had nothing to do with this. We were just waiting for people to start buying airplanes again. In this case, we could be wrong in one of two places. Either the airline industry doesn't rebound and people are permanently traveling less, or Airbus could kick Boeing's butt. Neither is really management's fault. It's rare that management does something so stupid that it really screws you up, though it happens. It usually happens when they make acquisitions at too high of a valuation.

Kazanjian: *Do you spend time with management before buying a stock?*

Pzena: We spend a day visiting with them. We're mostly trying to figure out what they're doing. We know a lot of what's going on in the company from talking to other people. We'd like to hear their own assessment of the future prospects and what they're trying to do to turn things around. Don't forget, we're buying companies in the depths of problems and typically the turnaround is not imminent. Management has to make an impact two to five years from now, and we're trying to make an assessment as to whether their plans make sense. Companies that are imminently going to turn around aren't really cheap.

Kazanjian: *Are there any industries or sectors you absolutely won't touch?*

Pzena: We won't buy things where we can't really figure them out, like fashion or hot technology products. HP is more of a franchise than a hot product. Sun Microsystems might be a hot product. We look for franchises and try and avoid those where we can't figure out whether there's a franchise. But there are no specific industries we categorically avoid.

Kazanjian: *What if a company is really cheap, but you don't like the management team. Is that enough to keep you away?*

Pzena: No. If management told us they were going to flush money down the toilet, we probably wouldn't buy it. That's pretty rare though. This goes back a few years, but when Edward Brennan was running Sears in the early 1990s, he had a bad reputation. Everybody said he didn't know what he was doing. We went and visited him as the company's whole retail operation had imploded into the red. We asked him a simple question about what was wrong and what he was going to do about it. His response was, "I don't really know. Our systems aren't good enough for us to figure out where we're making money and where we're losing money, which stores are profitable, which departments are profitable. But we're working on it. Six months from now we'll know and we'll make the right adjustments." Now, most people wouldn't invest in that, right? We did. This was back in my Sanford Bernstein days. We thought it was a great franchise and that they would figure out what makes money and what doesn't. Lo and behold they found things that were shocking back then. They were making no money in the hardware department and in the appliance business, and lots of money in women's apparel. They made changes in the stores and it worked.

Kazanjian: *We talked a lot about valuation and normalized earnings, but what about a company's balance sheet? Do you look very closely at that?*

Pzena: We're looking for a high probability that they can make it through the downturn. That's basically it. Of course, we want to avoid deep financial stress. And the lower the debt, the better.

Kazanjian: *Value investing has done very well over the last few years. Do you expect that to continue?*

Pzena: If you look at any of the academic studies, they show that buying low price-to-book stocks wins over any other kind of strategy over the long run, except when the spreads between growth and value are really narrow. Generally, wide is good because value stocks are cheaper. If you get wide spreads you'll make a lot of money. If you have narrow spreads, you might say that value investing won't be as attractive. Right now we're sort of in the middle. I would say we should expect normal returns going forward, and normal returns favor value over growth.

Kazanjian: *What are "normal" returns to you, in absolute terms?*

Pzena: Around 10 percent annualized.

Kazanjian: *How do you define value investing?*

Pzena: I define it as buying good business at very attractive prices relative to their long-term normal earnings.

Kazanjian: *You talked about having the toughest years of your career in the late 1990s when value was out of favor and high-flying Internet stocks were all the rage. Were you tempted to change your discipline back then and join the aggressive growth party?*

Pzena: I just didn't get what was going on. You don't know how many meetings I had where I sat across from clients who told me that their grandmother was a better investor than me, and all you've got to do is buy Cisco. I'd do the arithmetic on Cisco and show that with a $500 billion market cap, if you want to make 15 percent a year, the company has to earn $75 billion a year. It was only making $1 billion. To get to $75 was a real stretch. So I was never tempted to change. There were a lot of really cheap stocks to buy.

Pzena, who has been a private pilot for the past 17 years, insists it shouldn't be that hard for active managers to beat the indexes. If that's true, I wondered, why do the majority underperform the market over time? "Because they don't follow their discipline and get sucked into what's working at the moment," Pzena offers. "They're always a day late and a dollar short." In his mind, the secret to beating the averages is staying true to your strategy no matter what, even when you look completely out of step with the rest of Wall Street.

JOHN SCHNEIDER

PEA Capital

Although John Schneider's dad wasn't in the investment business, he frequently talked with John and his older brother, Arnie, about stocks. He certainly must have made a strong impression, since after college both John and Arnie wound up working as portfolio managers. Although the two brothers spent a short period of time working together, they've spent most of their careers at separate firms, yet both have built incredible track records, consistently showing up at the top of their respective peer categories.

Schneider has shown an impressive ability to spot attractive stocks in all areas of the stock market. He runs both the large-cap-dominated PIMCO PEA Value and the mid-cap-oriented PIMCO PEA Renaissance funds out of his office in New York City. John began working for Wilmington Capital Management after graduating from Lehigh University. After helping brother Arnie set up his own shop, he was recruited to join the team at PEA, a division of fund giant PIMCO, where he has been since 1999.

Schneider closely follows a list of around 400 companies, in search of undervalued gems that have fallen out of favor but sport favorable long-term prospects. The 40-year-old manager overlays his own brand of quantitative analysis with homegrown fundamental work, looking for positive trends working in the company's favor that the rest of Wall Street has apparently ignored.

Incidentally, right as this book went to press, Schneider called to let me know he was leaving PEA Capital to go out on his own. His new firm, JS Asset Management LLC, is headquartered in West Conshohocken, Pennsylvania. In addition to managing money for institutional accounts, he hopes to soon start running two new mutual funds following the same strategies as those he ran at PEA.

Kazanjian: *Given that both you and your brother wound up in the investment business, did you have some familial influence as boys that created this interest in the stock market?*

Schneider: Well, my dad was an individual investor, and we would always talk about stocks around the dinner table. He did help get me involved in the market early on. I had a paper portfolio where I made stock trades, but it was like real money to me.

Kazanjian: *At what point did you decide to get into the investment business as a profession?*

Schneider: I knew it was what I wanted to do when I took my first business class in college. Coming out of undergraduate school, I worked for Wilmington Capital Management in Wilmington, Delaware. That's where I started to learn my investment approach and began buying individual stocks.

Kazanjian: *Wilmington is a real value shop. Is that where you picked up your value philosophy?*

Schneider: I always knew I wanted to work for a value shop, but it didn't really gel until I started at Wilmington. I think it's really part of one's personality, and it's ingrained in you. You can tell whether a person believes in growth or value based on their lifestyle.

Kazanjian: *Does that mean you look for bargains and clip coupons in your personal life?*

Schneider: Exactly. I don't want to come off as cheap, but I don't have a fancy house or a fancy car.

Kazanjian: *What did you do at Wilmington?*

Schneider: I was an analyst. The firm managed about $1.3 billion, which was a decent size back in 1986. Money was run using a committee approach, and I was the most junior of seven investment professionals. We would each write up a report on a company and present it to the group for discussion. At age 25, Wilmington made me a partner in the firm and offered me stock.

Kazanjian: *How long were you there?*

Schneider: For about five years. The senior partners were near retirement age and decided to sell the business to Wilmington Trust, a local bank. I didn't really want to work for a bank so I left to work for another value shop outside of Philadelphia. I was there for about five years, then I worked for my brother for three years helping him to start his firm, and have been at PEA Capital ever since.

Kazanjian: *Why didn't you and your brother just keep working together?*

Schneider: I got a call out of the blue offering me an opportunity to be the value portfolio manager for a new boutique asset management business for PIMCO. The opportunity just sounded great in terms of having complete autonomy. I started here in 1999 and began running the Renaissance Fund right away. They gave me the Value Fund about a year later.

Kazanjian: *What's the primary difference between the Value and Renaissance funds?*

Schneider: Renaissance is an all-cap fund, with the bulk of its assets in mid-caps. Value is a large-cap fund.

Kazanjian: *So between the two funds, you can buy stocks of just about any market capitalization.*

Schneider: I am a believer that you want to create as few walls as possible. When I started the Renaissance Fund, they intended it to be focused on large-caps. I said I wanted to make it an all-cap fund so I could move around.

Kazanjian: *When you begin the process of putting a portfolio together, do you pay attention to the economy and overall stock market?*

Schneider: I do look at some macro variables, including the economy, but I'm very much a bottom-up guy. As for the economy, it plays more of a role in terms of weightings. In other words, if a cyclical stock looks really cheap, yet I'm concerned the economy is going into a recession, I might not make it quite as big a weighting in the portfolio.

Kazanjian: *Based on reading some of your recent writings, it seems to me that you're a pretty pessimistic guy about the prospect for the stock market over the next few years.*

Schneider: Yes. Some of that pessimism is probably because I'm a value guy, but I'm a little worried about some big macro items. I think stock market returns over the next few years will be less than the historical 10 to 11 percent.

Kazanjian: *Such as?*

Schneider: For example, people have been talking about budget and trade deficits since Ronald Reagan, but I wasn't very worried about it 20 years ago. Now that we're five years away from the beginning of the Baby Boomers turning 65, the reality of this is upon us. Same thing with the trade deficit. We need to keep the dollar weaker to close the trade deficit.

Kazanjian: *Are stocks best avoided in this kind of environment?*

Schneider: It's not so much that I'm bearish, it's more that my concerns about these issues influence what sectors or stocks I buy. For instance, I think there's a bit of a housing bubble and that the consumer is overleveraged. That makes me a bit more bearish on retail. The fact that we've got a trade deficit and will need a weak dollar for exports makes me more optimistic about U.S. manufacturing.

Kazanjian: *Let's talk more about the process you go through to find investment ideas.*

Schneider: I make fun of screening because I think a lot of the names that screen out are the most interesting. I start with an approach where I try to come up with creative new ideas and put them on what I call my monitor list. I have a monitor list of about 400 companies. These 400 companies serve as a very broad cross section of the economy and are interesting individual companies. I have a price target for all 400 of these stocks. I then rank them from most attractive to least attractive, based on price. In other words, I'll say this stock's worth $10 and it's now $7, so it has a 40 percent upside. I take the most attractive names, do more fundamental work, and tighten up the numbers. My analysts build models and talk to the management of those companies we find most attractive. If it's an industry we haven't been following in a while, we'll talk to Wall Street, not for buy or sell recommendations, but for informational purposes. We want to get up to speed and identify the company's earnings power. Another word some people use for that is normalized earnings or recovery earnings. A lot of the companies we're buying are in situations where earnings are currently depressed. In such cases, we look out two or three years, take our forward earnings number, and multiply it by a PE target to get our price target. Finally, we have to come up with a catalyst that will make the stock become better appreciated or less cheap in the marketplace.

Kazanjian: *How do you come to a decision about how much stock is worth?*

Schneider: A vast majority of the valuation models are earnings based. We will look at a company and say we think it has a certain dollar amount of earnings power, and should sell at an assumed PE. For instance, if it has $1 per share of earnings power, and we think it should sell for 10 times earnings, you get a stock price of $10. I should say that in this analysis, we hit a lot of dead ends. We'll do a lot of work and find out that our number is wrong, or that we can't find a catalyst. In such cases, we have to wait. So certain names can stay on the watch list a long time.

Kazanjian: *Can you go into more depth, in terms of what type of drill-down work you do after spotting stocks that look good on a valuation basis?*

Schneider: Let's assume it's a stock I haven't followed before. I will get a bunch of analysts to bring me up to speed. This is really the only time I use external Wall Street research. I'll get a quick understanding of what's going on in the industry and with these companies. At that point I turn off what Wall Street's got to say and do my own work. My analysts start to talk to the company. Often we'll also talk to competitors. Frequently we find stocks through other means. One company will tell us about another one. We then build models on all our companies focused on a longer time horizon than Wall Street. Wall Street seems to have a one- or two-quarter time horizon. I look out 24 months. Sometimes I'll own a stock for a shorter time period, often I'll own it longer, but that's my time horizon. We're building a model to show what a company can earn assuming A, B, and C happen. Besides being cheap on our normalized earnings, we also are trying to identify the catalysts, for lack of a better word, that will enable the company to earn that number.

Kazanjian: *Are most of the companies you grow interested in indeed in the midst of some transition or trouble?*

Schneider: Very much so. They have either trouble or a perception of trouble. That's why we look at how bad things can get. I'm trying to buy at the inflection point where things are going to get better.

Kazanjian: *Are growth investors so impatient that they just dump these stocks out at the first sign of disappointment, giving them to you at a cheaper price?*

Schneider: That's a good chunk of it. There's a trade-off between patience and—I keep coming back to it—this catalyst. As long as the fundamentals and the catalyst are still in place, even if the stock's going down, even if the company reports a disappointing quarter, I will continue to hold or maybe buy more. Momentum investors look at charts to tell them when to buy. That's not what I'm doing. I'm often buying in the uncomfortable period before the stock's price movement starts.

Kazanjian: *Is there any difference in the analysis you do for a larger company versus a smaller one?*

Schneider: The process is exactly the same, although a large company often has multiple divisions you have to look at, which can make the model a bit more complicated.

Kazanjian: *When looking at a huge company, do you still feel a need to talk to management, or is that more important with smaller firms?*

Schneider: We talk to the vast majority of our companies. In a small company you get to talk to the president. In a big company sometimes it's the CFO, division head, or investor relations person. But we almost always talk to management.

Kazanjian: *Do you pay attention to sector diversification in the portfolio? My guess is companies in the same sectors will all show up on your list at the same time.*

Schneider: When it comes to putting the portfolio together, I'm really looking at three things: liquidity, level of confidence, and diversification. I do try to stay diversified among sectors, although when I have confidence in a particular area, I'm willing to overweight it relative to our benchmarks.

Kazanjian: *How many stocks do you tend to hold in the portfolio?*

Schneider: The Value Fund has around 40 or 50 names. The Renaissance Fund has 70 or 80, since it owns smaller stocks.

Kazanjian: *Let's give our readers a real-life example of your process in action. I notice you've owned JC Penney for a few years now. How did you find that stock?*

Schneider: Before I owned JC Penney in 1998, it was a $78 stock and people were excited about it because the company had dropped a lot of its hard goods to focus on soft goods. The stock was projected to earn over $4, and was selling at almost 20 times that number. Then you got into a water torture situation, where earnings projections went from $4 to $3 to $2. During this period, the stock was put on my monitor list. Every time I looked at the company, the fundamentals kept faltering. Then when the stock got in the $20s, it started looking pretty cheap. However, I couldn't identify the catalyst that would get the company out of this downward spiral. The catalyst finally came when JC Penney hired Allen Questrom as CEO in the fall of 2000. When Questrom got in, he said, "I'm not going to talk to Wall Street for six months or so. I'm just going to go off and figure out what I need to do to fix things." We updated our work and looked at JC Penney's two main businesses: JC Penney stores and Eckerd, the drugstore chain. We looked at what the company's margins could be, assuming it was just average versus its peers and gave that number somewhat of a haircut. We finally came up with an earnings power of $3 a share. We got there by putting margins on sales for the two different divisions. There was a shortage of pharmacists and therefore a limit on the number of new drugstores the competitors of Eckerd could build. So we thought that business could get better. The department stores still had merchandise buyers at each store as opposed to centralized purchasing, which was about to change. We started buying the stock in the fourth quarter of 2000, and it actually went down at first. My average cost was $12.

Kazanjian: *When did the story start to take hold?*

Schneider: Around April 2001, JC Penney had an analyst meeting and started putting out margin targets for the company's two main businesses that looked very much like ours. As it turned out, JC Penney wound up selling Eckerd to CVS and a Canadian company in August 2004 for $3.5 billion. The company will use those proceeds to buy back stock and pay down debt. But the overall process is very much coming along and looks the way we originally envisioned. Wall Street's consensus earnings for the stock for next year is now $3 a share. That's a pretty good example of what I try to do. I looked out further than the Street, modeled a normalized earnings number, and saw several catalysts.

Kazanjian: *At what point will you sell the stock?*

Schneider: As soon as it hits our price target, but as earnings improve, so does that target. Once it hits the target, we will begin to systematically sell it.

Kazanjian: *JC Penney worked, but I'm sure you've had some misses along the way.*

Schneider: Conseco is one. In the summer of 1999 it was about a $30 stock. We thought it could earn around $3, and was therefore selling at 10 times earnings. The company was too leveraged but had tremendous cash flow. The catalyst was that management was going to pay down debt, and we felt it would ultimately become an acquisition story. There were all sorts of excuses about why the company missed its earnings. By the fall of that year the stock was trading at about $20 when it announced it was going to have a secondary offering. If the company was a free cash flow generator, which was part of my original catalyst, why did it need to issue more stock? The stock actually went up because everybody got excited and said this would resolve Conseco's problems. I felt something was wrong and sold out at $23. It was obviously a loss, but the company ultimately went bankrupt.

Kazanjian: *Actually that sounds more like a success story.*

Schneider: Going from $30 to $23 is not a success story.

Kazanjian: *No, but it's better than zero. You were pretty early to get out. What's the biggest lesson you've learned from your mistakes over the years?*

Schneider: A lot of people believe that if a stock goes down X percent you should automatically sell. I don't buy that because it seems to me that is a way to get yourself whipsawed. If the catalyst and the fundamentals are still in place, I'll often buy more on the way down. My system fails when the financials are falsified.

Kazanjian: *How can you protect yourself against that kind of fraud?*

Schneider: There's a good amount of academic work that shows if earnings are somehow magically staying up but cash flows are dropping off, that's a red flag. But the bottom line is if somebody's going to commit a criminal act and falsify financial statements, it's hard for us to catch that. If accountants, who have access to a great deal of nonpublic information, can be fooled, clearly a portfolio manager can, too.

Kazanjian: *Are balance sheets becoming more honest, given all that's happened in corporate America over the last few years?*

Schneider: When people go to jail, that usually puts people on notice. There's also a bit of cyclicality to this. If you go back in time and look at when these failures happened, it's often around economic downturns and recessions. The pile under the rug gets to be big and finally reveals itself during the downturn.

Kazanjian: *It would probably be hard for the average investor to build sophisticated earnings models like the ones you use. The most readily available valuation metric is the PE ratio, which is easily obtained online and in many newspapers. Is this a good valuation gauge to use when determining the relative value of a stock?*

Schneider: There are a lot of academic studies over all sorts of periods showing that absolute low PE investing does work. If you buy low PE stocks, in the lowest decile or lowest quintile, you should outperform the markets over long periods of time. But low PE investing can perform poorly over short stretches, including 1996–1999, when value was out of favor. That's why I think finding the catalysts is what has allowed me to outperform my benchmark. Also, going back to my comment about the failure of screening alone, I've made great returns buying stocks with depressed earnings. The final danger in looking just at low PEs is that you may buy just when the E is peaking. You certainly don't want to buy a company at four times earnings when the earnings are about to roll over.

Kazanjian: *While you held up well in the late 1990s, as growth stocks shot like a rocket, did you ever question your value discipline during these unusual times? After all, I remember some people proclaiming that value investing was dead forever.*

Schneider: It was frustrating, and you are sometimes tempted to deviate from your strategy. But I didn't. In fact, that's what created a literally once-in-a-generation opportunity for value investing starting in 2000. So many people couldn't endure the pain after living through what I call value hell from 1996 to 1999. You had outflows from value stocks, and individual portfolio managers who couldn't endure the pain capitulated and bought tech stocks. I stuck to what I knew would ultimately work, which took a great deal of fortitude.

Kazanjian: *Do you stay fully invested at all times?*

Schneider: I generally don't go above 10 percent cash.

Kazanjian: *As far as size is concerned, small- and mid-caps have performed better than large-caps over the last several years. Do you see this trend reversing itself?*

Schneider: Small-caps have outperformed large-caps for five consecutive years. In 2003, the Russell 2000 had its best performance since the creation of the index. If you took the total market and broke it down by market capitalization in 1999, the PEs of mega-cap stocks were twice the PEs of micro-cap stocks. Small-cap stocks now sell for somewhere between two and three PE points more than large-cap stocks. If you bring that back to 1983, when small-cap stocks peaked during the last cycle, small-cap stocks got to a three-PE-point premium. So I think the outperformance of small-cap stocks is near the end.

Kazanjian: *For an investor buying individual stocks, how many names do you think they need to own to be properly diversified, especially among value stocks?*

Schneider: There are studies that say you can be diversified with as few as 12 stocks. I think the average mutual fund and the average investor is over-diversified. Warren Buffett once said he'd rather have a bumpy 15 percent return than a smooth 12 percent (fewer stocks create a bumpier ride, but the potential for higher returns). I agree with that completely.

Kazanjian: *A lot of investment consultants say you need to own both growth and value funds in your portfolio. Do you agree with that?*

Schneider: I don't personally own any growth funds, although I do own a small percentage of international funds.

Kazanjian: *Do you think we can get into another stock market bubble like we did a few years ago?*

Schneider: I guarantee you we will see it. It might not be in the same order of magnitude, but it will happen. That's what capitalism is all about. A market is made up of fear and greed, and sometimes the greed gets to be what you would call a bubble.

Kazanjian: *What do you think of index funds?*

Schneider: I think index funds are fine. The problem I have is with what I call the quasi-index fund. It's the fund that's charging high management fees to perform like an index fund. It's bound to underperform because of the high costs.

Kazanjian: *Isn't that a good case for just owning low-cost index funds, especially since you're only expecting single-digit stock market turns for the coming years?*

Schneider: Jack Bogle [founder of the Vanguard Group] makes a great case for investing in index funds. I tend to agree with much of what he says. Studies show that 70 percent of all managers underperform the indexes. I believe my strategy of buying a concentrated portfolio of my best ideas [and having] a longer time horizon has passed the test of time. Many port-folios look like a quasi-index. Those funds will just keep muddling along. Yes, I'd rather own an index fund than a fund like that.

In one of his recent writings, Schneider said he believes investors should prepare for the possibility that we've returned to what he describes as a 1970s-type market. "The next decade probably won't be the bull market of the 1980s and 1990s, and we will have to take a different approach to in-vesting than one many relied on in the past two decades," he wrote. "However, along with its challenges, this 'new market order' is also likely to present some significant opportunities." Finding those opportunities through smart stock picking is what, in Schneider's mind, will lead to stel-lar returns going forward.

SUSAN SUVALL

Trust Company of the West

When Susan Suvall first started looking for work in the 1980s, not many women were in high-level positions on Wall Street. She wasn't about to let that stop her, though. Through tenacity and hard work, Suvall not only found a job at Morgan Stanley, she soon created an even more prestigious role for herself. In 1985, she landed a job managing money at Trust Company of the West (TCW) and has been there ever since.

Today Suvall is the firm's co-director of small- and mid-cap investing. In addition to running a slew of institutional accounts, Suvall is lead manager of the TCW Galileo Value Opportunities Fund. Her specialty is stocks with market capitalizations below $10 billion.

Suvall's main thesis is that valuation matters. She looks for stocks sporting one of three primary characteristics: turnarounds, unrecognized asset values, and undervalued growth. Turnarounds are companies with sound balance sheets selling at a significant discount to estimated sustainable earnings over the next two years. Unrecognized assets include securities selling below probable liquidation or private market value. Undervalued growth companies have strong balance sheets and potential growth rates of 10 to 20 percent, yet sell at a market multiple below the rest of their peer group.

By combining these attributes of growth and value, Suvall's portfolios have historically managed to shine, even during periods when value seems to be out of favor. More importantly, Suvall insists that she never strays from her discipline, which keeps her focused and prevents her from being tempted to change her stripes based on whatever may be hot in the market at any given time. She also has some good advice for those looking to enter the money management profession. It's savvy counsel from someone who really had to work hard to get to the top.

Kazanjian: *When did you get started in the investment business?*

Suvall: Back in 1981. As you may recall, it was a very strange time for the stock market. The Dow was at about 800, and it was just before the bull market took off. Business wasn't good, and it wasn't easy to get a job in the investment business. I went to the University of Pennsylvania, but it really didn't matter. At the time, every interviewer I talked with asked how many words I could type.

Kazanjian: *What was your major in college?*

Suvall: International relations. Majoring in international relations was like liberal arts. I had a very high grade point average, but it was very tough for women to break into the business back then. I know it sounds terrible, but they really did just want to know how many words I could type. I figured I could get into publishing or advertising, but I really wanted to work on Wall Street. I was always interested in making money because I grew up in a poor environment, and money was constantly a major issue. I wanted to be in a profession where I could be rewarded if I was good. I eventually landed a job as a sales assistant at Morgan Stanley in New York.

Kazanjian: *How was your typing?*

Suvall: Very funny. It was pretty good, though I did more tasks like handling calls on the desk and sitting on the trading floor. I worked in the options area, so I got to learn about the options business. I've never been one to just sit around. I'm always trying to learn more. I quickly moved from being a sales assistant on the options trading desk to trading odd lots in about three months. I didn't do any major trading, but I sat on the desk, took orders, and worked orders on the floor with different brokers. It was a really good way to learn and understand trading. I was at Morgan Stanley for two years, and then went to another sell-side firm. I never did find the sell-side to be very intellectual. Even when I was an options trader, I kept being hit on the back by these cigar-smoking guys asking me to get them a cup of coffee. The sell-side just wasn't an agreeable environment to me.

Kazanjian: *For readers who don't know, what exactly do you mean by the sell-side?*

Suvall: Sell-side refers to investment bankers, as opposed to money managers (firms that sell and trade stocks, versus those that invest money in them). I knew at that point I really did want to do something more than just sitting on a trading desk. What I really liked about investing was that you had to know a little bit about everything. You had to be up to speed on politics, economics, you name it. The more I learned about the market, the more I saw it was really about psychology. In fact, psychology is probably the best major for this business.

I next got a job at an investment bank that no longer exists. I was supposed to work with the salesperson, but wound up going to research meetings and taking very good notes on what the analysts were saying. I got to see that if you couldn't summarize a stock idea in about a paragraph, it's probably too complicated. I wrote up what every analyst said in a very condensed form and distributed these notes to the entire sales force. In turn, I basically created a new job for myself. I went from helping this salesperson and being the liaison for his clients to being the research liaison for the firm. It got to the point where they couldn't take it when I was out of the office. This was a fresh concept, and it was before e-mail. I get morning notes like this by e-mail all the time now, but it was a new concept in the early 1980s. While I enjoyed this, I knew I wanted to get on the buy-side. I didn't want to be the person who regurgitates information I hear from somebody else. I also started to see that the sell-side wasn't a pure place to be because investment banking got in the way. If the firm wanted your investment banking business, which of course it did because it's very profitable, an analyst might recommend your stock just because they'd possibly get your business. It wasn't really an objective way of looking at the world. But it was a great experience because I got to learn about a lot of different industries. I also got to see there were all different types of investors: growth investors, value investors, momentum investors, and those that just looked at technical analysis.

Kazanjian: *How and when did you make the leap over to the buy-side?*

Suvall: I really began to look heavily in different places. I tried to network to find out about any available opportunities. When it rains, it pours. I got four opportunities presented to me all at the same time after looking for almost a year. I ended up hooking up with a man who I believe was the greatest teacher I've ever had in this business, Boniface "Buzz" Zaino.

Kazanjian: *Isn't he with The Royce Funds now?*

Suvall: He is. He had a reputation at the time of being a legend in small-cap investing, and he is a really lovely man. He was looking for a research analyst who could speak to the Street, help narrow down the ideas that were presented to him, and do work on the companies. I interviewed and got the job in 1985. It was just Buzz, me, and another person in Los Angeles, Nicholas (Nick) Galuccio. He taught me a lot.

Kazanjian: *Was this at Trust Company of the West?*

Suvall: Exactly. Buzz came to TCW from Lehman Brothers in early 1985. Robert Day, the chairman of TCW, found the best money managers in whatever area they were in and hired them. Nick had worked with Buzz at Lehman and told Robert Day about him. Buzz left TCW about six years ago, and Nick and I were left with the business. We had about $900 million under management, although the Value Opportunities Fund was very small, with less than $30 million. It was still incubating.

Kazanjian: *Prior to taking over the fund, were you managing mostly institutional accounts?*

Suvall: It was all institutional accounts. The Value Opportunities Fund started as an institutional account. I've been very fortunate in my 19 years here. I learned this business from one of the best, and had his attention for a decade. Buzz is a value investor, although his style is a little different from the way Nick and I manage money today. We took his style and built on it. We look at the world in a slightly different way. It's not better or worse, but a little more aggressive in a lot of ways. Nick and I now co-manage more than $6 billion in the small- and mid-cap area. Nick is the lead manager of small-cap and I'm the lead manager of mid-cap, which is the Value Opportunities Fund.

Kazanjian: *Before we go on, one of the most frequent questions I get from readers and at investment conferences is, "How can I break into the investment business?" Your story illustrates one of the best answers, which is to get in the door doing whatever you have to, and then work your way up.*

Suvall: That's exactly right. I had no connections. My father worked in the garment industry. I got in wherever I could. If you are of average intelligence or above, want to get ahead, and want to learn, you can do it even if you start in the mailroom. I truly believe that. Over the years I have encouraged people who worked for me as assistants to move on and do more. I've told them to use this as an opportunity to learn and grow. Get an understanding of where you want to be in this business, be it in marketing, as a portfolio manager, an analyst, or on the sell-side. Better yet, do it all and figure out what you like best.

Kazanjian: *Does that upward mobility still exist in the business today?*

Suvall: That opportunity is totally there. Listen, if I did it when there were no women in the business, anybody can. The business is definitely much more open to women today. It's not a boy's business like it used to be. I never clawed my way to get ahead. I just always did more than was required of me. I kept asking, "What else can I do?" That question will really help you to get ahead. Most people just don't bother to do more.

Kazanjian: *You also mentioned that psychology is a great discipline to study for those wanting to get into the investment business. What really creates bull and bear markets? Is it as simple as being the psychology of the masses at any point in time?*

Suvall: I think it's clearly fear or greed. The market will go up in an improving economy, and down in a declining economy. There are these defined cycles. But the levels to which they go up or down are determined by greed or fear. We saw that in the late 1990s, when greed ruled. By 2000, it started being run by fear. In 2002 everything was being thrown out. In markets like that, it's crucial to understand the businesses you own, know that you hold quality companies, and stick to fundamentals. Be an investor, not a speculator, and wait for the greed to come back.

Kazanjian: *It just so happens that on the morning you and I are talking, the market is having a lousy day. Technology stocks are being hit especially hard. On days like* *this, the average investor is no doubt frustrated seeing their portfolio go down. How do you as a professional handle negative days like this?*

Suvall: It's never fun to see the market go down, but I always come back to the fundamentals. What are the companies I own? What do they do? Where are they? Do they have a preeminent market position and proprietary products? Why did I buy the stock to begin with? In general, in a market like this I put blinders on. You want to pay attention to the big picture, but there's a disconnect between what's going on in the markets and with the stocks. Often it's on days like these you find stocks to buy. I react in the opposite way of the market, and that's why I've been able to make money over the years. Human mentality says that when the market is down, something must be wrong, so let's sell. I like to look more deeply and closely at what I own. If the reason I bought the stock still exists, but the price is now cheaper, I'll just buy more. That's exactly what I did in 2002 when investors were just throwing everything out. In 2002, National Semiconductor was selling for $8.50 a share (the stock has split since then) and had almost $5 a share in cash. You could buy a great company with several dollars in earnings power for around $4, once you took out the cash. To me it was a no-brainer. There were other examples like that. It looked like the world was coming to an end. In truth, when the world looks like it's coming to an end, that's the time to invest.

Kazanjian: *Does the overall market environment have any impact on how you invest? In other words, if the market looks overheated, are you more likely to raise your cash levels?*

Suvall: No. Cash is a residual of the investment process. I'm being paid to manage stocks according to my value approach. I would rather have very little cash on hand. The last time I had a lot of cash was at the end of 2001, when everybody started pouring into value stocks and they got expensive. I had cash because I couldn't find anything to buy. Every time I've tried to guess about the direction of the market, it hasn't worked. I know better than to do that.

Kazanjian: *You're focused primarily on smaller stocks. What market capitalization range are you normally interested in?*

Suvall: I generally go from $100 million to $10 billion. We monitor over 3,000 stocks. The average market cap of stocks in the Value Opportunities Fund is around $4.5 billion.

Kazanjian: *With 3,000 names to choose from, how do you narrow that list down?*

Suvall: It starts with a quantitative analysis. We're looking for companies selling at low price-to-book and low market cap-to-sales ratios. The low market cap-to-sales ratio is important because we want to buy companies trading at two times sales or less. The reason is that we're buying companies with depressed margins or depressed revenues. When the margins or revenues improve, you get big leverage on the bottom line. That is the leverage ratio. We're looking for companies with very good balance sheets, because we want to avoid permanent capital loss. The portfolio is full of turnarounds, so the managements really have to focus on fixing their businesses. You don't want them to be worried about the banks coming after them. We also look for companies selling at the low end of their historical range, specifically the last three to four years, depending on whether the company's business has changed.

Kazanjian: *When you say historical range, are you talking about the historical PE ratio, or actual share price?*

Suvall: The share price. I look at the PE, too, but that comes later. All this preliminary work is done to figure out what the normalized earnings power of a company will be. When I say normalized earnings power, I mean the earnings a company can achieve within a 2- to 3-year period when business is back on track. Not when business is at its peak, but when business is back on track. We're opportunistic value managers. I'm looking for companies going through temporary situations that have led to some kind of an earnings trauma. The fallen angels, if you will. We really try to determine a company's intrinsic value based on the assets, normalized earnings power, or potential growth rate of the company. If a company looks good statistically, we'll then take it through a qualitative analysis. Actually, our process is probably more qualitative than quantitative.

Kazanjian: *You talked about trying to figure out what a company will earn once things get back on track. How do you come up with that number?*

Suvall: It's done based on what a company has done in the past, what it's doing now, and what the industry looks like. When we go from the quantitative to the qualitative analysis stage, we spend a lot of time poring over the financial statements—the 10-Qs, the 10-Ks, the proxies—everything that's available, including reports on the industry and competition. You read anything you can, you visit with companies and vendors, all in an effort to see what's going on and try to figure out what problems the company is having. You look for certain things, like whether earnings can turn around, or whether margin expansion is possible. Do company insiders own stock? That's very important because you want them to be on your side. We're looking at companies through three lenses: undervalued assets, turnarounds, and undervalued growth. This is a very fluid way to look at value, and is different from most other value managers.

Kazanjian: *It sounds like a more flexible approach that gives you the chance to per-form well in both value and growth markets.*

Suvall: Exactly. We let the market tell us where the value is. When we finally find an idea, we'll see if it fits into the undervalued asset, turnaround, or un-dervalued growth category. Undervalued assets are simply companies selling below their liquidation value, or book value. Turnarounds are companies having problems as a result of internal problems. In other words, the issues aren't macro related. Often the trouble comes when a company makes too many acquisitions and can't assimilate them as quickly as the market would like. Or perhaps earnings are temporarily hurt when a company is no longer able to sell an old product and, although it has come up with a new product, no one is buying it yet. Undervalued growth is really a fun category. It adds a lot of alpha to the portfolio. Every company will have some sort of problem at one point in its history. When that happens, growth investors will have to sell the stock. Such stocks can be down 30 to 40 percent in one day. Those kinds of stocks fit into our undervalued growth category.

Kazanjian: *Do you try to keep a certain percentage of the overall portfolio in each of these categories?*

Suvall: No, it really depends on the market. For instance, in 1998 we had the Asian crisis and decided that the thing to do was rotate the portfolio mostly into undervalued growth. We concluded that if the world didn't come to an end, which we suspected it wouldn't, those stocks would ben-efit most. We had a big technology bias in 1998, which worked out very well. In 1999 you had the beginning of the technology bubble. Stocks started getting multiples that were unbelievable. The portfolio was doing really well. Just as we buy stocks when they're statistically cheap, we also sell when they reach full value. The definition of full value differs depend-ing on each of the three categories, but in general it's when a stock gets to a PE multiple of one times the growth rate on normalized earnings. In other words, if we own a company that we believe can earn $1 a share, and it's growing at 15 percent a year, when the stock gets to $15, we would consider it to be fully valued, even though that's when most growth investors would start to buy.

We left a lot of money on the table in 1999. We were up 26 percent or so. Had we let our winners run, we would have been up over 100 percent. But we stick to our style and over time it has always helped us. So we were selling tech and buying financials. At that point interest rates were going up and financial stocks were selling at very low valuations, where they were in the early 1990s during the banking crisis. We felt these were good companies selling at low multiples just because rates were going up. It was a temporary margin compression. It proved to be a good move because during the tech wreck in 2000, we were up 40 percent.

Kazanjian: *Yet 2002 was a tough year for you. What happened?*

Suvall: In 2002 business was really bad. We didn't know when it would improve, but we knew stocks were too cheap to not buy. Money was really pouring into value funds, while growth investors were getting nothing but liquidations. It was exactly the opposite of what you saw in the late 1990s. We had a very big weighting in the undervalued growth category, with a large bias toward technology. Even though we do our analysis on a stock-by-stock basis, we do pay attention to the big picture. In the first quarter of 2002, GDP was up 5 percent and companies were telling us that business was getting better. We felt it was the right time to rotate out of the more defensive and financial positions into undervalued growth. Then you had the 100-year flood. You had two wars and corporate governance problems, which really blew the market away and created a lot of chaos and fear. The price of oil went up to $37 a barrel for the first time, which was shocking, and you had a pause in the economy. Our portfolio just rolled over. So do you run and sell and rotate into stocks that are more defensive? That's not our strategy. We stick to fundamental analysis and bought all of these companies that we knew we would eventually make money on. We didn't know when business would get better. We just knew it would. We always try to have a catalyst in every investment we make. In 2002, the catalyst was simply resumption of growth. It happened in 2003. As a result, we ended 2002 down 26 percent, but were up 49 percent in 2003.

Kazanjian: *Given your strategy, it seems like you've always got to keep an eye on what could possibly go wrong.*

Suvall: Precisely. My job as a portfolio manager is to really find the hole in every story. When you talk to companies they're always telling you good stuff and putting on a more positive spin. My job is to look at the negative, which is easy for me. I was brought up by a grandmother who lived through the Depression. She gave me a Depression mentality, where I'm always looking for the worst-case scenario. It's a good way to be. You look at the situation, figure out the worst case and the likelihood of that happening, and how we'll get from this point to the end point. After doing this for a number of years, you find that the variables that turn stocks around are usually the same. You get a new management team; the company sells off a money-losing division, buys back stock, or pays down debt. The bottom line is that the price you pay for a company is what matters, along with whether it has a good balance sheet, not to mention a preeminent market position or proprietary product.

Kazanjian: *Regarding turnarounds, how can you really tell whether a company is positioned to dig itself out of a problematic situation? Does it come down to competent management?*

Suvall: Management is always very important, but that's changed over the years. When I started out, there was a mentality that management didn't matter. If the company had good products, it would turn itself around. Good management is important in any of the three categories, but especially with undervalued growth.

Kazanjian: *You own some household names in your fund that seem like very successful growth companies, such as Southwest Airlines. This is one of the premier names in the industry. How did that get into your portfolio?*

Suvall: That's a good observation. After 9/11, you had a big selloff, especially in the tourist-related stocks. Southwest Airlines was really getting hit. The stock got under $12 a share with $1.20-plus in normalized earnings power. It had a great balance sheet, excellent management, and really the only business model at the time that was really working out. We liked the business model and the fact that the government was going to financially help out the airlines. We knew Southwest didn't need the help, but would get the money anyway. That's why we bought it. We made money on it and sold a little. But it has come down a bit lately, which is why we still own it.

Kazanjian: *So you bought Southwest when it was under a temporary cloud and have continued to hold on? What about when a story doesn't play out as you intended? At what point do you decide to pull the trigger and get rid of the stock?*

Suvall: When there is a secular change in the story. If the story is shaping as expected, we'll hold on, even if the share prices falls. If not, the stock will be sold.

Kazanjian: *How diversified do you keep your portfolio?*

Suvall: There are approximately 60 stocks in the portfolio. The minimum is 50 and the maximum is 75, although it always seems to stay around 60.

Kazanjian: *Some people talk about there being market cycles where small- and mid-caps outperform large-caps, and vice versa. Do you believe in this?*

Suvall: I do. Having said that, the way that I look at the world and the way I invest doesn't really take these cycles into account much. I'm really buying companies that are established. Yes, they may be in the mid-cap area, but I'm buying the stock based on valuation.

Kazanjian: *When you make a mistake, say you buy a turnaround that doesn't come to fruition, what's the most common reason for the story not panning out?*

Suvall: It's usually management. Turnarounds take a long time. Nothing ever happens as fast as you want it to. But if what management tells me is happening doesn't occur quarter after quarter, that's when I'll get rid of the stock.

Kazanjian: *With smaller companies, you can usually get access directly to the CEO and other key decision makers. Do you ever try to use this access to gain influence and suggest courses of action for them to follow? In other words, are you an active investor?*

Suvall: We're definitely hands off. We don't get involved with that at all.

Kazanjian: *How closely do you watch and monitor your investments?*

Suvall: Every day. Being located in New York is an advantage because companies are always coming through here. We're constantly in contact with management. The world has changed a bit because of the new regulations. In the old days we used to sit across from management and get a lot of information, but now they can't tell us as much. Our reason for meeting with them now is to get a general idea of the business model. We also listen to the quarterly conference calls, although we're more interested in how a company will be doing a year or two from now.

Kazanjian: *How do you invest your own money?*

Suvall: All of the money that I have in the stock market is in both of our funds. I trust this investment process of buying solid businesses at a discount. To me, that's the only way that makes sense. It's really the way I live my life. I don't go to Neiman Marcus to buy an outfit. I'll go to a store that has the same stuff at a discount.

Kazanjian: *In other words, you're a value investor at heart. Does this mean you have all of your stock market money invested in small- and mid-cap stocks?*

Suvall: Yes.

Kazanjian: *Do you think that's wise for the average investor?*

Suvall: No. I think everybody should be diversified among small-, mid-, and large-cap equities. I think every portfolio should have a bond element to it as well. It's always best to be diversified.

Kazanjian: *On the equity side, should investors own both growth and value?*

Suvall: Definitely because everything reverts to the mean. Value has its day, and then growth has its day. I feel like we're value investors who can also buy undervalued growth stocks. In other words, I'm buying growth at value prices. The main problem I have with growth investing is that if you buy a company selling at five to six times market cap-to-sales, it has a lot of downside potential. If you buy a company at two times market cap-to-sales or less, you don't have that much fluff built in the price. I feel like I can be a growth investor without taking on the risk of a growth investor. I may have to wait longer for it to pay off, but I have less risk. That's really what I'm always looking for. I don't want to lose money.

Kazanjian: *What percentage of your stock ideas don't work out?*

Suvall: I would say over time about 10 to 15 percent.

Kazanjian: *That's a pretty good batting average.*

Suvall: Yeah, it's not bad. This doesn't mean that at any point in time the stock might not be down, but it's usually in the money by the time it's sold.

Kazanjian: *In years like 2002 when your performance doesn't look so great, do you feel pressure to perform? In other words, are you tempted to try new strategies to pump up performance in order to please shareholders and your bosses?*

Suvall: I feel pressure to perform, but I still stick to my strategy. I always feel a pressure to perform. In good years, you worry about what you'll buy next. You should never get overly confident. It's best to always be humble. Of course clients usually react in a way that's the opposite of what they should. In 2002, when we had a bad year, money left the mutual fund after pouring in following a great year in 2001. It should have been pouring in during 2002. I always want to do better and better and better. Again, the key is sticking to your style.

Suvall is quick to point out that this doesn't mean you can't refine your style based on your experiences in the market. She admits that even her own process has evolved over time. For instance, early on she adhered to a much deeper value approach. Now she has a more fluid way of looking at stocks, while still following her strict discipline. Sticking to your guns is what will keep you out of trouble, she says. "Had we changed our stripes when the market wasn't going our way in 2002, we would never have come back so strongly—if at all—in the years that followed," Suvall adds.

PART THREE

The GLOBAL GLOBETROTTERS

SARAH KETTERER

Causeway Capital Management

As a young girl, Sarah Ketterer had a front-row view of the investment management world. Her dad, John Hotchkis, is an industry veteran. He's one of the original founders of Trust Company of the West, and started the value boutique Hotchkis and Wiley, with partner George Wiley, in 1980.

Although Ketterer worked for her father for a short time during college, she never planned to get into the investment management business. After earning her business degree at Dartmouth, Ketterer spent a few years at Banker's Trust, mostly on the banking side. Not long after leaving to start her own database business, Ketterer's dad talked her into joining his firm, and helping to lead their upstart international money management division. Ketterer accepted, began honing her investment skills, and has been trolling the worldwide waters looking for undervalued companies ever since.

She and her colleagues initially posted excellent returns running international portfolios for Hotchkis and Wiley. After the firm was sold to Merrill Lynch in the 1990s, Ketterer and several of her team members decided to jump ship and form their own firm in 2001. They named it Causeway Capital Management, after the 40-million-year-old Giants Causeway in Northern Ireland.

Although it's been around only a short time, the Causeway International Value Fund has been a standout performer since inception. The 43-year-old manager has actually proven her skills over a much longer period, though. And as you'll soon discover, she builds her portfolio one company—and country—at a time.

Kazanjian: *Were you always hoping to follow in your dad's footsteps by getting into the investment business?*

Ketterer: Growing up, I always knew I wanted to be in business, but I wasn't quite sure what I wanted to do. I think that's why 90 percent of people go to business school. They hope to have an incredible number of job opportunities thrown at their feet. When I finished graduate school at Dartmouth, I went to work for Banker's Trust. It was the first offer that came in the door. I got to work in a number of different areas. The one that fascinated me most was working in the merchant banking department, largely on behalf of U.S. clients making overseas acquisitions, particularly in Europe. I did a tremendous amount of data gathering and analysis of foreign company financial statements. It dawned on me then, which was the late 1980s, how inadequate that data was. So after three years at Banker's Trust, and plenty of time in New York City, I left and started an international database business, hoping to sell the data to some of the people I was best connected with, including my father John Hotchkis and his partner George Wiley, who had founded Hotchkis and Wiley.

Kazanjian: *Was your dad a willing client?*

Ketterer: He was. So I flew from New York to Los Angeles a few times in the early 1990s to talk to them about the data. They had just hired a very experienced investment professional from the Capital Group who was close to retirement to start an international equity product. At this point, I had no intention whatsoever of being in the investment management industry. As I did some consulting for my dad's firm and helped them get their minds sorted about how they wanted to approach the non-U.S. markets, within two months I had received a full-time offer to come work for them. The thought of returning to Southern California after having spent three years in New York was so appealing that I took it immediately.

Kazanjian: *You had never worked for your father before this time?*

Ketterer: Well, I did have this horrible summer in college when my father asked me to come work for him as he was starting Hotchkis and Wiley. To my chagrin, he put me in the back room. There were only three people working there at the time. I filed what were then called S&P tearsheets, which is the most mind-numbing job on this planet. You take the tearsheet, which comes in a huge stack in the mail, and you stick it in a binder. I lasted a couple of weeks and then just begged to do anything else.

Kazanjian: *So you began managing money for international accounts in 1990?*

Ketterer: Yes. I started in May, and by December we had our first multimillion-dollar account. It grew from there. We then hired an extremely experienced and incredibly talented colleague, Harry Hartford, who is still my partner today. He was working at the Bank of Ireland and moved his family from Dublin to Los Angeles. Five years into this, the partners of Hotchkis and Wiley, and particularly George Wiley, who was turning 70, were anxious to see some liquidity for their investment. By late 1996, they had officially sold their firm to Merrill Lynch. Merrill Lynch recognized the international equity business was growing rapidly at Hotchkis and Wiley, and gave us fairly substantial contracts with inducements to stick around. We got to know the Merrill Lynch organization very well because it was evolving from a retail-oriented investment management business based out of Princeton, New Jersey, to one with a more international or global focus through their subsequent $5.5 billion acquisition in 1997 of Mercury Asset Management. Mercury dwarfed Hotchkis and Wiley in size. My colleagues and I went from feeling sort of important to completely neglected in a fairly short period of time.

Kazanjian: *Is that when you decided to go out on your own?*

Ketterer: It wasn't quite that simple. I had always wanted to be on my own. I noticed the great satisfaction my father had from his independent, employee-owned firm. You don't answer to anyone. I had more bosses over the years who just didn't understand the investing business. The primary tenets of investment management are stability, continuity, and consistency of return. That seemed to escape them. The brokerage and investment banking business is very different. It's one of transactions and climbing up the organization. It's the complete opposite of investment management. My clients expect me to be doing the same thing every day, forever. They correlate change with any bobble in performance. So why did I leave? The writing was on the wall with the Mercury acquisition as Hotchkis and Wiley seemed increasingly less relevant. By the late 1990s, value investing was very much out of style. Everybody, even our most level-headed client, was beginning to wonder if they made a huge error by not having more growth managers in their lineup. We were considered heretics by many competitors. The other mainstream investment managers were very concerned about business risk and kept a close eye on funds that strayed too far from owning all the big TMT stocks—telecommunications, media, and technology—because they were the dominant force in the markets. We did something entirely different. Our approach was pure bottom-up. The belief has been, and will always be, that we can identify undervalued stocks across a variety of market cap ranges, even in a hostile environment where investors think earnings are going to be depressed. For some of the industries we look at, those were tough times.

In early 2001, Merrill Lynch said, "We don't think we want you anymore." They planned to sell Hotchkis and Wiley. The most interested buyer was a growth manager with tremendous internal conflict of its own. My colleagues and I couldn't bear the idea of having to go to our loyal clients and tell them it made sense for them to sign up with a subsidiary of a huge growth manager. So Harry and another portfolio manager, Jamie Doyle, and I met nights and weekends to construct a business plan. We then gave Merrill Lynch our notice. They gave us a couple of days and told us to leave. When we did, a total of 21 other employees followed us. We started Causeway in a matter of days, opening in June 2001.

Kazanjian: *Let's go back to your early days at Hotchkis and Wiley. You were really thrown into a situation where you went from data collector to investment manager. Did you learn how to pick stocks from scratch?*

Ketterer: Purely from scratch. I had investment banking training and spent a lot of time doing valuation work, including detailed financial modeling, the forensic dissemination of balance sheets and income statements, and making projections. Much of my work at Banker's Trust involved discus-

sions with company management about their business, how many widgets
they could sell, what the margins looked like, anything relative to the industry. You'd work out all the numbers to get down to operating income
and any other deductions to get the nirvana number, which is free cash
flow. This is cash flow the business generates after paying all its bills. Management can reinvest that free cash in the business—perhaps via acquisitions—or return it to shareholders. In my last two years at Banker's Trust, I
did this kind of valuation work for non-U.S. companies. That's what really
gave me a start looking at international markets. They were grossly ineffi-
ciently priced in the early 1990s relative to their peers in the United
States. Stocks all over Europe and in parts of Asia, including Japan, Hong
Kong, Singapore, and Australia were so mispriced that it wasn't too difficult to take some financial tools, a reasonable set of investment disciplines,
and screens that I'd inherited from the domestic equity business at
Hotchkis and Wiley and adapt them for evaluating international stocks. I
just kept turnover low and emphasized companies paying dividends, growing those dividends, and growing book value. That was more than half of
the battle. Most of my competitors at the time were still closet indexing.
There was very little concept of the unshackled international manager
who could construct a portfolio without concerns about variance from
the benchmark.

Kazanjian: *Did this value orientation come from the fact that Hotchkis and Wiley
was a value shop?*

Ketterer: Yes, although I think investment managers are born one way
or another. They come right out of the box with an investment style.
When we interview young inexperienced MBAs, they already sort of
know what they want. They either want to chase growth stocks, because
they're mesmerized by momentum, or they have a calmer demeanor
with enough maturity to look out beyond the cycle we're in now. In
house hunting, it's the difference between the person who just sees the
ramshackle disaster in front, as opposed to the other who can actually
look behind it all and see it renovated.

Kazanjian: *What is the case for international investing today? After all, there seems
to be an increasing correlation between U.S. and world markets.*

Ketterer: The number-one reason has been and will always be diversification. What does diversification do for an investor? It lowers risk, which
I define as volatility of return. Why do we care about volatility? Because

returns that fluctuate modestly allow one to sleep better at night. Calm investors are less likely to make poor decisions because they will have returns that are consistent and more predictable. Human nature is to swing big, but we usually do it at the wrong time. I guess history is strewn with examples of people who sold their holdings right at the bottom and bought them all back at the top. So diversification is crucial. Yes, correlations have been inching up between the non-U.S. markets, as measured by some of the standard international indices like EAFE (the Europe, Australasia, and Far East Index, which is designed to measure the overall performance of overseas markets), and the United States. But maybe more reassuring is the fact that the foreign markets, again measured by these large international indices, have had lower volatility than the U.S. market over the past five years. If you think about it, when you mix a lower volatility asset class with your U.S. holdings, you're lowering the overall volatility of your portfolio. That's exactly what we profess to do for our clients. We reduce the volatility of return, which allows for more consistent returns and the potential for greater gains. There are times when international equities have been fantastic. The more recent past is a good example. Since the United States came off the boil at the end of our bubble period in early 2000, international markets have surpassed the U.S. market. I think people forget that. The 1980s were a time when international stole the show, largely due to the bubble in Japan. I'd say where investors will do quite well in the future is with international value. I'm not just tooting my own horn, but we've looked at the studies. Even our institutional clients are always asking us why they should bother with international. We're able to show them they are adding returns through international value, while bringing the risk down.

Kazanjian: *It's true that international, as measured by the EAFE index, did well in the 1980s. But you would have suffered owning international in the 1990s.*

Ketterer: Not if you held on into the next decade. Part of what held back international in the 1990s was all this enthusiasm about the U.S. market. This brought a lot of money to the United States, and these enormous capital flows supported the dollar and made it very strong. That's another obstacle dollar-based international investors faced when going overseas in the latter half of the 1990s. They had this headwind of currency. Many of the stocks we follow do quite well when their local currency depreciates because it gives them a competitive cost advantage. So all is not lost when foreign currencies are weak. It just means the portfolio upside has to over-come this translation loss.

Kazanjian: *Another argument against international investing is that many U.S. companies, especially the large multinationals, are global in nature, and get a large percentage of revenues overseas. As a result, you don't have to leave our borders for international exposure.*

Ketterer: This just isn't correct. The same types of companies and indus-tries are valued extremely differently in all of our markets. Regional or lo-cal investors have a great amount of influence. Sure, you can buy Coca-Cola, which has all these operations all over the world, and get in-ternational exposure. But you won't have a diversified portfolio because Coke will crumble when the U.S. market crumbles. However, Cadbury Schweppes, which is listed on the London stock exchange, is in a very similar business and won't be nearly as affected by slow sales in the United States because it's listed in the United Kingdom.

Kazanjian: *Still, it is true that if we see the U.S. market fall, we're likely to see for-eign markets follow the next day. At least that's the normal trend.*

Ketterer: The point I want to leave you with is don't own the market. That is the lesson I learned on my first day of work in 1990. The whole idea be-hind active management is that investors are holding a subset of the market that's been hand selected, ideally from the bottom up. We construct our portfolios with both return and risk criteria, so that all the stocks blend to-gether, leading to the lowest-risk portfolio and one that also has the high-est expected return. Yes, the anecdotal evidence exists of markets moving together, but you're not holding the markets. You're holding a portfolio that ideally doesn't have a particularly high correlation with the market.

Kazanjian: *I assume then that you're not a fan of indexing.*

Ketterer: For international markets? You might as well just put your money in a drawer.

Kazanjian: *If you were to take a diversified international stock portfolio, put it next to a diversified U.S. stock portfolio, and ignore it for 10 years, would you expect the foreign or U.S. portfolio to be worth more at the end of that time period?*

Ketterer: Over a longer stretch, up to a decade or more, I do think this in-efficient pricing we see internationally, which isn't as evident in the United States, gives foreign equities a bit of an advantage. The caveat is, you would need to own a value portfolio of stocks, as opposed to just the market.

Kazanjian: *Why won't a growth approach work in foreign markets?*

Ketterer: It's not just unique to foreign markets. The value investor is buy-ing stocks right down at base camp, which is sometimes very painful, and then holding the stock as you ascend half-way or three-quarters of the way up the mountain. The growth investor is buying once earnings have been regenerated and everything is going well. That's the point when everyone wants to own the stock. As you're getting close to the precipice, the risk level increases rather rapidly. Growth investors sort of know they're playing with fire. If anything goes wrong, all the good news is already priced into the stock, and they've gone right over the edge.

Kazanjian: *What percentage of a stock portfolio do you think U.S. investors should have internationally?*

Ketterer: For institutions we recommend 50-plus percent to really get the full benefit.

Kazanjian: *Fifty percent? That seems kind of high.*

Ketterer: For individuals, I think if you have under 10 overseas it sort of doesn't matter. I'm not sure it will make enough of a difference. It's up to individuals' willingness to take risk. The more time you have before you need the money, the more you might be willing to take on international exposure. In the event that something goes awry, it gives the portfolio more time to right itself. But I do think that 30 to 40 percent international probably feels about right for individuals.

Kazanjian: *What percentage of your own portfolio do you keep internationally?*

Ketterer: About 80 percent. I'm a big believer.

Kazanjian: *Do you keep that money in your fund, or buy individual stocks?*

Ketterer: No, I've never understood in all my years of doing this how my peers could possibly be trading for their own portfolio. There's not enough time in the day. When you're covering a 70-stock portfolio, and you've got another 10 under research, you can spend every waking mo-ment on those stocks.

Kazanjian: *Will you invest in almost any country?*

Ketterer: We specialize in the developed world, so there are 24 markets we consider to be developed. And 24 is usually enough. If you can't find value in these 24 countries, you might as well pack up and go home. Those are the European markets plus Australia, New Zealand, Canada, Japan, Hong

Kong, Singapore, Korea, and Taiwan, although the latter two are not generally considered developed. I'm not a big fan of the emerging markets. I don't even recommend them. I think the risks are too high and you don't need them.

Kazanjian: *When you start the investment process, do you begin by looking at companies or countries?*

Ketterer: We start from the bottom. We look at 3,400 stocks in those 24 markets, all with a market capitalization above $1 billion. We don't buy any small-caps.

Kazanjian: *I assume you run these through your computer screens. What sorts of variables are you looking for?*

Ketterer: The screens are like a sieve that dips through all these stocks. Our quantitative specialists test the criteria we screen for to identify stocks that are already biased to outperform their markets, based on a series of back tests. The stocks that make it through the screens with the greatest amount of potency tend to be winners over the long term. So if we're going to focus our research effort on any group of stocks, clearly we want to do so on those that pass the screen with flying colors.

Kazanjian: *What exactly are you screening for?*

Ketterer: We screen within country and then within the industry. It's a two-prong screen. Within each country, we screen stocks for their prospective earnings yield, defined as the ratio of earnings per share over price per share, or every increment of earnings the stock can deliver for the price you're paying for it. That earnings yield has to exceed the country's 10-year government bond yield. Think of the bond yield as the risk-free alternative investment. We want to buy equities with a risk premium of at least 200 basis points (2 percent), which is lower than the long-term averages for equity risk premiums in all of our markets. But it works as an effective screen. As bond yields rise, we must find stocks with an even higher earnings yield. In other words, stock prices must fall to where the earnings yield exceeds this hurdle. To think about it in another way, if earnings yield equates to the ratio of earnings to price, the reciprocal is the PE ratio. High earnings yield stocks are also low PE stocks. So we know these are value stocks because they have low PEs. At the same time they have a payout yield in excess of the market average. Payout yield, as we define it, is just dividend yield plus share buybacks. We turn the buybacks into a yield by taking the average of the last couple of years of buybacks over the market

cap. Some companies prefer to buy back stock instead of paying dividends, which helps shareholders through improvement in earnings per
share by reducing shares outstanding. We like to see that. The intersection
of the two—the high earnings yield and payout yield above the market
average—tends to be a very effective screen. At the same time, we look
for the intersection of two criteria within industries. One is earnings revisions, which we like to see. We use an outside service for this. Analyst
earnings revisions reach a turning point then start to move up. So that's
very reassuring. We combine this with a price-to-cash flow ratio that's less
than the industry average. This happens to be one of the few criteria you
can compare across borders. When we start looking within industries,
we're now comparing stocks in Spain to stocks in Singapore and Switzer-
land, all of which have different accounting methods. In fact we define
price-to-cash flow as enterprise value to EBITDA. Enterprise value is just
market cap plus the company's debt, less cash over earnings before interest, taxes, depreciation, and amortization, which is sort of like cash flow.
When that price-to-cash flow number is less than the industry average, it
means the stock is undervalued compared to its industry peers. We have
stocks that pass our screen within countries and industries, although a
stock needs to pass only one or the other to be included in the next step
of the research process.

Kazanjian: *Since these screens are so reliant on financial results, are you able to trust
the numbers coming from these other countries, given the vast differences in accounting standards?*

Ketterer: That's one of the beauties of screening within a country, because
all of the comparisons are done within the same accounting standards.

Kazanjian: *From this initial 3,400 list, how many will generally pop out for further
examination?*

Ketterer: On average we'll see 400 each week that pass the criteria. That's a
lot of stocks. But of those we may see 20 to 30 that we didn't see in the
prior week. The fresh water in the tide pool is pretty modest.

Kazanjian: *Are you then focusing your efforts on the fresh water?*

Ketterer: Yes. The very next step is a financial strength score. We go
through each stock and reject those that we consider to have inadequate
financial strength. This is particularly critical for deep cyclicals. In order to
be patient we must have financial strength. We need to own those technology companies and the bottom of the tech cycle with net cash on the bal-

ance sheet and so much financial flexibility that no matter how grim it gets, they'll be alive two years from now.

Kazanjian: *How do you define financial strength?*

Ketterer: It depends on the industry. We used to do it by country. We gave up on those about four years ago and evolved to industry scores. For different industries certain criteria are meaningful. We assess overall creditworthiness and fixed charges. We look for outstanding debt balances. In stable businesses, like pharmaceuticals, it's surprising to see any of these companies with a lot of debt, given all the cash they generate. If they do have debt, you start to wonder why. It rings alarm bells.

Kazanjian: *What's the next step?*

Ketterer: Competitive analysis. What really makes a winning stock from a value perspective is a company with a fairly benign competitive environment. Conversely, what challenges management and seems to hinder their ability to improve earnings growth is overwhelming amounts of competition. Once we've assessed the competition and strength of the competition, we move to the remainder of what we call 360-degree analysis. When you've talked to the competition you're only part of the way there. The next step is talking to the customers, suppliers, and rest of the chain. They can be very revealing. We'll see something in the financials that will be corroborated by discussions with suppliers and competitors. And all of that goes into the electronic notebooks that we keep as analysts, and that we funnel into building financial projections on the company. Assessing that fair value is the most important criterion. It's the most important step in this entire fundamental research process. And it's the most difficult because there's so much art that couples with the science.

Kazanjian: *How do you decide what something is worth?*

Ketterer: We sometimes end up with a range but more often than not we build all of our projections based on assumptions. For instance, we bought GlaxoSmithKline. This isn't exactly your hideaway stock. It's a huge, $100 billion–plus market cap constituent of the FTSE 100, the largest stocks in the United Kingdom stock exchange index. Why is it a value stock? Because investors hate it. They think the company is just one enormous pincushion for the generic drug firms. My assumptions are that somewhere in that R&D pipeline there's some value because very little of it has been priced into the stock today. If I'm wrong, we've overpaid. But if I'm right,

I can quantify the upside. As we go through bouts of pessimism, when investors give up on the stock and knock it down by a pound or more, we have the conviction to go in and buy more because we have assessed its fair value. We've taken a stick and we've drawn a line in the sand and said, "This is fair value." And every time the stock drops 5, 10, 15 percent below fair value, we're going to buy a little more. And that's what disciplined investing is all about. It's when you take your emotions and lock them up in the closet.

Kazanjian: *Do you buy the GlaxoSmithKline American Depositary Receipts available here in the United States, or do you strictly buy the foreign securities on local foreign exchanges?*

Ketterer: All of the securities we buy are foreign listed.

Kazanjian: *You currently have roughly 31 percent of the portfolio invested in the United Kingdom. Is that because you like the United Kingdom, or merely where the best-valued companies happen to be located?*

Ketterer: It's entirely residual of that bottom–up stock collection process.

Kazanjian: *What if all the stocks you liked were in the United Kingdom? Would you put your entire portfolio there, or expand your horizons to make it more diversified?*

Ketterer: We do make sure we're diversified among countries. If you try to overload any one country or industry, the risk model will catch it. As a safety check, we won't have more than 30 percent in any one country except for the United Kingdom, which we cap at 35 percent because it's the second largest stock market outside the United States and particularly deep and broad.

Kazanjian: *How many stocks do you tend to hold in the portfolio?*

Ketterer: Between 60 and 80.

Kazanjian: *Most of the variables in stock selection we've talked about so far are quantitative. What about on the fundamental side? Do you meet with management, for instance?*

Ketterer: We do. We're all on the road every couple of months for about a week at a time. Some foreign funds do that work by having everybody located all over the world. I think that's a mistake because nobody talks to each other. You can find all these wonderful ideas and then you're all in different time zones, so nobody communicates and nothing ever happens. The approach that we've taken is to keep the entire investment team on one floor of one office. We're all sort of crammed together for a reason, so that we meet frequently and exchange information. Meeting with a company is not a prerequisite, but some sort of contact is necessary, such as a conference call. Usually we're already familiar with the company and the management. It's just now, because the share price has come down for whatever reason, we can buy the stock.

Kazanjian: *What makes you decide to sell a stock?*

Ketterer: One of the most helpful features of having a live ranking of stocks on a risk-adjusted return basis is that we can see how the stocks rank relative to each other. As a stock performs, and the share price rises, all other things being equal, it will descend in the ranking. We divide this list of 150 stocks into tiers. For every tier it falls, we'll take another 25 basis points or so off the weighting. We take profits based on a relative value. In other words, relative to the other potential investment candidates listed on this ranking, how does this stock compare? If it's now in the 50th percentile, we'll cut the weight in half. By the time it goes to the bottom, we're out and we've recycled the proceeds back into higher-ranking candidates.

Kazanjian: *How long are you willing to wait for an idea to work out?*

Ketterer: When you're a value investor, you're a patient investor. You've probably bought the stock too early, and you've probably suffered a little pain. You had to buy more just to get the average weighted book price down to some level where you're not embarrassed to show it to the client. And you're going to be holding it for a very long time. You're collecting dividends, meeting with management, crossing your fingers, whatever it takes. Management may require a few years to improve the business and revive earnings. And we'll be patient. So it takes a long time and our portfolio turnover is quite low as a result.

Kazanjian: *Is it possible for an individual investor in the United States to easily buy these foreign securities?*

Ketterer: It's possible, though they're probably more likely to do it through ADRs. (ADRs, or American Depositary Receipts, are proxies for foreign stocks sold on the New York Stock Exchange and denominated in dollars.) It's hard for individuals to buy securities directly on the foreign exchanges. Even if you did, it's important to be highly diversified, which can be expensive unless you have huge amounts of money. The reason we're constructing a portfolio of 60-plus stocks is because it's the blend of those stocks that gets us to the outcome we want. Incidentally, ADRs are unfortunate animals, as far as I'm concerned. They're generally less liquid than their cousins trading in the local market. So you get less liquidity and the currency fluctuation is embedded in the share price.

Kazanjian: *Speaking of currency, do you hedge your holdings to protect yourself from local market currency fluctuations?*

Ketterer: Generally we don't hedge. We'll only hedge portions of the portfolio for defensive reasons, and that happens very infrequently. We hedged Hong Kong dollars and yen during the Asian crisis. We will hedge only when currencies are under speculative attack, and we still want to own the underlying equity. We're building and maintaining the portfolio with an eye to currency in the following way. All of our stocks are analyzed using the current spot rate. We can't tell you which way the currency will go. Nobody can. But at least we know what to expect.

Kazanjian: *So investing in a fund like yours is also somewhat of a currency play.*

Ketterer: Well, you certainly are exposed. Currency is one of the factors that we use in our risk model. If we were to overly concentrate in any one currency, we would see that effect in the expected risk for the portfolio. So we're measuring it, we're monitoring it, but we're typically not hedging it. One of the reasons my colleagues and I have a philosophical dislike for currency hedging is that we try to keep as little cash as possible. We're being paid to put money into stocks. Once you start a big hedging program, you've got to raise cash in order to mark the positions to market. Some months the positions will be positive, and other months negative. They may be negative or positive for a prolonged period of time. But if you have to keep raising cash by selling stocks in order to settle your hedges, that's taking money away from the main engine or driver of performance. As we look at performance attribution over time, by far the single greatest contributor is stock, not currency or country, selection.

Kazanjian: *Looking ahead over the next few years, what's your outlook for international markets vis-à-vis the United States?*

Ketterer: I don't see any reason why in the next couple of years we should see demonstrably better performance out of non-U.S. versus U.S. markets. When you get down to the value manager who's working from the bottom up and identifying undervalued stocks, then I could see a difference. As I mentioned before, I think non-U.S. stocks are often priced less efficiently than the United States and that provides a real opportunity for the international value manager. Those comments apply to the developed world. In the developing markets, it's hard to say.

So what kind of returns is Ketterer anticipating from the market? On the assumption that bond yields rise to between 5 and 6 percent, and adding in the typical long-term equity risk premium of around 3 percent, she sees U.S. and international stocks returning around 9 percent over the next 5 to 10 years. "If you get 10 percent, you ought to go running to the bank," Ketterer says, adding value managers successful at identifying unpopular stocks might be able to do a bit better than that.

RUDOLPH-RIAD YOUNES

Julius Baer Investment Management

For Riad Younes, the world is literally his oyster. As manager of the Julius Baer International Fund, he's able to buy companies of all sizes anywhere on the planet. While Younes got into international investing almost by accident, it's a perfect fit for his eclectic background. Although he was born in Nigeria, he spent most of his life in Lebanon, before moving to the United States to attend college.

After earning an engineering degree and working in the field for a short time, Younes went back to school for an MBA and wound up in the investment business—first on the fixed-income side, and later as an international analyst and portfolio manager.

As you'll discover, Younes relies heavily on his instincts when it comes to making investment decisions, although he pays careful attention to a company's valuation and growth prospects. While he's most optimistic about the prospects for central Europe, Younes feels that international markets in general are much more attractive than the United States and will remain so for at least the next decade.

Younes, who characteristically refuses to give out his age, is a big believer in diversification and often keeps up to 300 stocks in his fund. And while he's willing to own anything, small and emerging markets stocks have to climb a much higher barrier to make it into the portfolio.

Kazanjian: *You're originally from Lebanon and moved to the United States in 1981. Tell me a bit about your younger years.*

Younes: I grew up during the war and think this experience helped and readied me for the volatility of the financial markets. When you have bombs exploding and people dying next to you, yet you still have to focus and study and worry about exams, it takes a lot of mental toughness. In a sense, you have to manage risk while keeping your head cool.

Kazanjian: *Did you go to college in Lebanon?*

Younes: Yes. I came to the States for my last two years of college. I finished my undergraduate degree in engineering at Columbia, and also did my master's there. After a short stint in engineering I realized that was not my calling in life. It wasn't interesting to me. So I went to business school, at the Yale School of Management, and completed my MBA in 1991.

Kazanjian: *Is that when you decided to get into the investment industry?*

Younes: I never even thought about investment management, although I was always very good with numbers. I was mostly interested either in investment banking or consulting. Because of my strong quantitative background, I was hired by Swiss Bank Corporation to help the senior global fixed-income manager develop spreadsheet and valuation models. I worked mostly in currencies and bonds. Two years later, the head of international equity at Swiss Bank, which is now UBS, was hired by Julius Baer in New York. Although I didn't work for the guy, he was seemingly impressed by my results. He called a few months later and asked if I would like to join him. I had some reservations, but was getting bored with fixed income. I figured if I could get into equities I'd consider it. He met all my demands so I decided to take the opportunity. This was in 1993. At the time I was not very familiar with Julius Baer. It turned out to be a very good organization with almost no politics. It's family owned and run.

Kazanjian: *Did you start out on the equity side at Julius Baer?*

Younes: No, I worked in all asset classes. In 1995 we restructured the group, divided management into different asset classes, and each person became responsible for one asset class. I chose to focus on international equities.

Kazanjian: *Why did you want to concentrate on international stocks?*

Younes: For several reasons. One, I felt that's where the bank's strength was. Two, because of my very diverse background, I felt comfortable dealing with different markets and their cultures. Three, I felt the international equity markets were much less efficient than the United States. If you really want to have high returns, high alpha, it pays much more to be active in an inefficient market.

Kazanjian: *You've been investing in international equities with great success for about a decade now. How did you develop the investment process you follow today?*

Younes: Let me warn you from the start that there is no holy grail! My partner Richard Pell and I had the luxury of not having a legacy process built by others to follow. Sometimes your weakness becomes your strength. Many times in life we do things because we are told to do them. In the west, we eat with a fork, for example, because that's how everyone eats, though there may be a more efficient way.

In developing our process, we went to basics. An optimal process is one that is built on a philosophy that understands the role and tasks of the portfolio manager. A common misperception in the market is that to be a great manager one needs to be a great analyst. In reality, a portfolio manager's role is not one dimensional. He or she is a strategist, an analyst, and a trader simultaneously. And to be a great portfolio manager one needs to be just above average in each function because the synergies are humongous. It seems a simple task, but in reality it is a difficult feat.

The strategist part is needed because the job and duty of the portfolio manager is to see the big picture at the country and sector level. The analyst part is needed because one must understand accounting and how to value companies—valuation does matter. The trader part is needed because risk management is key not only to a trader's survival, but also to a portfolio manager's survival. Money management is a combination of dogmatism and pragmatism. And pragmatism is nothing but risk management, knowing when to fight the trend and when to go with it. It's knowing when to ride your winners, take your profits, or cut your losses.

In biological terms, the strategist is your right brain, the analyst is your left brain, and the trader is your discipline. If you are able to use your full brain in a disciplined manner you are going to succeed. That is the essence of portfolio management—it is as simple as that.

Our process is also built on the understanding and respect of the laws of gravity that govern equities.

Kazanjian: *What do you mean by the laws of gravity?*

Younes: The history of equity investing is very interesting. Let's go back to the South Sea bubble during Sir Isaac Newton's time in the 1720s. He invested a ton of his wealth in the equity market during that euphoria and almost lost it all. He said, "I can calculate the motion of heavenly bodies but not the madness of people." In his time people had no idea how to value equities. Early in this century investors required dividend yields to be higher than bond yields, on the belief that since equities are riskier than bonds one should ask for a higher dividend yield to own a stock. If you look at the stock market before the 1950s, dividend yields were considerably higher than bond yields. The relationship later reversed itself as investors realized that growth more than compensates for the risk. It is now very common to see dividend yields well below bond yields. The new school of thought, which is currently the most predominant one, is that since equities have historically returned about 9 percent above Treasury bills, investors should continue to expect to earn 9 percent above Treasury bills from equities. To me this is heresy. What if people lost money in equities for the last 80 years? Does that mean people should expect to lose money when they invest in equities? It all comes down to the laws of gravity. One of the laws is that no asset class in the world can grow above the GDP rate for an indefinite period. Whether you're investing in bonds, equities, or real estate, over time it has to grow below or at GDP. The same laws apply to earnings. Can the earnings of a corporation grow above GDP rate forever? No.

One main law of gravity is that the long-term earnings growth of a company is below that of nominal GDP. If earnings were to grow indefinitely at a higher rate than nominal GDP, then, at one point in time, they would become larger than GDP. If earnings of existing companies were to grow indefinitely at the rate of GDP, then one has to assume there is no new business formation—which is highly unlikely. There are always new industries and leading companies that are emerging from the pack. As a result, corporate earnings should grow at a rate slightly below GDP. So, as time goes by, today's performance leaders will slowly fade and be displaced by tomorrow's new leaders. Studies have shown that new entrants, on the aggregate, generate about 15 percent of industry sales within five years from entry.

One of the laws of nature is the law of terminal velocity. That is the maximum speed a falling object can reach. In nature, as an object falls, its speed increases and causes an increase in air resistance. The falling object continues to accelerate until air resistance equals gravity. At that point the object stops accelerating and continues to fall at a constant speed—terminal velocity. Shape, mass, and density of the object, along with gravity, determine terminal velocity.

Fast-growing companies and sectors in the financial jungle are also governed by the law of terminal velocity. We call it the law of terminal valuation. When an industry or a company grows above GDP it creates friction. Corporate dominance invites regulatory scrutiny, and fat margins and opportunities in a certain sector attract new players to the space. Ultimately, because of such frictions, a fast-growing industry would cease to grow faster than GDP. Otherwise it becomes larger than the economy. A company growing at a faster rate than its industry (won't keep growing at that rate forever). Otherwise its market share would become larger than 100 percent.

Barriers to entry, the industry's potential peak market share of GDP, the company's potential peak market share within the industry, along with the industry's obsolescence rate determine terminal valuation. The higher the barriers to entry are, the higher the company's margin and hence the higher its terminal valuation. The more the industry can increase its share of GDP, the higher the company's terminal valuation. The higher the company's peak market share of the industry, the higher its terminal valuation. And the slower an industry becomes obsolete in the post-growth period, the slower companies decay relative to GDP, and hence the higher the valuation. Eventually industries decay, as their importance in the economy diminishes. Over the last century, the agriculture sector gave way to manufacturing, which in turn is giving way to the service sector. The trick is figuring out what the long-term GDP growth is.

Kazanjian: *Especially since the GDP rate is always changing.*

Younes: GDP rates indeed fluctuate. You have to estimate the long-term GDP growth rate, because today's rate doesn't matter. How do you determine that? By relying on another law of gravity: The 30-year Treasury bond yield is the best indicator of expected long-term nominal GDP growth. In the early 1980s we had high inflation, so expectations for long-term nominal GDP growth were high. The opposite was true in the 1950s; we had low inflation and thus expected low growth.

Kazanjian: *As we speak, that's a little under 5 percent if I'm not mistaken.*

Younes: Today the market expects long-term growth of 5 percent because we are in a very low inflation environment. In the 1980s, when the long bond yield was 10 to 14 percent, the market expected normal GDP of 10 to 14 percent because inflation was 6 to 10 percent. Therefore, based on today's expectations, we should expect earnings growth of around 5 percent.

Kazanjian: *This seems like a fairly low and achievable number.*

Younes: No. That's misleading. If you look at statistics for S&P 500 earnings over the last 50 years, they have grown below the GDP rate, despite the fact that the index is always replacing slow-growers with very high-growth companies.

Kazanjian: *That's a bit surprising. I think most people assume companies grow at a faster rate than that.*

Younes: Yes, because investors listen to the spin of Wall Street. As I mentioned earlier, if you look at the facts you will find that U.S. GDP grew by 7.1 percent annually during 1950–2002, while S&P 500 reported earnings per share grew by 5.20 percent annually. Despite the fact that the index frequently replaces slow-growing members with fast-growers, it has failed to have its earnings grow at the rate of GDP.

Kazanjian: *Given that, what characteristics are you looking for when evaluating stocks?*

Younes: Valuing stocks in theory is very easy but in practice extremely cumbersome. Very simply, the price of a stock should reflect the present value of the perpetual stream of expected cash flows. The problem with discount models is they are too sensitive to the inputs. If one were to tweak some of the inputs such as the growth rate or the discount rate, one may end up with a price anywhere between zero and infinity. Another problem with commonly used discount models is that they are too complex with so many variables they cease to be intuitive. And that is very important, because intuition, that is, common sense, is our *last line* of defense.

Our philosophy is to keep things simple. Simplicity helps one preserve intuition, common sense, and sanity. Of all the equity valuation models used today, dividend discount models are the simplest. They are also very powerful if the inputs are reasonable. The inputs are few but can be easily manipulated to get any answer desired.

The reason we were and still are in a bubble is because the quality of the consensus input is poor, not [because of] the models. The quality of the output is not dependent on the complexity of the models but rather on the quality of the input. So if we can keep the models simple, the task of improving the quality of input becomes much easier, and hence the output. In a two-stage dividend discount model there are four main inputs: the initial dividend, the discount rate, the growth rate in the first stage, and the growth rate in the second stage.

We have resorted to the "laws of gravity" that govern equities to restrict our freedom and prevent us from making heroic assumptions to support our conclusions, and therefore help us avoid the garbage-in, garbage-out syndrome. We have heavily relied on the very strong relationship among nominal GDP growth, the long-term government bond yield, and earnings growth. This relationship has enabled us to transform the dividend discount model into a powerful tool.

The law that links the long-term Treasury bond yield to long-term nominal GDP growth also prevents us from increasing the growth rate without simultaneously increasing the discount rate. In other words, it restrains our freedom to manipulate output.

The two most common applications for the model are to calculate the implied growth rate for a stock or a sector, or the implied risk premium for the market in general.

Kazanjian: *How do you decide how much you're willing to pay for the stock?*

Younes: Theoretically, one should rely only on valuation discount models. But because of their high sensitivities to input, and the unnecessary complexities that suffocate intuition, analysts and portfolio managers are relying more and more on financial and operational ratios for guidance either instead of the models or for support—a sanity check, if you will. But one has to be aware that these ratios are merely a rule of thumb—a lazy way to determine valuations. They are relatively powerful at the country and sector levels. They are also sometimes powerful for the average company, but are generally misleading for the very good or bad ones.

We rely on discount models and financial ratios when valuing companies. But in order to determine what to rely on and how, one needs to ask why one is buying the stock. For simplicity, you buy a stock for three reasons: either for its past, its present, or its future.

You buy a stock for its past when its best days are behind it. At that stage, a company usually destroys value and tends to be worthless as a going concern and is therefore worth more dead than alive. In such cases discount models are not useful since they reflect its valuation as a going concern. Hence asset-based valuation metrics that reflect the stock's liquidation value are much more relevant. If there is a catalyst, such as change in management, then we consider a 30 percent discount to assets as attractive. If we have to wait for a catalyst, then we may require a 50 percent discount or more.

If you are buying a stock for its present, then most likely you are buying an average company in an average-growth industry. In such cases financial and operational ratios such as PE or EV (enterprise value)/EBITDA are powerful rules of thumb and are heavily relied on for a sanity check. We limit the scope of comparisons using those metrics to peers within the same industry.

If you are buying a stock for its future, the discount model is the most relevant tool. Asset-based valuations tend to be irrelevant, but financial ratios remain somehow relevant, especially price/sales—usually a price/sales above five is a warning signal that we may be in hallucination territory. The most frequent use of the discount model is to calculate the implied growth rate. How much do earnings need to grow over the next 10 years to justify today's price? We then make sure that the growth rate is reasonable and does not violate the laws of gravity.

Kazanjian: *How do you figure out what those reasonable expectations are?*

Younes: As I said earlier, there are three factors in the economy that will determine a company's growth rate: the company's market share, the industry's ultimate market share of the economy, and the entry barriers to that industry. So when you calculate the implied growth you need to subject it to the scrutiny of gravity and common sense. Sometimes it is obvious; other times it's not. I'll give you an example of when it was obvious. In March 2000, the Nasdaq was above 5,000. If you calculated the implied growth rates required to justify that level, you would have found out that earnings needed to grow by 20 percent over the next 20 years. Not a grotesque number for tech junkies. But for that to happen, one has to believe that in 20 years the Nasdaq's profit would be equal to 7 percent of GDP. The problem is that historically, the whole private sector's profit has averaged about 5.4 percent of GDP. Yet the current members of Nasdaq are expected in 20 years to have cumulative profits equal to 7 percent of GDP.

Kazanjian: *It definitely sounds like there's a lot of intuition involved in your process. What percentage of your approach is quantitative versus qualitative, especially in determining value?*

Younes: If you look at the human brain, the left brain is logical, sequential, rational, analytical, and objective. The right brain is random, intuitive, holistic, and subjective. In investment terms, the left brain is like a quantitative or bottom-up approach, the right brain is more qualitative or top-down driven. Whenever you are on one side or the other, in general I think you're using only half your brain to beat the market. I believe that we are slaves to information. Sometimes the useful information that comes to us is top-down and we use it. Sometimes it's company specific. Sometimes you find oil by looking for seepage, other times you get it by drilling. For example, our decision to invest in central and eastern Europe was mainly driven by the political decision of western Europe to expand eastward and include the region in the European Union. And recently, Turkey is one of our latest ventures because of its improving prospects of getting an invitation to join the European Union.

Kazanjian: *Are you looking to buy a stock at a certain percentage below what you think it's worth?*

Younes: Because we are not dealing with a precise science, we don't usually have exact price targets. We deal with ranges mostly. If we are buying a company for its past, we are looking to buy at a 30 to 50 percent discount to net asset value. If we are buying for its present, we are targeting a 10 to 20 percent discount to peer multiples. And if we are buying for its future, we are looking for reasonable and achievable implied growth rates.

Kazanjian: *Given that you don't go in with a specific target price, how do you know when it's time to sell a stock?*

Younes: When the financial ratios start to get stretched, you take a close look. When long-term growth rates begin to get near or above the GDP growth rate, it tells you you're starting to fight gravity. As long as the growth rate for a stock stays within the GDP range, you feel it's sustainable because it's easy to grow below GDP for very long periods of time. It's very difficult to grow above GDP for a sustainable period because you're creating lots of friction.

Kazanjian: *What about on the downside? If a stock is falling in price, what makes you decide it isn't working out and you've made a mistake?*

Younes: Selling is done for several reasons. Sometimes we sell to reduce risk. I could have a 1 percent position that has tripled and becomes 3 percent of the portfolio. That's too high, so I'll reduce the position. The second reason is if our thesis is proven wrong, and I'm wrong a lot. Sometimes because of underperformance, we might decide to reduce our exposure, even if the fundamentals still look okay. We won't necessarily go against our fundamental convictions, but we will reduce our bet and wait until either things go our way or we get convinced we were wrong.

Kazanjian: *How many stocks do you tend to own in the portfolio?*

Younes: In the beginning we were always criticized for having too many stocks. There is a saying that there is no free lunch in the market. In reality there is only one free lunch and that is diversification. It's a free insurance. If you want to buy insurance in the real world you have to pay for it. In the financial markets, the more you're diversified, the more you reduce your risk, and it doesn't cost a thing. For me, if I could have 1 million companies in the portfolio, I would have 1 million companies. Generally, I find it very practical to have somewhere between 200 and 300 companies. The number depends on what the opportunities are. If we find more opportunities in smaller companies or in high-risk sectors, the number of names in the portfolio has to be very large. If the valuation discrepancy is more in the large-cap names, then you'll see the portfolio closer to 150 names than 300.

Kazanjian: *So you'll buy companies of all market caps?*

Younes: Yes. We are mostly large-cap managers, but we can buy anything under the sun. Of course, we do have different entry barriers depending on the size of the company. A large blue-chip name needs an expected return of 10 percent to qualify into the portfolio. A mid-cap name needs a return of 20 to 25 percent to qualify. A small-cap name needs an expected return of 30 to 50 percent. A micro-cap needs a double or triple. The less liquid the name, the harder it is to sell us on the idea, and therefore justify getting it into the portfolio.

Kazanjian: *You can basically buy any company anywhere in the world.*

Younes: Exactly. Why artificially constrain yourself?

Kazanjian: *Given that your starting point is so broad, how do you make a decision on which companies and countries to own?*

Younes: Our investible universe is more than 10,000 stocks. How can we follow them? A common practice in the industry is to first reduce the stock universe into a manageable number through screening. Usually, simple financial ratios such as dividend yields and PE ratios are used to reduce the number from a few thousand names to a couple of hundred. Then, an army of analysts reduces the number to about 100 names. Amazing! A simple task of screening that could have been undertaken by a fifth-grader has already done more than 90 percent of the work. We decided to reverse the process.

We wanted to be responsible for 90 percent of the work while keeping it simple, powerful, and intuitive. A simple process that is not powerful and intuitive loses its relevance, so we tend to focus on sector dynamics in the developed world, macroeconomic factors in the emerging world, and on dynamic information at the company level. In other words, we're looking for seepage with selective drilling.

Kazanjian: *Do you start off by saying, "I think Europe is the most attractive place to be, so I want most of my money there, while I don't like Japan, so I'm not going to put much in that country"?*

Younes: In Europe we tend to be sector driven, because it is a solid and well-developed economy and macroeconomic conditions have little effect on the vitality of the private sector. We are great believers in what's known as the Porter Model and the factors that shape an industry's prospects: the power of suppliers, the power of customers, the barriers to entry and exit, the degree of rivalry in the industry, and the threat of substitutes. As these factors change, an industry's profitability and prospects dramatically change.

The same cannot be said about the emerging markets. Because of financial mismanagement 101 at both the private and government level, any economic weakness could lead to a crisis. The main source of this instability is the mismatch of debt with revenue. While most of the emerging-market companies earn their revenue in local currency, the bulk of their debt is in hard currency. A little devaluation could and has led to a mass wave of bankruptcies.

In Japan we use a hybrid approach. The domestic sector is heavily affected by macroeconomic conditions while the export sector is analyzed along industry dynamics.

Kazanjian: *Is there any country you absolutely will not invest in?*

Younes: That's a very big mistake. Everything is investable. To paraphrase an insurance industry philosophy, "There is no such thing as a bad risk, though there are bad premiums." No country, sector, or stock is too risky. The only questions are: How much should you buy and what price should you pay? If I were to avoid anything today, it would be technology—because the premiums are too high, not because they are too risky.

Kazanjian: *You have said that in the emerging-market countries, you prefer to be an early settler, not a pioneer. What do you mean by that?*

Younes: I was using an old American adage. What's the difference between a pioneer and an early settler? The pioneers got arrows in their backs. In pharmaceuticals, you want to be the first one who discovers molecules because you will get the patent. In a land mine, you want to be the last one walking out, so everything will be safe in front of you. In life, sometimes you have a first-mover advantage and sometimes you have a last-mover advantage. The growth rate will be higher there over the long term, so you should be able to make more money. But we haven't made money there yet. In the emerging markets, so far we have been in a pioneering era, like those Americans who came early and got scalped. The trick is to know which emerging markets are entering the early settler era. For us, central and eastern Europe was a clear case of a region leaving the pioneering era and entering the early settler era, so we invested significantly there. When you look at the emerging markets in Latin America, Asia, or Africa, the vast majority are still in the pioneering era, which means you have to go in with a trading mentality. They have not been a buy-and-hold market as of yet.

Kazanjian: *Looking ahead 3 to 5 years, which countries do you think will be most attractive for investors?*

Younes: If Turkey gets unconditional support from the EU for its aspiration to join the club, it could be the best-performing equity market in the world over the next 3 to 5 years. After that, I still feel central Europe and Russia are very attractive investments for the long haul.

Kazanjian: *What about Asia, and specifically China? People keep talking about how fast the population there is growing and how that will be fertile ground for investors.*

Younes: I don't much agree with them. People have to separate China's economic and equity investment prospects. These are two different issues. We saw a huge traffic explosion in telecommunications and the Internet in the United States, yet many technology and telecommunications companies got decimated and went bankrupt. This goes back to the brain. Most people are right handed and it seems to me also right brained. Many analysts, when recommending a stock, tend to focus on one thing—the demand and growth side of the story. They say, "Go invest in the Internet because demand is going to be up 100 percent a year and everybody's using it." Few ask, "What is the price of this company and how hard is it for anybody to open a web site?" When you find out it only takes $500 to have your own web site and learn that many of these companies are trading at 30 to 40 times sales, your left brain tells you it's not as exciting as people are claiming. If you were to rely solely on your right brain, you would have mortgaged your house and bought all these stocks.

I have no doubt that we are at the beginning of a big structural change where China is becoming more manufacturing based. But if everybody overbuilt in China, nobody would make money. The only way you make money is when demand exceeds supply. If demand goes up 10-fold, but supply increases 20-fold, are you going to make money? For me the best investment in China would be to buy real estate. You know that at the end of the game, labor and wages will rise, translating into higher real estate prices. If I were to invest in China's equity market, I would buy only infrastructure plays—utility and electric companies. I think you're going to see many companies there go bankrupt.

Kazanjian: *What are your feelings about Japan?*

Younes: Japan has the most improving geographic but the worst demographics. Over the last 10 years there has been a quantum leap change in China, as it became a huge economic power on the global scene. Today Japan is benefiting tremendously from this very close neighbor (China) by investing in it, selling to it, and trading with it. The growth in Japan you see today is driven more by the emergence of China than by any internal development in Japan. And, I still think the Japanese equity market is very expensive.

Kazanjian: *Do you spend a lot of time traveling to visit these companies?*

Youne: If I were investing in the 1920s, I would never be in my office because information did not travel. To know what the Exchange was doing in New York, people used smoke signals. Today, information, in general, is very much available, especially for large companies. Going and visiting these big companies adds very little value. In addition, analysts and companies visit our offices daily. I spend only about 10 percent of my time traveling, but mostly to visit remote counties and companies that are not widely followed.

There are two ways to make money in the market. Either you're smarter than the average investor, or you're better at finding where the market is inefficient. The bottleneck today is in knowing how to translate this avalanche of information into knowledge, how to translate the knowledge into wisdom, and how to translate wisdom into alpha. That is why the bulk of our energy is spent on filtering and processing information—not on collecting it.

Kazanjian: *Let's talk about the case for international investing today. Given that the global markets are more correlated than ever before, why should U.S. investors put any of their equity money overseas?*

Younes: Why not? Why should you have a small menu to choose from? When you start with a smaller universe, you start with a suboptimal universe. The reasons for international investing are many. First, we expect higher cyclical growth overseas. Today the United States is less than 5 percent of world population, yet its GDP is about 35 percent of world GDP. Our GDP per capita is about 7 times bigger than the rest of the world. Globalization is economic democratization. Over time the gap between the "haves" and the "have nots" will narrow dramatically. Second, foreign companies are less efficient and have worse corporate governance. In order to compete with U.S. companies in a globalized economy they have no choice but to emulate the American corporate culture, and therefore offer better prospects for structural growth. Third, valuations overseas are much cheaper by almost any metric. And finally, you get diversification. Not all sectors are global, not all regions are synchronized with the U.S. economic cycle, and not all global leaders are U.S. companies.

Kazanjian: *Are you more bullish on international markets than on the United States looking out over the next several years?*

Younes: Definitely, especially if you're looking at some of the pockets of opportunity in eastern Europe, Russia, and Turkey. But in the short-term, as you have suggested, if the U.S. economy goes through a bad time, the whole world will have a painful adjustment and you may lose money in equities no matter where you are.

Kazanjian: *Isn't that an argument against international investing?*

Younes: No, because you'll lose less money internationally. The correlation is very strong short term because you have the same investors. Over time the law of gravity rules. We believe that over the next 30 to 40 years you'll see higher growth in international markets driven by the cyclical and structural forces mentioned earlier.

Not only is Younes more bullish on international markets, his outlook for the United States over the next several years is rather grim. He believes that, based on the laws of gravity, fair value for the S&P 500 is around 600 to 800, while he thinks the Nasdaq (which he compares to the stock bubble in Japan during the late 1980s) should trade around 500 to 800. That's because he's convinced we have a major earnings quality problem and huge structural imbalances in this country that will take some time to work themselves out. Investors, he maintains, remain far too optimistic about future prospects, and therefore expect U.S. companies to grow much faster than they possibly can in today's competitive global environment.

PART FOUR

The SECTOR SPECIALISTS

DAVID CHAN

Jennison Associates

Although David Chan has less experience than most of the other Masters featured in this book, he has by far the most eclectic background. Chan originally started out as a pre-med student at Harvard, which seemed logical since his father and brother were both doctors. He ultimately got a degree in biochemistry. And while that sounds like pretty good training for the eventual manager of a healthcare sector fund, getting into the investment business was the furthest thing from Chan's mind. Instead, after graduation he worked for the public television station in Boston, enrolled in film school, and ultimately made several short movies.

Chan soon realized, however, that the entertainment industry wasn't quite right for him. He went back to school, earned an MBA from Columbia University, and landed a job with the Boston Consulting Group in 1989. He consulted on projects in a variety of industries, including healthcare and investment management. While interviewing money managers in the course of a consulting gig for a large brokerage firm, he realized what a great job they had.

At that point, he set his sights on leaving consulting and moving into the investment business. Thanks to a chance connection with someone at Jennison Associates, he landed a job as a research analyst following medical devices and restaurants. Over time he became the senior healthcare analyst for Jennison and when the firm launched its own sector funds in 1999, Chan was tapped to run the Health Sciences portfolio.

Chan invests most of the fund's money in pharmaceutical and biotech companies, although his universe is the entire healthcare sector. And although healthcare has historically been a very profitable area for investors, Chan emphasizes that this is one area of the market that requires a constant watchful eye, given the continuous change in the industry.

Kazanjian: *You certainly have quite a unique and diverse background. I think you're the only investment manager I've ever interviewed who is also a former filmmaker.*

Chan: Granted, I didn't follow the normal career trajectory for someone in the investment business. But I've actually been interested in stocks since I was a kid. I was introduced to investing by my father, who invested and speculated in coins, stamps, stocks, and options. When I was in film school, I remember writing my own stock charting programs on an old Commodore 64 computer.

Kazanjian: *I understand you got your undergraduate degree in biochemistry, which is actually fitting for the manager of a healthcare fund.*

Chan: Right. I was a pre-med student for several years. I wasn't sure exactly what I wanted to do after college. Eventually I got an MBA and went to work in management consulting for a couple of years.

Kazanjian: *Before that, though, you went to film school. Did you get to work as a professional in the industry?*

Chan: I did. After college I worked for the public television station in Boston for a while. I really had aspirations of being filmmaker. I got some grants and made a couple of documentaries that were shown on public television. One was on a jazz pianist and another was a short fiction film. But at some point it became clear that this wasn't going to be a career for me.

Kazanjian: *After about 18 months in the entertainment business, you got an MBA and joined the Boston Consulting Group. What kind of work were you doing there?*

Chan: Like most consultants early on in their career, I worked on a variety of consulting projects for a number of different industries. One of our largest clients was a large pharmaceutical firm. I got to do a number of projects for them, including evaluating the prospects for a particular therapeutic area or general issues like how to optimally organize the research and development department to get new drugs out in a more timely fashion. That stuff is obviously all related to what I do now.

I guess the genesis of how I got into this business came when we were working on a project for the old Kidder Peabody. As part of that project, Kidder Peabody was trying to figure out why it had such a low rating compared to others in the industry. As part of my work, I interviewed all of the firm's clients, including a number of money managers. After interviewing two dozen or so different money managers, I realized what a great job they had. That was the moment I decided that this business was much more interesting and fun than what I was doing as a consultant. So I decided I wanted to get a job in the investment industry.

Kazanjian: *How long were you at Boston Consulting?*

Chan: About three years.

Kazanjian: *Did you just start sending out resumes to investment firms?*

Chan: I talked to everybody I knew who might have a relationship in this area. I think the ultimate connection came from an alumnus of the Columbia Business School who, through sheer luck, hooked me up with somebody who worked at Jennison. I was able to sweet talk them into hiring someone without experience. For that I'll always be grateful.

Kazanjian: *You began working at Jennison in 1992. What was your original job?*

Chan: I started off as an analyst covering medical devices and restaurants. From there I gradually became more of a specialized healthcare analyst. A few years later, during the Hillary Clinton era when everyone thought it was all over for good for healthcare companies, our pharmaceutical analyst, who had been here for 20 years and was a legend in his time, decided to retire. They gave me that job, covering the much bigger and more important pharmaceutical and biotech sectors. The pharmaceutical stocks bottomed around then and we did well in the sector during the recovery. So a few years later, when the healthcare sector fund was started, it was logical that I would be tapped to manage it. My main role at Jennison is still as the healthcare analyst for large-cap growth stocks.

Kazanjian: *As far as the fund is concerned, how do you define the healthcare area? What industries do you concentrate on?*

Chan: We'll look at anything that's health related in any market capitalization, including pharmaceuticals, biotech, and medical devices and services. This product has the unusual freedom to do almost anything. We short stocks, do private placements, and even use options. We can also keep up to 20 percent of the portfolio outside of healthcare if we find something that is compelling.

Kazanjian: *Do you buy both foreign and domestic securities?*

Chan: Yes, although the foreign component tends to be relatively small. In general, I tend to mostly own product companies, either in the pharmaceutical or biotechnology industries. That just happens to be the area where I think there are always a lot of great investment opportunities.

Kazanjian: *As far as foreign versus domestic companies, do foreign companies have any advantage over their U.S. counterparts, or vice versa, especially in the pharmaceutical industry?*

Chan: I wouldn't say so. It's a very global business. There are only six large-cap U.S. pharmaceutical companies left. If you want to own large-cap pharmaceutical stocks, you're limited to about a dozen worldwide. The relative attractiveness of one over the other is based on their product life cycles. Where a company is headquartered doesn't really matter.

Kazanjian: *Do foreign companies have the same types of regulations and hurdles to jump through?*

Chan: The process of getting a product approved in the United States is exactly the same whether you're a U.S. or British company. There's no real difference.

Kazanjian: *When looking at demographics, people say healthcare is a great place to be because the Baby Boomers are getting older and will need more medical services. What is your opinion? How do you view the healthcare sector over the next 5 to 10 years?*

Chan: That's a tough one. People absolutely consume more healthcare products and services as they age, but the bigger unknown is how much pricing pressure there will be. There's a lot outside the United States, and you have only to pick up the newspaper to know that it's also here in America. I think the environment for pharmaceutical companies is becoming much tougher. At the same time the path for generics is much easier. The environment in which you could buy these big pharmaceutical companies and hold on for 10 years is gone. That said, there's a huge variety of companies in the healthcare space, and I believe there are always good investment opportunities. Typically the macroenvironment matters less for that smaller company launching a hot new product. It is certainly tougher right now for the traditional big pharmaceutical companies because of all the political heat on drug prices, including why drugs cost more in the United States than in Canada.

Kazanjian: *That debate will no doubt continue. Healthcare is clearly a political football. What impact will any actions by the government have on these companies?*

Chan: It's impossible to say. It's easy to conclude that the pressures are there and that the environment for these companies will get tougher and tougher. Exactly how it plays out, I'm not sure. In the rest of the world, the government sets the prices for drugs. It's only in the United States that there's still a relatively free market. One could imagine an extreme scenario where the government starts setting prices here as well. I hope that doesn't happen because it would probably be very bad for innovation in the industry. But it's certainly a possibility. Regardless, a lot of pressure on pricing will remain.

Kazanjian: *Does this political noise have any influence on your investment process or the kinds of stocks you want to own?*

Chan: It's obviously an underlying backdrop. It means I'm less likely to own huge positions in big-cap pharmaceutical companies and more likely to look for opportunities in small- and mid-cap companies, where the positive dynamics can far outweigh any negative macro factors.

Kazanjian: *Looking through your portfolio, you clearly have the largest percentage of the fund's money in a combination of pharmaceutical and biotech product companies, which you've already said were your favorite areas of the market. Let's begin with the pharmaceutical companies. What do you look for when evaluating these companies?*

Chan: Finding these companies is easy. As I mentioned, there aren't that many large ones. Even in the small- and mid-cap area, it's quite a definable universe. I probably track 30 to 40 pharmaceutical and specialty pharmaceutical companies, and maybe 70 to 100 biotech companies. That's my defined universe. In an ideal world, I'm looking for a company with some new product that no one's paid attention to or has been underestimated to some extent. Then, as new data come out or the product makes it to market and launches well, you can get some very large moves in the stock. That's what you hope for.

Kazanjian: *Specifically, what are you looking for in making this determination for pharmaceutical companies?*

Chan: I look at everything, trying to pull the whole picture together. I focus a lot on new products. If you have a big mature company, like Pfizer, it's hard to figure out for sure how much a big product like Lipitor will grow in a given year. And even if you get that right, you're not adding a lot of value because there's no leverage. But if you can find a new product in a smaller company that will be a $1 billion product a few years out, you can add a lot of value figuring that out. New products have more positive leverage on a company than you can imagine. There are a lot of fixed costs in this business, namely research and development and the general infrastructure. Drugs are very high gross margin products. A lot of the gross margin of a new product can potentially go right down to the bottom line.

Kazanjian: *How do you figure out whether a new product will be successful?*

Chan: You do a lot of research. My team and I meet with companies, go to medical meetings, talk to physicians, and do physician surveys. We try to keep abreast of what's going on in every therapeutic area and figure out where there are unmet medical needs. We look for products with characteristics that doctors would like and could use. When we find these products, we evaluate where it could be priced and see how many patients have this condition to determine how big the product could be.

Kazanjian: *From a valuation perspective, do you look at what the stock is selling for to determine whether it's a good time to buy?*

Chan: We do look at valuation because if everybody already knows this is a great product and the opportunity is more than priced into the stock, it's probably not a great stock even though it's a great story. We don't really have a hard formula, such as it must be X times the PE relative to the growth rate. We just want to get a sense of whether the full opportunity is already priced into the stock.

Kazanjian: *The big pharmaceutical companies have been laggards in recent years. Many of them are plagued with expiring patents, and the generics have really been stealing the show.*

Chan: It's definitely been true in the last few years that the small guys have had more leverage. As you alluded to, there's just too much baggage among many of the large-cap companies right now.

Kazanjian: *Does that mean you're focusing your investments in some of the smaller names?*

Chan: Yes.

Kazanjian: *But how do these smaller companies compete, especially in terms of marketing? It can be very expensive to go out and bring these drugs to market.*

Chan: It's kind of ironic. If you have a really good product, the marketing matters less. If, for instance, you have a cancer product that really makes a difference, it doesn't matter that you're up against a very big company. It's an overstatement to say your product will sell itself, but you only have to worry about who has the biggest, most effective sales force when there are five companies all competing with an identical kind of drug. If you've got the one cure nobody else has, people will find you.

Kazanjian: *Before we leave the subject of pharmaceutical stocks, last year we saw Merck recall its popular arthritis drug Vioxx after testing showed it could increase the risk of heart attacks in patients taking it on a regular basis. Now the company faces countless potential lawsuits. This action also dragged many of Merck's competitors down as well. What are your thoughts on this, as well as the future implications this development might have for both Merck and the other big pharmaceutical stocks?*

Chan: The withdrawal of Vioxx, like the prior withdrawals of Rezulin, Baycol, and Redux, will likely have a short- and medium-term chilling impact on drug sentiment and fundamentals. The impact on sentiment is pretty straightforward: Investors will probably demand an increased risk premium for the chance that on any given day a high-profile drug might be withdrawn. From a fundamental basis, it also could have an impact on FDA drug approvals. With all the calls for Congressional investigations and the like, I would think the FDA, at the margin, will be a little more cautious in approving new drugs, particularly those with safety signals and in therapeutic categories where there are already good alternatives. It's yet another headwind for the industry. However, not all drugs will be equally affected. For instance, the approval risk and timing for a novel cancer drug probably won't be any different now than before the Vioxx withdrawal.

Kazanjian: *Another concern is that the large pharmaceutical companies don't seem to have any big blockbusters in the immediate pipeline. Do you see any significant drugs coming out in the coming years that investors should pay attention to, and that might reenergize the sector?*

Chan: I don't want to be too specific here, but there are absolutely some potential blockbuster drugs that I'm tracking closely in areas such as multiple sclerosis, obesity, cardiovascular disease, diabetes, and cancer. I think the industry is still capable of producing new drugs. The tougher part is protecting their current sales base from the utilization, pricing, and generic pressures we talked about earlier.

Kazanjian: *Now let's spend a few minutes talking about biotech. Most people think of this as one of the riskiest areas of market. A lot of biotech companies are in a developmental stage, and often don't even have any marketable products. They're raising money in many cases to try and create a product. How do you evaluate these companies, especially those ones at an earlier stage of development?*

Chan: First of all, there are many profitable biotech companies now, and fewer at that earlier stage of development, unlike several years ago. That said, it's really the same type of evaluation as with the pharmaceutical companies. You evaluate a new biotech product like you would any new drug product. I don't really differentiate between the drug and biotech industries. The only difference is there tends to be more early stage single-product companies in the biotech industry. I'm often a little more cautious in that area, and maybe won't make as big a bet for a very early stage company, even if I like the product, because it's inherently more volatile and riskier, as you pointed out.

Kazanjian: *When you hear a biotech company is working on some new innovation, how do you check the story out to determine whether there really is a market for it?*

Chan: By doing all of the things I previously described. We try to understand from the thought leaders in medicine whether the product makes sense. Most of the companies we own are at a later stage of development, and there's actual clinical data you can evaluate to see whether the product is effective and safe.

Kazanjian: *What about such factors as insider stock sales? We've seen many cases in recent years where insiders of biotech companies have sold huge chunks of stock days before a product was ultimately rejected by the FDA.*

Chan: I monitor that activity, but it normally isn't a big swing factor. It's obviously a red flag though if all the insiders are selling before a key decision. In such cases, you want to go back and understand why they're selling and question your own assumptions. There are many reasons for insider sales of stock. On the flip side, it's a big vote of confidence for these very few companies whose management hasn't sold the stock for years.

Kazanjian: *What makes you sell a stock?*

Chan: You buy a stock with a certain thesis in mind. The main reason to sell is because the thesis doesn't develop the way you hoped. Sometimes you get unfavorable clinical data, or maybe the earnings leverage you hoped for isn't there. In either case, if the thesis doesn't play out, you sell. Alternatively, if the stock has gone up, you feel the price fairly reflects what you understand about the company, and you find a better place to invest your money, you'll sell as well.

Kazanjian: *Do you buy IPOs?*

Chan: Sure.

Kazanjian: *How do you evaluate those differently from more established companies?*

Chan: We evaluate them exactly the same way. Sometimes you don't hear about the company until a few weeks before it actually goes public, which makes evaluating and completing a full due diligence very difficult. But the evaluation process is pretty much the same. I try to meet with the managements of every IPO in my sector, even if the deal doesn't look promising in the near term, because a company's prospects can change dramatically. For instance, one of my biggest winners in 2004 was a company that went public the previous year. I declined to invest then because of what I thought was a very risky clinical trial result ahead of them. But in 2004, to my surprise, they reported that the trial succeeded, and I was familiar enough with the company and the management to be able to take a large position, even though the stock was up more than 70 percent that day. The stock more than doubled in the few months since then.

Kazanjian: *What's one of the most exciting areas of the healthcare sector right now?*

Chan: I really do think the generic drug companies are a fascinating area of their own. They are in the business of challenging the patents of branded companies, so you're trying to figure out how strong their legal case could be and what the upside is if they win. The way the rules work, if you successfully challenge a branded company's patent, you get a six-month period in which you are the exclusive seller of that generic drug. It can be an enormous windfall. We spend time with legal experts as well as consultants trying to figure that out. Obviously this analysis also plays a part in our analysis of the pharmaceutical companies. If we think they have large products that are vulnerable, obviously that's something you want to stay away from.

Kazanjian: *Do you think the best opportunities going forward are with the generic manufacturers, as opposed to those developing new medications? After all, a lot of insurance companies are steering patients to generics whenever possible, because those drugs are so much cheaper.*

Chan: It's hard to say. Some generic drug companies are unattractive, and some branded companies are attractive. I don't necessarily think one is better off than the other per se. It is also a function of where the stock prices are. In other words, for a while generic drug manufacturers were doing extremely well and had very high PEs. If you asked me this question six months ago, I would have said the upside success for these companies is already reflected in the stock price. Since then we've had some pricing issues in the generic drug industry, and the prices of these stocks have collapsed, making them more attractive. Healthcare is a very volatile area.

Kazanjian: *Does that mean you constantly have to move in and out of these names to make money?*

Chan: I hate to say it, but the honest truth is because of this volatility, the answer is yes. I think the era where one could just buy one quality company and ride it for 10 years is gone. There's just such extreme volatility in these names, and the businesses themselves can also change very quickly.

Kazanjian: *Given this inherent volatility, how many stocks do you keep in your portfolio?*

Chan: Right now I own well over 60 names. The portfolio is quite diversified in terms of the number of securities.

Kazanjian: *And you trade around those names a lot?*

Chan: Always.

Kazanjian: *What's your average holding period?*

Chan: Sometimes a company can suddenly become popular and the stock will run up a lot. If I determine there's no longer a good risk-reward ratio. I will sell the stock, knowing it could suddenly be unpopular four months from now. The turnover is well over 100 percent, although that's not because our strategy is to purposely trade a lot. Generally when I buy a name I plan to hold it for multiyear periods. But if the stock goes up 50 percent, suddenly the return doesn't look as attractive for the next two years and something else could look better.

Kazanjian: *What if it goes down 50 percent instead?*

Chan: If the stock has gone down and there's no fundamental reason and I'm confident in the story, I'll typically buy more.

Kazanjian: *Do you buy any nursing home or related stocks?*

Chan: I do occasionally invest in healthcare providers. It's a much tougher area to evaluate because I don't think the business is inherently attractive. Every now and then these stocks get cheap enough or there's a turn in the business that's enough for me to want to play. But I don't really like those businesses that much.

Kazanjian: *Why?*

Chan: I'll give you an answer that's a generalization for all healthcare providers. A lot of these businesses are dependent on the government. On any day you could wake up and literally with one stroke of a pen, either the agency that runs Medicare or some random bill in Congress could decide that reimbursements are going down, and you can get killed. It's very hard to make forecasts for these businesses. On the flip side, sometimes it works out the other way as well. Reimbursements can get a little bump up and be better than you expected. But it's a hard way to make money.

Kazanjian: *Do you run computer screens, or is most of your process for finding stocks bottom-up?*

Chan: It's mostly bottom-up. I look at tables of PE multiples, but I don't really have any kind of black box.

Kazanjian: *Where do you find most of your new ideas?*

Chan: A lot of these are companies I already know because I've been following them so long. But I get new ideas through frequent meetings with companies, sell-side analysts, and other buy-side colleagues with whom I frequently trade ideas. Mostly, I know the universe and am just always looking for some opportunity to buy. This opportunity can come because a stock is down a lot and I believe it shouldn't be, or because of some catalyst. Perhaps a stock has been out of favor for a while and people have forgotten about it. A very frequent scenario in biotech is a lead product will fail, the stock will blow up and go down 70 percent, and then you'll come back to it a year later. There will be a second or third product that's progressing nicely that people forgot about and aren't paying attention to. But then people start to notice and the stock can recover, sometimes dramatically.

Kazanjian: *You mentioned earlier that you're able to short stocks. How often do you do that?*

Chan: Very rarely. I only do it for fundamental reasons when I believe it to be a sure thing.

Kazanjian: *What is a "sure thing" to you?*

Chan: When I believe there's blatant fraud or the stock is up on really bad data.

Kazanjian: *How do you know whether there's been fraud? That's often hard to detect until everyone else knows about it.*

Chan: You don't know, but you get a sense that the numbers don't add up, or you've been in situations where management has lied to you in the past. You're right. It's not easy to detect, and often you find out too late.

Kazanjian: *While your fund has been a real standout in the healthcare category, you and your peers all had a tough time in 2002. What happened?*

Chan: On the product side it was just a year when it seemed like the FDA wasn't going to approve anything. You had a couple of notable product failures in the clinic, and there were a few areas where it just seemed like the FDA was unreceptive to approving any new drugs. The FDA is almost like a pendulum. On the one hand they're always worried about whether Americans are getting access to the newest and best drugs as fast as everybody else in the world, creating periods when they're rushing to approve new things. On the flip side, if you get a couple of well-publicized drug recalls, the attitude shifts to one where they are extra cautious about making sure no unsafe drugs ever get out. The reality is no drug is truly 100 percent safe. There's just a ratio of benefit to risk.

Kazanjian: *Is the FDA getting faster about making decisions?*

Chan: Things started to get better in 2003. The pendulum is beginning to swing back the other way again, though not in all areas. Clearly the FDA is showing a lot of interest in getting new cancer drugs to market.

Kazanjian: *Are there any primary forces out there that will determine the direction of healthcare stocks going forward?*

Chan: I'd say the industry is facing a sort of headwind right now, and it's increasingly harder for undifferentiated products to do well. There was a time 10 years ago when you could truly have a me-too drug, get it to the market, and sell it for the same price as the first guy. I think those days are gone forever. But, that said, healthcare has been a great area to be in over the last decade.

Given that they are on the frontlines of all the latest research and testing, you'd think that doctors would be perfectly positioned to pick winning healthcare stocks. However, as Chan points out, doctors have historically proven themselves to be rather poor investors. Perhaps that's because they're always looking for the big hits, rather than sticking to what they know.

That said, Chan insists he learned some very valuable lessons during the tough environment for healthcare stocks in 2002. Specifically, he often tempers the volatility in the sector caused by binary events such as the release of crucial clinical data and pending FDA decisions by using options to hedge his exposure in front of key decisions. While this can mute some of the upside gain if all goes well, it also lowers his downside in case his companies face an unfavorable outcome.

ANDREW DAVIS

Davis Advisors

Few would argue that Andrew Davis was destined to get into the investment industry. After all, his father and grandfather are both legendary figures in the business. Grandfather Shelby Cullom Davis advised governors and presidents and saw his own initial $100,000 investment in the late 1940s grow into more than $800 million over a 40-year period. Dad Shelby M.C. Davis founded the predecessor to what is now Davis Advisors in 1969 and created one of the top records on Wall Street running the firm's flagship New York Venture Fund.

Davis certainly didn't have your average childhood. Discussions at the

dinner table often revolved around the stock market, family vacations included company visits, and *Wall $treet Week* was required weekly viewing.
Still, Davis didn't originally intend to follow in his father's footsteps. Instead, he planned to get into psychology, which is what he studied in his
early years at Colby College where he ultimately changed to a double major in economics and business. After graduation, Davis wound up going to
work for a bank, and has been involved in the financial industry ever since.

He joined the firm where his dad was a partner in 1993, after eight
years at PaineWebber. Today, the 41-year-old manager runs both the Davis
Appreciation & Income Fund, which specializes in convertible securities,
and the Davis Real Estate Fund. Unlike some other real estate funds, Davis
invests almost exclusively in REITs (real estate investment trusts). And he
has a unique approach for figuring out which ones are most attractive at
any given time.

Kazanjian: *What was it like growing up in a family of investment legends?*

Davis: Certainly we were not the usual family, and the interest my father
and grandfather had in the markets definitely shaped my youth. We had
lots of dinnertime conversations about what PE multiples were, the cost of
spending, and the value of compounding. We went to the occasional baseball game, but there was definitely a financial impetus in our family. I remember the first financial lesson I ever learned from my father when I was
about six years old. He asked whether I wanted a dollar a day for the rest
of my life or a penny that doubles every day for the rest of my life. Like
every first grader, I was thinking about the packs of bubble gum I could
get, so I wanted the dollar, not considering that the penny would be worth
so much more over time.

Kazanjian: *I also understand that when your fifth-grade teacher asked the class to
prepare a research paper on an interesting subject, you chose to write a report on
Memorex.*

Davis: I'm still wondering what my fifth-grade teacher must have thought
about that. Memorex turned out to be a pretty good lesson for my father
as an investor. He made a lot of money in Memorex and then lost most of
it as the company went from a huge valuation to bankruptcy, much like
other tech stocks at that time. The same thing happened with many Internet stocks in the late 1990s. Before I wrote the paper, my father had
showed me Memorex's annual report, which I read and then wrote about.

The teacher had said we could write about anything, and doing a report on Memorex seemed to make sense. It's a great example of the apple not falling far from the tree, I suppose. A lot of people wrote about hockey and baseball players. I wrote about the rise of a company.

Kazanjian: *It sort of sounds a bit abnormal for kids to be so interested in stocks at such a young age. Did you resent this constant exposure to the markets, or were you an aspiring stock analyst almost from birth?*

Davis: I think when I was young, the lessons were more subtle than they were by the time I got into high school and then college. I remember sitting around as a teenager with my brother at our dinner table, and my father would turn on this little black-and-white TV on Friday night because it was time for *Wall $treet Week* and *Washington Week*. Nothing infuriated me more at that time in my life. There was a time into my early years in college when I actually thought I was going to be a psychologist and studied a fair amount of psychology. But I took a few business and economics classes my sophomore year and I found it just plain interesting. But it wasn't as if I planned to get into investing and join the family business. Remember, there was no Davis Selected Advisers (the firm's previous name) until 1994. My father was a partner in a small mutual fund company called Venture Advisers. Before that he worked for Fiduciary Trust in New York City, so I certainly never expected to be working with my father.

As time went by, my interest in economics and my interest in business administration grew. It really fascinated me how some people were extremely good at managing businesses, while others rose to the occasion initially and then just really made a mess of things. I had wonderful professors throughout my years at Colby College who did an extraordinary job helping to mold this interest, and I had great mentors coming out of school.

Kazanjian: *Plus, I suppose those psychology courses came in handy when trying to make sense of business and the stock market.*

Davis: Absolutely. You need that knowledge to understand the investment world.

Kazanjian: *So you studied economics and business at Colby College, got a liberal arts degree, and then what happened?*

Davis: I went straight to work for Shawmut Bank in Boston. I was trying to get any job I could. I had worked every summer since I was probably 17 on the stock market floor as a specialist clerk. I was there for the first 100 million share day on Wall Street, which sounds like nothing now. After about eight months, I got a call from a guy at PaineWebber in New York named Peter Marcus, who was the best securities analyst covering non-precious metal stocks, like steel, aluminum, and copper. I originally interviewed with him right before I started with Shawmut. He offered me a job working as his research assistant and I figured why not. I resigned my position at Shawmut, moved to New York, and started working for Peter. I worked with him for around five years, and slowly but surely got my arms around the steel and aluminum industries. He was an extraordinary mentor, doling out praise with a thimble but teaching like a professor. I eventually wrote most of his reports. To me he was and is a mad scientist genius. I owe him a lot.

I then became a securities analyst at PaineWebber covering closed-end bond funds, before adding coverage of convertible securities. After three years, I left PaineWebber, moved to Santa Fe, New Mexico, and took over managing what was then called the Retirement Planning Funds of America Convertible Securities Fund, which was run by Venture Advisers, the firm where my father was a partner.

Kazanjian: *Was it just a coincidence that you took over a fund run by your father's firm?*

Davis: Not a coincidence; more a merger of needs. I obviously had lengthy talks with Dad about convertible securities before I decided to take the job. By this time, around 1990, I had proven to him that these securities were immensely attractive. That was the number-one reason I took the position. It was certainly not your traditional analyst post. Most analysts follow an industry. This was very different in that I was following a type of investment vehicle with all sorts of industries within it. There were 500 companies at the time from 35 different industries. I liked this broad spectrum because I wanted to eventually become a portfolio manager and I didn't want to be pigeonholed in one industry. I learned from Peter Marcus that when your industry goes out of favor, nobody wants to talk to you, and that's not so good for one's success as a sell-side analyst. I had talked to my father about this and he thought that it might be a good idea to start a convertible fund at Venture Advisers. So he got it up and running and managed it. I like to think that he was my best customer while I was running PaineWebber's convertible research department. I left PaineWebber, ultimately, because I couldn't get the institutional salesmen to believe in the ideas of a 27-year-old vice president and head of a department, despite my successful track record. I thought it would be helpful to leave PaineWebber, become a portfolio manager for a couple of years, and then return to PaineWebber with a good *audited* track record. Well, I never returned. I stayed with Venture Advisers, having been hired by the senior partner at the firm to manage its convertible securities fund.

Kazanjian: *I know that to this day you still do a lot of work in the area of convertible securities. What's so attractive to you about this area of the market?*

Davis: It's the potential it offers for asymmetrical returns. That's a fancy way of saying the potential for getting lots of upside return relative to the risk one takes in buying the common stock. If I do my job well and the common stock is up 20 percent, you can get the lion's share of this return, 16 or 17 percent, through the convertible. On the other hand, if the common stock goes down 20 percent, you're going to be down only half as much. It's what we call the 80–50 rule. It's easy to focus only on the upside. But God help you when things go wrong. And as we've seen over the last few years, things can go very wrong. Over the 11 or so years I've been running what's now called the Davis Appreciation & Income Fund (we changed the name from the Davis Convertible Securities Fund in 2003), we're up about 102 percent of the S&P 500, while we've cut the average volatility by more than one-third. That's what makes convertibles attractive. They also have a yield component, which is attractive to many.

Kazanjian: *Do you analyze a convertible the same way you analyze a common stock?*

Davis: No, we analyze both but separately. Of course, you always have to understand the common stock. But the convertible adds an additional layer of complexity, because you need to know how it will behave if the common stock goes up or down. The key is finding those that are in that sweet spot, which is this 80–50 area. Figuring this out is admittedly subjective. There's no black box to tell you how it's going work. However, we think we have developed a system over time that gives us a pretty good read on how the convertibles will react.

Kazanjian: *When did you start focusing on real estate?*

Davis: As I was leaving PaineWebber in 1993, REITs first started to come around again. The first IPO of this REIT generation was in 1991. My interest in REITs stemmed from the fact that they are similar to convertibles. They are a yielding, equity-like instrument. On top of that, what really got me excited about real estate was that, during the savings-and-loan financial crisis of the early 1990s, banks, insurance companies, and pension funds wound up unintentionally owning a lot of real estate that they had to get rid of. This offered tremendous opportunity—even a generational opportunity—to buy real estate at very low valuations. So we started the Real Estate Fund in 1994.

Kazanjian: *What exactly are REITs?*

Davis: REITs are actually very simple to understand. A REIT, or real estate investment trust, is like a mutual fund of real estate holdings instead of stocks or bonds. A REIT is a publicly traded company on any one of the stock exchanges that is comprised of income-producing real estate properties, such as office buildings, apartment complexes, industrial space, or self-storage units. All of that income—rent less expenses—is passed through to the shareholders of the REIT in the form of dividends that are not taxed at the corporate level.

Kazanjian: *REITs tend to have very high dividend yields. I suppose that's because of this pass-through feature.*

Davis: That's exactly right. REITs tend to have high dividend yields because they generally pay out more than they earn in terms of net income. And they do that because real estate has huge depreciation, which is a non-cash charge. The rule is that REITs have to pay out 90 percent of their REIT taxable income. That's one of the hoops REITs have to jump through in order to get this single-taxation status. Because REITs have huge amounts of depreciation on the books as well, they tend to have much more cash flow than net income, so they pay out more. REITs generally pay out anywhere from 60 to 100 percent of their free cash flow each year.

Kazanjian: *From what you've said, REITs are a fairly new instrument, since they only date back to the 1990s.*

Davis: Well, let's say this is the first successful generation of REITs. The REITs of today that started in the 1990s are really a third generation of the original instrument. The iteration of REITs in the 1970s was primarily mortgage REITs, most of which no longer exist. Those REITs were mostly yield curve surfers and that kind of thing always seems to end badly. The 1980s had another iteration of REITs that suffered from conflicts of interest between shareholders and management. Many REIT management teams owned very little stock in the very REITs they were managing and used the REITs as vehicles for dumping overvalued acquisitions. It was a disaster. However, the 1990s brought this whole concept of self-managed, fully integrated REITs, which became businesses that used real estate to generate profits. Management was fully motivated because, on average, a management team owned about 12 percent of the company the REIT managed. Also, the tax laws changed. The 1986 tax act under Ronald Reagan took away many of the existing real estate income tax shelters. Now buildings were being built for a tenant, rather than just for a tax advantage. This helped the supply–demand equation stay much more in balance. So it was a very good slew of events that ended up making real estate into what we believe is no longer a boom/bust vehicle, but rather a vehicle that merits investment at any point in the cycle.

Kazanjian: *But how should you view REITs? I mean, technically they're stocks, but they represent the real estate sector. Is owning a REIT more like owning a stock or piece of property?*

Davis: That's a great question and the answer is that it's really somewhere in between. Real estate stocks and S&P 500 stocks are correlated only about maybe 0.2 or 0.3 on a scale of +1.0 (perfect positive correlation) to 0.0 (no correlation) to −0.1 (perfect negative correlation).

Kazanjian: *In periods where real estate prices are going through the roof, yet stock prices are going down, how would REITs be expected to perform?*

Davis: Certainly they'll be affected by the negative market. Buying a REIT stock is definitely not the same as buying a building. However, there's no question that the earnings of a REIT are made up of the earnings from a building. Over time, the performance of the earnings of those buildings will determine how well the earnings of the REIT will grow. In my mind, it ultimately comes down to whether these REITs are capable of growing revenue and rents over time, keeping their buildings fully occupied, and managing expenses prudently. That's why we look for the very best management teams.

Kazanjian: *If an individual already owns a home, or even some rentals and commercial property, is going out and buying REITs simply an overlap to asset classes they already have in their portfolio?*

Davis: To some degree, but not with a single-family home. Home ownership is a speculative investment in that you don't collect any income from it. If you own the house that you're living in, you'll only realize any kind of monetary value when you sell it. But REITs are very similar to owning commercial or investment property with one big difference: liquidity. Selling a building is time consuming and can be difficult. A REIT is much easier to buy and sell.

Kazanjian: *Assuming someone doesn't own any outside commercial property, what is the role of REITs in an overall stock portfolio?*

Davis: I think when you look at an overall portfolio, you've got the growth elements, the income elements, and elements that lie somewhere in between. That's where REITs seem to be in my mind. You have a growth characteristic because over the last 30 or 40 years real estate's been a pretty good investment from a capital growth standpoint. On top of that you have income growth, which is what I think will drive REIT valuations over the next five years. The dividend growth alone in these REITs could be 3 to 7 percent a year. In a yield-starved environment, such as the one we're in right now, REITs make great sense.

Kazanjian: *What type of yields are REITs paying right now?*

Davis: Yields on REITs range anywhere from 5 to 9 percent and are growing about 3 to 7 percent per year. There are outliers both below and above those numbers, but that's generally where you'll find them. Again, our argument is that nothing yields 9 percent for no reason. The risk associated with a 9 percent yield is palpable. We would rather buy the 5 and 6 percent yield with a growth element attached to it and watch that dividend grow (this is where the penny-per-day compound-earnings lesson from my childhood applies). That way you get the capital appreciation as well. Years from now you might actually have a 9 percent yielding vehicle, yet you never took the risk of owning a 9 percent yielding company.

Kazanjian: *So for someone with a 100 percent equity portfolio, what percentage of that would you recommend they keep in REITs?*

Davis: I think that number should be anywhere from 5 to 15 percent.

Kazanjian: *For younger investors and those not needing income, what's the point of having REITs?*

Davis: Anything not correlated with the return of common stocks over time is going to be a risk reducer for an overall portfolio. By definition, that's got to be good.

Kazanjian: *Those living on a fixed income and looking at CD yields of 3 percent or less these days are probably reading about these REIT yields and salivating. Would you recommend that those in need of a steady stream of income buy REITs for the generous dividend yields, or are they too risky for that purpose?*

Davis: We're looking at REITs now as a bond alternative. Fixed-income instruments make me much more nervous than REITs right now. A lot would have to go wrong for REIT income streams to be in jeopardy. In the past four years, we've had a significant recession and terrorist attack that shut down the economy, yet very few REITs cut their dividends. So I feel pretty good owning REITs for income, though you need to understand you are still taking stock market risk. This is not the same as buying a T-bill.

Kazanjian: *One issue regarding real estate is the concern we could be in the midst of a bubble, especially in certain parts of the country. If that proves to be true, and real estate prices suddenly fell, how would that impact REITs?*

Davis: The primary bubble that we talk about in real estate is in the single-family home market, particularly on both coasts. I would suggest that the bubble is reasonably unrelated to commercial real estate as a whole. But there is some bubbling in the commercial real estate market. How will that impact REITs? It must be bad, right? Well, the answer is yes and no. REITs have the great advantage of being able to sell real estate into the bubble. That's taking advantage of the real estate market.

Kazanjian: *Presumably they'll sell into a higher market, hold onto the cash, and buy back when prices come down?*

Davis: Either that or they can take the cash and pay it out as a dividend to shareholders. They can also take the cash to purchase property in areas that aren't in a bubble. That's another big difference about today's REITs. The 1980s version REIT was all about creating a large collection of properties. The model today is buy or build, improve value with solid management of the real estate asset, and then eventually sell. We call this managing the entire real estate investment cycle. If this is done properly, one can potentially make money during all points of the cycle.

Kazanjian: *So the fact that we may be in the midst of a real estate bubble doesn't impact your decision on whether to be invested in REITs?*

Davis: It impacts my decision only if the REITs are buying properties at bubble prices or building properties in bubble markets. If that's not happening, then I feel very comfortable owning them as they can use the bubble to their advantage.

Kazanjian: *REITs have outperformed the S&P 500 for several years in a row. Can this great performance possibly continue, especially given that we've come so far and interest rates are clearly on the rise?*

Davis: Let's first talk about interest rates, which are less important to REITs fundamentally than they are psychologically. Psychologically, it seems that when interest rates go up, it's as if the dinner bell sounds and everybody divests REITs. But the real killer of real estate is a supply–demand imbalance, that is, having many excess empty buildings in a given market. That's the fundamental crusher of real estate valuation. As interest rates move back up, there's less supply built because the money isn't cheap and easy to borrow. If there's less supply, that's good news. This means that real estate owners and REIT managers are much happier campers. Just about all REIT CEOs I've spoken with lately tell me they'd love to see interest rates about 2 percent higher, because that should create less supply. Also, higher interest rates imply that the economy's a bit stronger, and that's got to be good for demand. Finally, if interest rates are higher, presumably there might be a little inflation as the economy heats up, and inflation has always been good for real estate. The negative side of this is that if a REIT's balance sheet has floating rate debt or debt that needs refinancing, higher interest rates will lead to higher interest expense on the REIT's income statement and ultimately result in lower earnings. But there isn't a REIT CEO out there unwilling to have that hit of a nickel or dime to annual earnings if it means not having that speculative building built across the street.

Kazanjian: *From a stock perspective, don't higher interest rates make REITs less competitive as an asset class if people can get a higher yield on other, safer instruments?*

Davis: That's a fair observation. Certainly higher rates will mean that other vehicles might look more attractive at the margin. But again, when you're talking about yields of 6 or 7 percent versus a money market yield of 2 percent, REITs are still attractive. Moreover, the well-managed REIT has the potential for creating capital gains and we expect its yield to grow over time. Remember, REITs are a total return vehicle, not just a yield play.

Kazanjian: *But REITs have performed so well over the last few years. What are the implications of that for the future?*

Davis: I don't subscribe to the theory that just because something's been up for two or three years in a row that means it's necessarily going to be down the next three years. Over time, stocks move because of one thing alone, and that's growth of earnings. What's going to happen with real estate stocks in the next few years? In my mind the outlook is fairly good. We've got an improving economy, a supply situation that's relatively good, and interest rates backing up to make the supply situation potentially even better. All of this sounds pretty solid for real estate fundamentals. What's the bad news? Higher rates affect psychology and lower earnings growth to a degree. Plus, management teams could make poor decisions. Investing always involves risk taking, but I repeat that one should not subscribe to the concept that just because something's been up for a few years in a row that means it's got to come back down, particularly when one is talking about companies trading at maybe 8 to 14 times earnings versus the S&P 500 average of about 22 times.

Kazanjian: *But that's still a much higher level than REITs have historically sold at.*

Davis: Those immortally dangerous words on Wall Street, "This time it's different." I think this is a new breed of REITs that maybe are worth 12 to 15 times earnings. Are they worth 18 times earnings? No. But 12 times, in a market that's selling around 22, just doesn't sound that misvalued to me. That's not to say there won't be volatility, however.

Kazanjian: *And the third potential negative we should touch on is the fact that lots of money has flowed into the sector, especially in the last two years or so. That's usually a bad sign when everyone piles in at once.*

Davis: That is more troubling. I would not want to be managing the amount of money that some of our larger competitors are running today. The good news is our fund is a relatively manageable size. But it's still a concern. One positive is that we had an 18 percent correction in the sector in early 2004, and that shutdown flows into the sector pretty well. Despite these headwinds, I'm absolutely comfortable with the overall outlook for REITs going out five years. Over the next 12 months, I am less comfortable.

Kazanjian: *Now that we've explored the broad landscape, let's talk about how you evaluate individual REITs. How many total companies are there in the universe for you to choose from?*

Davis: About 250, and we're probably interested in about 130 of them.

Kazanjian: *That's a fairly small universe to choose from. How many stocks do you keep in the portfolio at any one time?*

Davis: Around 35.

Kazanjian: *So how do you find and evaluate those 35 stocks?*

Davis: That's a complicated question. We start by evaluating what geographic areas a REIT operates in. This gives us a good platform for seeing which REITs are operating in markets that seem to be improving. We call this our Geographic Information System model. Keep in mind we do this at the *submarket* level. For example, we don't just look at the market of Manhattan. We look at the submarkets: Midtown, Downtown, the West Side, and the East Side. All of these submarkets behave differently even though they're all part of Manhattan. For us it's very important to know how all of these different areas are performing. Further, our forecasts are based on rent, occupancy, absorption, and so forth. Since this basic information is obtained from an outside service and available to anyone, we go further by cross-checking the data with real-world observations. In other words, we read. We use computer technology to sift through some 13,000 publications, searching for relevant articles and commentary on the submarkets we are researching. We then use this color, compare it to the economic forecast, and make our adjustments. That's where I think we add a lot of value. Anybody can buy economic models, but adding, checking, and layering other information on top is where we really get confidence.

Kazanjian: *I suppose this list also helps you see which areas are deteriorating.*

Davis: That's really a crucial point. We always compare the new list to our older list, to see what the rate of change is. So there might be a company that used to be in the 13th most attractive position that's now number 7. That rate of change merits further investigation. This approach also helps us find out which companies have the most value. A REIT that's gone from 15 to 12 is probably a better value now than it was the previous month.

Kazanjian: *And if one goes from 6 to 12, that may be a reason to get rid of it.*

Davis: Exactly. We use this process for both buying and selling. Once we have these data, our next step is trying to determine the owner earnings of the businesses and their growth rates. We also value the assets and liabilities to the current market in order to calculate a liquidation value. This is important in understanding the worst-case scenario. It's easier to determine liquidation value for a real estate company than for companies in some other industries. Because there are so many private property transactions, it is possible to get a pretty good idea of what people are paying for similar properties in the portfolio. We then decide whether the stock seems to make sense from a value standpoint. Granted, there are a lot of little tricky factors involved in this decision. How do you value, vacant land, since it isn't generating any income? But if that land is one acre on the beachfront in Palm Beach, it is probably worth a lot more than one acre sitting in the middle of southern New Mexico.

Kazanjian: *The REITs must constantly be aware of how much their properties are worth. Can a potential investor call and ask for this number, to save the work of going through and making all these calculations and estimates themselves?*

Davis: The companies indeed know this number, but whether they'll share it with you is a different story because that number is a moving target and very subjective. Most companies won't give it out because of the litigious world we live in. It's also important to point out that knowing the liquidation value is far less important than deciphering what kind of earnings growth these assets are able to generate and how confident we are that those numbers actually will be met.

Kazanjian: *What about the management team?*

Davis: Management is very important in most businesses. In real estate, it's absolutely critical. We expect that management will make mistakes. We just don't want to see the same mistake repeated. If a management team is making the same mistake over and over again, they're not worth their salt. For this reason, we do a thorough review of management's philosophy, its history of decision making, and its plans for the future growth of earnings before we're ready to invest.

Kazanjian: *Are you looking to buy the REITs at a specific discount to your perceived value?*

Davis: We are, but there's no hard-and-fast rule. Having a specific number doesn't work for us because it ignores the quality of the company we're dealing with. For a great business I will buy at a much smaller discount than I will for a mediocre company.

Kazanjian: *Does the current dividend yield fit into your decision-making process?*

Davis: It does, although dividend growth is joined at the hip to earnings growth, so it's useless to count them separately. Too many investors focus on yield alone when making a purchase decision. I've been around this business long enough to have witnessed what happens when one becomes myopic in terms of dividend yield. It almost inevitably ends badly.

Kazanjian: *If an individual is looking to buy individual REITs, how many does he or she need to own for proper diversification?*

Davis: Diversification is important, but not at the cost of total return. There are some REITs that own real estate nationwide and there are some that focus on a specific region of the country. In the same way, there are some REITs that own only one type of property, while others own all different types of property. Total return, therefore, depends on the individual investor's risk appetite for diversification. In all instances, we want to maximize return for incurring an appropriate amount of risk.

Kazanjian: *You own a little bit of everything—retail, office properties, industrial. Do you purposely try to invest in all of these different areas?*

Davis: It is ironic that we seem to have a little bit of everything right now. This does not happen by design. Our investments are driven by the mantra of looking for companies that can manage the entire real estate investment cycle. It just so happens we have been able to find such companies in the industrial, retail, apartment, and office sectors. We never look at the index to see how it breaks down by sector, and we're certainly not trying to match it. The composition is just a matter of where our research leads us.

Kazanjian: *What is your sell discipline?*

Davis: It's the exact opposite of what we've been talking about. To summarize: In our submarket analysis we identify the REITs whose deteriorating performances have not yet been perceived in the companies' stock prices.

Davis says his average holding period for a stock is around four or five years, though he's owned some companies much longer. "Our ideal holding period is forever," he insists. "Keep in mind that if you look at the *Forbes 400*, there are a lot of real estate millionaires and billionaires on that list. They've held on for a long time, and they're obviously doing something right. Without question, real estate is a pretty good investment."

DAVID ELLISON

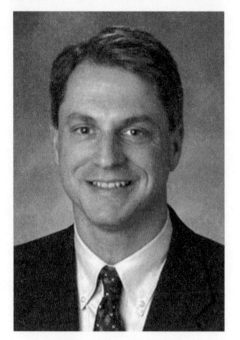

FBR Fund Advisors

As a young stock analyst in the 1980s, David Ellison had a chance to work with and learn from such esteemed fund managers as Peter Lynch, Morris Smith, and Bob Stansky at Fidelity Investments. Ellison joined Fidelity after getting his MBA, even though he had barely even heard of the company before. After a short stint in back-office operations, Ellison worked his way into the research department, ultimately becoming Fidelity's banking analyst.

In addition to researching small banks and thrifts, Fidelity ultimately gave him a shot at starting and running the Fidelity Select Home Finance

Fund. He remained at the helm of that fund for 11 years, which is almost unprecedented for a sector manager at Fidelity. In 1996 he was lured away to run the upstart mutual fund operation at Friedman, Billings, Ramsey Group.

Ellison now manages the FBR Small Cap Financial and Large Cap Financial funds, both of which have stood head and shoulders above the competition. The 46-year-old manager has especially found success buying many of the lesser-followed small regional banks that often get overlooked by the rest of Wall Street.

Now that interest rates are starting to rise, what does the future hold for the financial services industry? In Ellison's mind, the sector remains as attractive as ever, assuming you know what to buy and go back to the basics when analyzing companies in this area of the market.

Kazanjian: *When did you first develop an interest in investing?*

Ellison: My interest sort of started when I was in high school. I grew up in Middletown, New York, and took a history and economics course my senior year. It was back when Nixon was president and there was a lot of talk about inflation, the Federal Reserve, fiscal policy, and monetary policy. I was interested enough that when I went to St. Lawrence University in Canton, New York, I wound up majoring in economics.

Kazanjian: *What did you do after graduation?*

Ellison: I worked at a savings bank in Middletown called Middletown Savings Bank. I started as a teller. After being there for about six months, I went to business school to get to the next level. I got my MBA in 1983 from the Rochester Institute of Technology. Then, when I got out of school, I went to Boston to be with my girlfriend and started looking for jobs. I interviewed at a number of places and had an offer from Liberty Mutual and Fidelity. Both were investment related, though the one at Fidelity was less so in terms of what I really wanted to do. My girlfriend's father had been in the investment business for many years, so I asked what he thought. His suggestion was to go to Fidelity because it was a more vibrant story and they were doing interesting things. What's ironic is that the Fidelity job paid less money, and back then a couple of thousand dollars made a big difference.

Kazanjian: *What exactly were you hired to do at Fidelity?*

Ellison: At that time Fidelity brought its back office in-house as a cost-saving measure. They also started a discount brokerage operation. We were trying to figure out what to do with the trade confirmations and how to get them out as people started to trade. Basically it was a glorified service job. Fidelity wanted some MBAs like me to work there, partly because the economy wasn't great and they could hire MBAs for positions like that. The position gave me access to everybody in the research department. About seven months later, Fidelity was looking for people to hire into the research area. By then I was a known entity, had all the appropriate credentials, and was hired by the director of research. It just so happened they were looking for somebody to follow the small banks and thrifts. In the early 1980s there were a lot of thrift conversions happening across the country. A lot of analysts and fund managers didn't really understand it that well, and I had actually worked at a savings bank. They figured I must know everything. I was given the job of looking at all of these small thrift conversions. I remember the first company I called on was South Boston Savings Bank. Most of these companies were unknown to most analysts and were happy to talk to anybody. Plus, I was from Fidelity, a local investment house that could buy stock in the publicly traded company, so they were more than happy to speak to me, help me out, and teach me the business as they understood it. There were probably two or three companies like this a week that came public. I had piles and piles of prospectuses. The smaller banks were vastly undercapitalized and going public (with an initial public offering) was really a way for them to try to survive after a 10- to 20-year rise in rates started to reverse itself.

Kazanjian: *Let's talk more about an analyst's role at Fidelity. Were you doing research on these companies and then presenting your findings to the various fund managers with buy or sell recommendations?*

Ellison: Basically I was given all the small banks and thrifts to cover. My job was to do research and tell the fund managers which companies I liked and didn't like. Fidelity also used to have weekly meetings where you could talk about your group, what was happening, and what you liked and didn't like. Certain fund managers were very interested in this group, while others didn't care. Actually, Peter Lynch was one of the most interested fund managers in terms of investing in the names and trying to understand what was going on. My job was to help everybody understand what was happening, how the companies were doing relative to each other, who was going to do poorly, who was going to do better, and so on. It was a big process of compare and contrast. My universe was constantly expanding. I went from maybe having 20 companies to having 300 or 400. It was an interesting time. People were repairing the damage done to the industry by years of rising rates, and I was just there watching it. And the stocks performed well.

Kazanjian: *What was it like working with great managers like Peter Lynch?*

Ellison: I still speak with Peter every once in awhile. He was just a guy who wanted to understand how businesses operated, like a lot of the other Fidelity managers. I think Peter was able to get the best out of people. He always felt that the more people he talked to, the better he would understand what was going on. That's one of the things I learned from him. There were a lot of other good people at Fidelity then. These guys just didn't take anything for granted and always wanted to learn. It was a great transfer of intellectual wealth that happened during that period. When I got into the business you were either 23 like me or you were 43 or 50. There wasn't anybody in between because the market had done nothing for 10 or 15 years. So these mutual fund companies hadn't grown and hired anybody new.

Kazanjian: *You clearly got to learn the art of portfolio management from this incredible amalgamation of great fund managers you were working around.*

Ellison: Yes, although I didn't know it at the time. I think my collective understanding of the business goes back to that first call to South Boston Savings Bank. I didn't come into this knowing how a bank worked. What Peter gave me is an understanding of how to deal with the ups and downs of the market. You can talk about companies all day long, but you have to learn how not to lose your confidence. I think that's a big part of money management over a long period of time. There's a process to investing. The process I learned at Fidelity was to buy companies you understand at a decent valuation, and keep in touch with them as best you can so you're not blindsided. Avoid the blowups at all costs and make sure you understand what you own and the risks of those investments. Then, always reassess those risks. I remember we owned a lot of Fannie Mae and Freddie Mac, which I covered. Luckily the stocks did very well over time and made a lot of money for the shareholders. My thought was that everybody knows why we own them, so I sort of turned the tables and said let's find a reason to sell these stocks. In a sense, let's go in and talk to the companies and try to find things that could go wrong. The last thing you want to do is get married to something and not see it for what it really is because you're so excited about the upside.

Kazanjian: *You also got a shot at running your own fund. When did that come along?*

Ellison: In 1985 I helped write the prospectus and start the Fidelity Select Savings and Loan Fund. We changed the name to the Fidelity Home Finance Fund, which is still in existence today and is part of the Fidelity Select group of funds. I managed it through 1996, which is a pretty long time by Fidelity standards.

Kazanjian: *What made you leave Fidelity for FBR, your current firm?*

Ellison: It wasn't really any one thing. I could have stayed at Fidelity the rest of my career, but I really wanted a change. My feeling was I had built up a certain amount of knowledge of the industry and a track record, and I could either continue what I was doing at Fidelity or someplace else. I'd been running that sector fund for a long time, and they kept me because I was doing a reasonably good job and money was coming in. But the company changed. When I got there it was small, and it had grown very large. The people that I had been working with for many years had either retired or left. I went from being unmarried to married with three kids. I had known the principals at FBR for many years and they called and offered me a chance to do what I was doing there instead.

Kazanjian: *FBR didn't have any funds at the time. You were responsible for helping to build that whole operation, correct?*

Ellison: Right. I'm actually president of the FBR Funds. We now have six total funds. I manage the Small Cap Financial and Large Cap Financial funds, which started in 1997.

Kazanjian: *Which types of companies do you follow? Do you confine yourself to banks, or do you look at brokerage firms, insurers, and other financial-related businesses?*

Ellison: By prospectus it's pretty much anything in the financial services sector. In the small-cap fund, I primarily invest in the small bank and thrift universe. That's 99 percent of the portfolio. I would really call this more of a micro-cap fund, because they're quite small.

Kazanjian: *Are these like the tiny neighborhood banks with just a few branches?*

Ellison: Exactly, the neighborhood banks that serve coffee and doughnuts. There are plenty of those companies out there to choose from, at least 400 to 500. So it's a large universe.

Kazanjian: *The financial services sector overall has done really well over the last few years. Your funds have benefited from this, especially the one investing in smaller banks. But this has been during a period of declining interest rates. Now that rates are on the rise, how will the financial services industry be impacted going forward?*

Ellison: There are four things in a generic sense that drive the industry. One is interest rates. Next is credit and credit conditions within the economy. The third thing is accounting changes, meaning whether accounting rules are changed. And fourth is the regulatory environment. While we had regulatory and accounting issues in the late 1980s and early 1990s, and some credit issues in the early 1990s, the real issue now is interest rates. Frankly, I think interest rates generally are too low. From a fundamental point of view, banks obviously take money in at a certain rate and lend it out at another rate. As the lending rate approaches zero, it's difficult to make money because your deposit rates aren't going below zero. Over the last couple of years, it's been difficult for traditional banks because they've had to deal with a barrage of refinancings. Every time they turn around their yield on assets is dropping. Of course their cost of funds has dropped, but it gets to a point where you can't really drop it anymore and you start to see spread compression, meaning the difference between the yield on assets and cost of funds starts to come in. What's benefited them to a great degree is that credit has been very good.

Kazanjian: *You mentioned the trend in refinancings. You have a situation now where banks are lending out long-term money at 5 and 6 percent, while paying rates of maybe 2 or 3 percent. But what happens when rates go up, and banks start paying 6, 7, 8 percent for CDs, while holding all of these 5 percent loans on the books? Isn't that going to be a problem?*

Ellison: That's a great question. Most of these banks are now keeping only the adjustable-rate mortgages and selling off the fixed-rate loans to conduits such as Fannie Mae and Freddie Mac. It makes me wonder who is buying all these loans. The banking industry itself has thought through what you just pointed out, and is therefore in a good position for rising rates. They'd rather take a smaller spread now with the adjustable rates than lock in a low rate for 30 years and pray that rates stay low.

Kazanjian: *On the other side of the coin, in some areas we've seen housing prices skyrocket. As a result, people are taking out huge loans that they can afford only because of the low adjustable rates. But when rates go from 4 percent to 8 percent, they may no longer be able to afford those payments. Won't the banks be saddled with defaults?*

Ellison: That risk is certainly out there, but it's being mitigated. Banks that hold this kind of paper are requiring higher down payments and personal mortgage insurance where appropriate. But it's a question you have to ask on a bank-by-bank basis. Frankly, some of the guys I've spoken with haven't thought about what you just suggested. But I think the industry overall is generally much better managed than it was 20 years ago.

Kazanjian: *Are there enough safeguards in place to prevent another debacle like we had with the savings-and-loan industry in the early 1990s?*

Ellison: I think so, at least in the regulated parts of the financial services industry. The banks are in great shape on a relative basis. Regulators are tough and the accounting requirements are very good. Accounting for the banking industry used to be horrific when I first started following it. When I go back and look at some of these old prospectuses I have in my drawer, you wonder why everybody at the company didn't go to jail. It was just unbelievable. If you look across the various industries out there now, you've got the best accounting in the banking business, which is one reason you don't have any trouble. Accounting is all about three *C*'s: It should be *consistent* across all industries. It should be *comprehensible* in terms of how it works and how it fits into the business of what you're doing. The third and most important thing is it should be *conservative*. You should basically underreport your revenues and overreport your expenses as best you can so that earnings are understated and closely resemble the cash flow of the company.

Kazanjian: *In this smaller bank universe, given that you have around 400 names to choose from, how do you determine which names are most attractive for investment?*

Ellison: Since I'm following a value approach, I'm first looking for stocks selling at low price-to-book and price-to-earnings ratios. I'll maybe pick the top 50 from that universe and start looking at the individual companies. When examining individual names, I look at their capital ratios and at their lending strategies. Then you look at management. The banking business is really about assets and liabilities. On the asset side what you want is somebody who understands that making loans is about losing money. It's not about making money. You want a return on your money, but you must understand that when you make loans you can actually lose money. If you have that type of lending philosophy, you're probably going to be okay on the credit side. On the liability side, you want a company that understands liabilities are the true value of the company. In other words, that's where the jewels lie. You want to be working the liabilities side harder than the asset side in terms of trying to make it better. To put this into perspective, let's say I give you $1 million, put you out on the street with a table, and give you a sheet of paper for each person you loan money to saying that I owe you $1,000 and you can pay whenever you can. How long would it take you to give that money out? Very little time because people would be happy to take your money, especially when it says pay me back whenever you can. They'd take that $1,000 and go off and you'd never see them again, even though it was just a loan. That was basically the style of indiscriminate lending that was going on in the mid–1980s. Banks just threw money at these things. But let's say you did the reverse. You set up a table with a sign asking people to give you $1,000, for which you'll pay them 1 percent interest. How much money are you going to get? Barely enough for a cup of coffee. So anybody can lend money. At the end of the day, banks fail because their liabilities go bad, not because their loans go bad.

Kazanjian: *That's a really interesting point. So a bank's lending practices, and how loose they are in giving out money, are really crucial variables. You mentioned the starting point of looking at price-to-book and price-to-earnings ratios. Isn't it true that financial stocks by nature tend to have low PEs?*

Ellison: Yes, but not always. I find the lower valuations to be a good thing because they give you some downside protection. If you're at 80 times earnings, and something goes wrong, you've got a long way to go to get back up.

Kazanjian: *Do you analyze the larger financial services companies differently than smaller ones?*

Ellison: It's pretty much the same thing. At the end of the day, the simpler you keep it, the better. Banking is about the basics. It's understanding the risks on both sides. If you get caught up in some new branch format, or some new lending strategy, or some ad on TV, that's a mistake. I spend 20 percent of my time looking at companies and making sure what I think is happening really is happening. I spend the other 80 percent saying no to people who want me to buy the next new thing. The money trade business has been around for thousands of years and there's nothing new. You take money, you lend it out, you have FDIC insurance, you have branches, you have people to serve the community. But when you come down to it, it's really all about the people. There are good banks that have been destroyed by new managers who didn't intuitively understand what banks are all about. Banks are not growth companies. They are companies that are supposed to lend conservatively in good and bad times. They grow with the economy. At the end of the day you're buying a consistency of growth over a long period of time. You want to see book value growing and steady capital ratios. Obviously the bank may be growing and making more loans every year, but you want a conservative loan style. If you see that change, you should be worried. You want also to see a company that focuses a lot of its energy on building deposits. If my deposits cost 1 percent and yours cost 3 percent in this market because you're out there borrowing a lot of money or paying high CD rates because you need to get money, I have to work a lot less hard on the asset side to make loans in order to earn the same amount of money as you do.

Kazanjian: *Speaking of building assets, we've seen a huge trend of consolidation in the banking industry. Will that continue at such a fast pace in the future?*

Ellison: Consolidation is part of the business. It will be around forever, though it comes and goes in waves. I think that, generally speaking, consolidation is a shareholder value added for the smaller companies. For the bigger companies, it's a push—almost even a negative for shareholders. At the end of the day, when you get two big companies getting together, invariably shareholders don't make a lot of money. Those who make money are the investment bankers, lawyers, and the guys selling cigars at the golf club. These big deals are really about getting bigger. If you look at all the data, smaller companies generally earn better returns on equity and assets than bigger companies.

Kazanjian: *But how do these smaller companies compete with the big behemoths with millions to spend on marketing and advertising?*

Ellison: They compete with people and FDIC insurance. Remember, the key is to get money cheap enough to make a profit. The big companies tend to have more overhead. They have more senior vice presidents, executive vice presidents, first vice presidents, second vice presidents, and regional directors. These small banks can be quite lean with lower overall expenses, and they can price deposits at roughly the same amount. No, they don't have all the fancy services, like electronic bill paying. But at the end of the day the bulk of people out there in this economy are middle to lower-middle class and don't use those services anyway. The banking business primarily services those people who are 25 years old making $30,000 a year, who don't have five IRAs and an accountant doing the stapling.

Kazanjian: *I guess your point about the smaller banks being better for shareholders has come through in the performance of your funds as well. After all, the Small Cap Financial Fund has done much better than its larger brethren since inception.*

Ellison: That's a good point. There are really two primary reasons for that. One is clearly consolidation, and when smaller banks are taken over, the stock price usually goes up. The second is that smaller companies are more underfollowed. Therefore, as an analyst, I can add value in this area more easily. Another theory I have to explain the outperformance is one of safety. There's less of a terrorist threat, for instance, in these regional banks. Plus, they have generally done well fundamentally and the earnings have really come through.

Kazanjian: *How many stocks do you tend to own in the portfolio at any given time?*

Ellison: Between 45 and 70, depending on what's going on in the industry.

Kazanjian: *Moving on to some other areas, what's your opinion of the brokerage business?*

Ellison: The brokerage business, in my opinion, is all about having your expenses vary with revenues, because revenues are variable. It's a decent business. It's just volatile and therefore the stocks are volatile. As an analyst or investor you don't want to own them after there has been a clear out-performance in terms of revenues going up and business being good. The time to buy them is when things are ugly and have been ugly and the companies are struggling.

Kazanjian: *What about the insurance industry, especially in this post-9/11 world?*

Ellison: Insurance is tough because the fundamental benchmarks or buoys are very unknown. Unlike loans, where you can easily get your hands on the national average for a 30-year mortgage, it's hard to get a grasp on what's happening to commercial insurance rates in Chicago. And you often don't know you have lousy pricing until it's too late. Your ability to understand the business without significant research is dubious because you can't really verify anything you're being told by these companies unless you go out and do a lot of blocking and tackling. Even then you won't be able to get a lot of good information on the margin. Insurers are hard companies to analyze, so I typically don't keep a lot of money there.

Kazanjian: *We talked about some of the things you look for when buying a stock. What makes you sell?*

Ellison: Valuation. Stocks can become overpriced and you must have the discipline to say, "I bought it at $1\frac{1}{2}$ times book and now it's 3 times book. That's at the high end of where it has been historically," so you start peeling it back. Obviously you also look at PE and price-to-book. Then you watch for signs of a change in direction. Maybe there's a management change where they start focusing less on the wrong things. The real problems are on the credit side. That's really where you get the blowups. It doesn't matter if rates go up or down, but when credits blow up, forget it, especially with these small-cap names.

Kazanjian: *Some people reading this book are living on a fixed income and have watched CD rates plummet in recent years. Now that interest rates are moving higher, we're starting to see loan rates go up, but CDs still haven't budged much. Do you think banks will try to keep the rates paid on these time deposits artificially low, even as loan rates go up, in the hopes that people will just get used to earning less?*

Ellison: Banks have historically been slow to raise CD rates on the way up, just as they are very quick to lower them on the way down. But here's another way to look at this scenario: Would you rather get 1 percent in a CD this year, or be down 8 or 9 percent in the market? One of the things that can hurt you is a lack of patience. If I've seen anybody do poorly in the market over the years, it's always because of a lack of patience. I think people see the low rates, become impatient, and do something that's inappropriate for their risk profile. I feel people should forget about the yield and try to understand the risk. Ultimately investors get in trouble because they misunderstand risk as opposed to being disappointed about the yield. CDs are obviously a no-risk investment, but the returns are quite low right now. Still, that beats taking the risk of investing in an inappropriate asset class and losing some of your principal.

Kazanjian: *For the average investor putting a stock portfolio together, what role should a financial services sector fund like yours play in the overall scheme of things?*

Ellison: There are four big sectors in the overall economy where you can make money from an equity point of view: financial services, technology, healthcare, and energy. I run two funds that represent one of the four sectors. The point is if you're going to be in equities, you must be in one of those four sectors in some way. That's where you're going to get growth. The financial services sector just kind of always plods along. It's a growing business and demand for financial services is going up, not down. You need to be in that sector to be successful investing in the market as we know it today. You could say, "Why don't I just buy a big fund like the S&P 500?" where you're getting a diversified play that includes elements of the financial services sector. That's certainly one option. But a sector fund like mine is another diversified way to play one of the four big sectors. It shouldn't be your whole portfolio, but if you want to own financial services, this is a pretty safe way to do it. One approach investors can take is to invest in the best sector funds for each of these four areas. That's what a lot of financial advisors are doing these days. Instead of buying individual stocks, they buy sector funds to cover all of the broad areas.

Kazanjian: *If one decides to build a portfolio on a sector basis like this, what percentage should be in financial services, in your opinion?*

Ellison: It depends on one's individual understanding of that sector, but under my analysis it would be 25 percent. You'd have 25 percent in each sector, not knowing which one would do the best over a period of time. That's my own strategy.

In summing up his investment process, Ellison emphasizes that simplicity is essential. Like his mentor Peter Lynch, he believes that if you don't understand a company, you shouldn't own it. And, in the financial services sector, bigger isn't necessarily better. "I think understanding the people in charge is paramount in this industry," Ellison adds. "This is not a complicated industry. It's about balance. Own companies across the country and focus on what they're doing, as opposed to being so concerned about what's happening with the industry overall."

PAUL WICK

J. & W. Seligman & Co.

Paul Wick began investing in technology stocks long before the rest of Wall Street realized it was so cool. At just 26, he was handed the reigns of the Seligman Communications and Information Fund, one of the nation's first technology mutual funds, and by far among the largest. Although Wick didn't know much about tech stocks when he first started, he inherited a great track record, and proved to be a fast learner. In just a few short years, Wick found himself presiding over the top-performing fund in the country over just about every time period you examined.

Of course, technology became the "in" sector during the late 1990s, as a slew of new tech funds opened up shop, and investors of all stripes suddenly loaded up on a variety of high-tech names. While Wick also profited from the huge run-up, and even selectively bought some of the hot Internet IPOs, he never lost track of the fundamentals, which allowed him to suffer less damage than many competitors when the bubble finally burst.

A native of Buffalo, New York, Wick earned both a bachelor's degree in economics and an MBA from Duke University. He moved out to Palo Alto, California, in 1998, so he could work right in the heart of the Silicon Valley. He feels that gives him a better pulse on what's happening in the tech industry. It also allows him to see many of his portfolio holdings up close.

Wick's a technology manager who keeps a close eye on valuations. While the past few years have been quite challenging for tech investors, Wick sees better days ahead. The 41-year-old manager has plenty of advice on how to spot new ideas, and what to look for when evaluating the attractiveness of stocks in this very volatile market sector.

Kazanjian: *Did you start out at Seligman right after graduating from Duke?*

Wick: That's correct. I was assigned to work for Tom Nugent, who ran a whole bunch of things all at once. He managed Seligman Growth, a large-cap growth fund, Seligman Frontier, a small-cap growth fund, and the Seligman High Yield Bond Fund. He was doing way too many things. He hired me to be his assistant. Six months after I joined Seligman, Tom decided to make me a full-time high-yield debt credit analyst.

Kazanjian: *That doesn't sound like a very sexy job.*

Wick: It was actually fun and a great learning experience. This was in late 1987. When Tom left the firm in March 1989, I was the only person who knew much about the credits of these companies, so they made me manager of the junk bond fund. It had maybe $75 million in assets. We also had a $50 million pension junk bond account for Brunswick Corporation that got thrown into my lap. A trader on the junk bond fund became my co-manager. We did a great job in terms of performance. Our chief investment officer, Ron Schroeder, thought very highly of my potential. In late 1989, he tapped me to run the Communications and Information Fund. Cal Dooman, who managed the fund since its inception in 1983, was retiring. The guy who was originally going to take over that fund, Chuck Cadlek, had a change of heart at the last minute. They couldn't find anyone else to run the fund. It was like a $40 million fund then. It was very volatile and research intensive, and no one wanted it. The average age of the investment staff at Seligman in those days was probably 55 or 60. So it was an unusual confluence of circumstances that enabled me to end up running this fund when I was 26 years old.

Kazanjian: *Was that your first exposure to technology stocks?*

Wick: I'd had very modest exposure to it in the beginning when I was an assistant to Tom Nugent.

Kazanjian: *And you just happened to be available to run the Communications and Information Fund?*

Wick: I was available. I didn't know anything. It's the kind of thing that probably wouldn't happen nowadays. It was very much a trial by fire. I had one week with Cal before he retired for him to tell me about all the companies in the fund. Then he was gone, and suddenly the portfolio was in my lap.

Kazanjian: *Did you inherit a pretty good track record?*

Wick: I did. In fact, Cal had been here for over 20 years. He had a reputation for being the best fund manager at Seligman. In addition to running the Communications and Information Fund, which was almost like a sideline, he managed Tri-Continental, our big closed-end blue-chip fund. He had terrific results at Tri-Continental from 1985 to 1989.

Kazanjian: *Given that all of this was just thrown into your lap, how did you figure out how to invest in these technology stocks?*

Wick: It was very much a process of learning by doing, and very slowly getting to know who all the companies were. It was so much easier back then—there were far fewer companies. The software industry was a lot smaller, and you didn't have an Internet or cellular phone industry. You had far fewer public companies overall. Today there are probably a few hundred public semiconductor companies alone, and a whole lot of semiconductor equipment companies. Back in those days there were maybe 15 semiconductor equipment stocks, and it was a whole lot easier to get up to speed on the industry. Of course, the fund also had a mandate to invest in media and telecom stocks, so I had to learn those areas as well.

Kazanjian: *Indeed, the mandate for your fund is pretty broad.*

Wick: It can encompass, quoting from the prospectus, all areas of the communications and information and related industries. It's a pretty vague description. I remember when Cal ran the fund, at one point he owned Worlds of Wonder, the toy company. He justified it by telling me that they had a talking Teddy bear.

Kazanjian: *By 1995, your fund was at the top of the 3-, 5-, and 10-year performance charts for all mutual funds in the entire country. Here you were in your early 30s, you had only been managing the fund for about six years, and you were unquestionably the best-performing fund manager in the industry, at least judging by the numbers. What was that like?*

Wick: To be honest, it made me overconfident. So many things had gone right in such a short period of time that I started to feel like I could do no wrong. That whole feeling was punctured in the last two months of 1995 when chip stocks really fell out of bed. I'll never forget in November 1995, I went to a high-tech conference in Israel. When I left, the fund was up 75 percent year-to-date. Then Cirrus Logic suddenly blew up, triggering a chain reaction. All of a sudden, everything in the semiconductor industry started to fall apart. PC sales weren't quite as strong as people had expected. There were too many DRAM chips in inventory. Semiconductor equipment spending suddenly stopped. It just was awful. In six weeks, the fund went from being up 75 percent to being up 45 percent. It was such a shock. It certainly brought home the lesson that I didn't know everything, and that I was not infallible. It highlighted how dangerous investing in technology stocks can be.

Kazanjian: *Why are stocks in the technology sector so incredibly volatile?*

Wick: Well, not every area within technology is necessarily that volatile. In the electronics industry, in particular, what makes it volatile is that the psychology of buyers is always changing. You can have some pretty dramatic changes in a short period of time in terms of orders, pricing, and the willingness of people to hold inventory. That can quickly cause a dramatic change in earnings and the forward outlook. Parts of the electronics industry are also very cyclical. On top of that, you always have the persistent issue of technological change and an unrelenting competition. Some areas are more susceptible to that than others. Microsoft is arguably not that vulnerable to it, but most companies are.

I remember back in the early 1990s there was a company that invented the Ethernet bridge for the local area network. It went public, the technology took off in a big way, and the stock was a home run. Literally one year later Cisco went public and started to market routers. Routers made bridges completely obsolete. Within two years of Cisco having gone public, this other company either went bankrupt or was acquired for nothing. This kind of thing happens in technology. It doesn't happen as much in cable television or newspapers, where you don't have as much change. In technology, if you're a chip company and you have a dominant business in selling graphic decoder chips for decoding the images on a DVD disk, if another company comes a long with a better or cheaper chip, you can quickly get designed out. A company with a seemingly terrific franchise can lose it very easily overnight.

Kazanjian: *Is that because investors are always off looking for the next new hot thing in technology?*

Wick: Partly. It's mostly because consumers and purchasing agents are always looking for the next big thing. There are also events that happen within the industry to exacerbate these things. For instance, if the opportunities are better at another company and employees see the writing on the wall, they will leave. That just accentuates the changing fortunes you so often see in the high-tech industry. You don't see this in some areas. Take software, for instance. An architect using AutoCAD to design a residence or commercial building spends an awful lot of time learning that program and won't switch to some other design program at the drop of a hat just because it's cheaper or slightly better. But overall, the volatility in this sector is amazing, both in terms of stock prices and business fundamentals.

Kazanjian: *It's interesting that your fund stayed small for all those years, despite the great performance. In fact, investors didn't start piling into technology funds until the mid-1990s. At that point, it seemed like people wanted to own nothing but tech, leading to the now-infamous bubble. What, in your opinion, caused this bubble in the first place? Was it driven mostly by greed?*

Wick: I think the tremendous interest in technology in the late 1990s can be boiled down to a few things. Personal computers became pervasive in both the workplace and home. The Internet took off as a big-time consumer phenomenon. It drove people to want to go out and buy a new computer. The other big thing was that cell phones were becoming inexpensive and ubiquitous. Plus, corporations were getting tremendous productivity benefits by wiring their employees together into networks. Those four big trends all hit at once. I think it also started to dawn on people that there were some tremendous technology businesses. One thing that always puzzled the heck out of me was that during the early to mid-1990s, Intel rarely traded for more than 12 or 13 times earnings, yet the company generated a ton of cash flow from operations and had returns on capital in the top 5 percent of the S&P 500. It was such an incredible franchise. An awful lot of people had the mindset that this was a cyclical business. But for most of the 1990s, Intel was pretty much a secular growth story. It wasn't all that cyclical. A lot of people just didn't want to be bothered with the details.

Then you also had the mindset of a lot of mutual fund managers who kind of looked down their nose at technology and didn't want to try and understand it. It's the whole Warren Buffett view of the world, which I think is really stupid.

Kazanjian: *You mean the idea that you should only buy companies that you completely understand?*

Wick: Yes. I don't want to be bothered with trying to understand everything. That's such a copout. The technology industry arguably has far better growth prospects than the vast majority of the other sectors in the market.

Kazanjian: *But if you don't understand what a company's doing, doesn't it make it harder for you to analyze its future prospects?*

Wick: Given the extent of growth in the industry and how profitable some of these companies are, doesn't it behoove you as an interested observer to try and learn about this industry, so you can participate in it? Otherwise I think you're selling your investors short. Maybe that sentiment started to go away somewhat during the mid-1990s, helping to drive these gains. The other thing that happened is technology stocks had outperformed for such a long time. From 1991 through 1999, technology stocks and funds didn't have a single down year. Technology had become a much bigger piece of all the major indices, including the S&P. As the indexing trend became increasingly powerful, fund managers who might have otherwise looked askance at tech ended up being dragged kicking and screaming into the sector.

Kazanjian: *I must admit, it seemed like every growth fund manager I talked with in the 1990s—including some of the most respected names in the industry—was loading up on tech stocks. They even bought some of the now-bankrupt Internet companies that seemed to have unlimited potential. Did you, too, buy into all the Internet IPOs that were coming to market almost daily in the late 1990s and that immediately skyrocketed on day one?*

Wick: Our way of looking at the world has always been focused on the nuts-and-bolts fundamentals of high profitability, having solid cash flows from operations, and not paying an absurd amount of money for the companies that you're investing in. As a result, we very much have a growth-at-a-reasonable-price view of the world. The Internet really violated a lot of that. Those companies, for the most part, were losing money. They didn't even seem too concerned about ever making money. There was kind of this land grab mindset, and the valuations were insane. It was something that immediately struck us as highly dangerous. In this business you see fads come and go, and they end badly. We had done extremely well with America Online, which we sold far too soon because of our value bias. We were very skeptical of these Internet IPOs and wound up flipping almost all of them, which was a good decision in some instances and bad in others.

Kazanjian: *You mean you bought the IPOs and then sold out right away? Why would you buy them in the first place if you felt they didn't represent good value, given your discipline?*

Wick: It was like making free money back then, and I would have been violating my fiduciary duty to shareholders if I didn't let them partake in that. It was a red-hot IPO market. Even though we had a tremendous amount of skepticism about the long-term prospects of these companies, it would have been silly to just sit by and watch these stocks go up 50 percent, 100 percent, 300 percent in one hour's trading time.

Kazanjian: *So these were stocks you wouldn't have owned on a fundamental basis, but bought and flipped because of what was happening with the market?*

Wick: These were companies we would have owned at the IPO price, but when they immediately double in the aftermarket, you say to yourself, "There's no way I'm going to stick with this."

Kazanjian: *Were those huge stock price rises driven by institutions, or by individual investors who seemed to have such an insatiable desire to own these companies?*

Wick: I think the rise of day traders and individual investors participating in the market certainly played a role in that, but it was mostly just mutual funds, pension funds, and hedge funds cashing in on a craze.

Kazanjian: *While your fund certainly benefited from the run-up, you looked somewhat tame being up only 75 percent in 2000.*

Wick: What happened throughout the mutual fund industry, which caused some funds to have outrageous gains, is the SEC had not really cracked down on the way mutual funds distributed allocations of initial public offerings. If you were a mutual fund family and wanted to steer the hottest issues to one or two select funds, you would just not put the order in for some of your funds after you got the allocation. Let's say you had a $1 billion fund, a $50 million fund, and an allocation of only 50,000 shares. If that issue quadrupled, it would have no impact on the $1 billion fund, because it's such a small percentage of the assets. So you would instead put the allocation into the smaller $50 million fund, which would add several percentage points of performance just from flipping the deal. What happened is that firms with these small funds filled them with hot IPOs. My fund had almost $9 billion in late 1999. A hot IPO did little for my performance.

Kazanjian: *Of course, many of these hot funds that were pumped up by IPOs completely fell out of bed when the bubble burst. What do you think finally caused this frothy party to end?*

Wick: The pendulum had just swung too far. You got to a point during 2000 where Internet IPOs would immediately go up on the first day and then trade off pretty dramatically. There were so many companies going public that it became a joke. Managements were talking about how they didn't want to ever show a profit because then people will slap a PE ratio on the company.

Kazanjian: *There must have been a whole lot of greed out there. How else can you explain why the investment bankers took these things public in the first place?*

Wick: Exactly. There were hundreds and hundreds of companies going public. It overwhelmed the buying power of the market. All of these unprofitable companies that were cash flow negative had lots of venture capital investors who wanted liquidity. The amount of selling, in terms of IPOs and secondary issues, just went ballistic. It got to the point where the market couldn't handle it.

Kazanjian: *Let's get into some of the specifics of how you find and analyze companies for your portfolio.*

Wick: Given that I've been running the same fund for 15 years, I have more than a passing familiarity with quite a few of the companies that fall into our universe of coverage. One big difference between now and when I first started is that I've now got a pretty experienced group of people working with me. I've also been in California since 1998. I think that's a big advantage to investing in the tech industry. The way we go about doing things is the analysts who work with me are expected to become experts on the industry segment they're responsible for, and they follow that industry for a long time.

Kazanjian: *How do you find potential investment candidates?*

Wick: Through a little of everything. My analysts certainly talk to company management of the entire food chain and sample a whole lot of companies. We also read a prodigious amount of electronic and tech industry trade publications, including *Microprocessor Report, PC Magazine, InfoWorld,* and *Business Communications Review.* This helps us to have a better understanding of the product and the industry. I think it's important not to base your views of the world on sell-side research.

Kazanjian: *What are you looking for when reading these publications?*

Wick: General industry knowledge. We're trying to figure out what's going on, who's got good products, and how users view these products. Magazines and weekly periodicals like *Computer World* and *Network World* have all sorts of product reviews, plus articles on end-users and their perceptions of these companies. They talk about which products are better, and which ones consumers are interested in swapping out of. This information helps us to build a mosaic. We also talk to people that we know in the industry to a significant degree. One advantage of being here in Silicon Valley is that this is where probably two-thirds of the venture capitalists are, so you get a really good perspective on what's happening at private tech firms. A lot of times that gives you insight into the weaknesses of the existing public companies. Also, being here in Silicon Valley allows you to interact with people in many facets of the industry, whether it's the CEO, top marketing guy, or just an engineer in a company. All these people can help you understand what's going on and assess the strengths and weaknesses of various players in different areas of technology.

Kazanjian: *Is the technology itself more important, or are you more concerned with the management of these companies?*

Wick: Both are very important. You can have the smartest group of people in the world and if they don't have access to certain technologies because other companies hold all the patents to them, it's going to be a tough road. Similarly, you can have great technology, but if you don't have capable people making business decisions, you frequently fumble the football. That's why you really need both.

Kazanjian: *Do you invest in companies at all stages of development, or do you pre-fer more established businesses?*

Wick: The Communications and Information Fund has obviously become much larger than it was back in 1990, when it was a lot easier to be more focused on smaller-cap companies. Now we're kind of forced to gravitate mostly to companies with at least $700 million of market cap. You're typically looking at companies that are on the small side of mid-sized companies, all the way up to the largest. We think that the larger cap you go, the more efficiently priced companies are, so we tend to invest in companies with market caps between $750 million and $5 billion. That's where we spend the bulk of our time.

Kazanjian: *What do you look at when evaluating the prices of these stocks?*

Wick: We look at a whole bunch of things. First, we calculate the enterprise value of the company, which is the equity market cap minus cash plus debt. We then compare the cash flow from operations and operating earnings after taxes to the enterprise value of the company. We also compare those same valuation metrics to similar companies and the S&P 500 averages. We overlay that with our sense of how strong a company's franchise technologies are, how good the management team is, how good the products are, and what sort of growth we expect from the business over an investment time horizon of one to five years. We may also lay out our expectation for a company's cash flows over the next three or four years. In that case, we'd pick a terminal growth rate and compute a discounted cash flow for the company, again incorporating cash on the balance sheet as well as debt, and comparing that to the present value of the company to figure out whether the current share price is an opportunity.

Kazanjian: *Are any of these financial figures more important than others?*

Wick: Probably the least important one is just a straight PE because it can frequently be misleading. There are so many businesses where cash flow from operations is meaningfully unique from reported earnings. Therefore, enterprise value, free cash flows, and discounted cash flows are most important.

Kazanjian: *If readers are looking to buy one or two individual tech stocks for their portfolio, what would you say are the most important things they should consider before making such a purchase?*

Wick: First of all, is it a good business? That's the initial question you have to ask yourself. Then you need to figure out how different the technology and intellectual property is. Are there barriers around this business? That's really the key to a sustainable long-term investment in most technology companies. You next have to ask how profitable the company is, how high margins can get, and are we there yet or do we have a long way to go. Finally, given everything you know, you need to see whether the valuation is reasonable, attractive, or unfavorable.

When we're trying to make a decision on a given company, we try to stack the odds in our favor as much as possible. To do that, we look for companies with significant differentiated intellectual property, favorable new product cycles or an existing product portfolio that doesn't face increasing competition, and end markets with a reasonable amount of growth. We also like companies where product concentration isn't outrageously dangerous. In other words, a lot of companies that really blow up get 50 percent of revenues from one customer or one product. If you're a chip company, and all of your sales come from selling DVD decoder chips, if someone comes along with a better chip, they can design you out of your customers in a heartbeat.

Kazanjian: *What is the ideal company for you?*

Wick: The ideal company is Microsoft at one times earnings—in other words, a company with brilliant management, a fast growing end market, great intellectual property, high profit margins, and tremendous cash flows from operations, at an incredibly low valuation. That's the best-case scenario. Let's face it, you don't get those types of scenarios very often. The worst kind of scenario is to pay a huge amount of money for a lousy business that is hemorrhaging money, has dumb people running it, is in a brutally competitive area with no barriers to entry, and that's trading at a huge valuation.

Kazanjian: *That sounds like some of the Internet stocks we saw in the 1990s.*

Wick: Exactly. Or things like fuel cells and some of these other areas that are pie in the sky.

Kazanjian: *Given what you said about the rapid rate of change in technology, I assume you must have to follow your investments fairly closely and be willing to pull the trigger at any time.*

Wick: Absolutely.

Kazanjian:　*What makes you decide to sell an investment and how often do you trade around the names in your portfolio?*

Wick:　Turnover in the Communications and Information Fund has averaged around 100 percent annually over the last 15 years. We sell a stock when the risk-reward of owning it becomes unfavorable, meaning when we think the business has changed in a way that makes the likelihood of making money less probable over a time horizon of anywhere from three months to a year. Or, it could be that stock has done well and the valuation is now much more expensive than was previously the case. For instance, if you bought a company at 20 times forward earnings that was growing at 30 percent a year, but growth has now slowed down to 10 percent, you might want to find something else with more upside. Perhaps fundamental changes have taken place, and margins can't go up any higher, so sales growth is destined to slow. Maybe the market a company sells into is becoming more mature and decelerating. We look at all of those things.

Kazanjian:　*What about if the price of stock drops by a huge percentage, especially given how volatile these stocks are? Will you get out to avoid owning a falling knife?*

Wick:　I'm not a big fan of mechanical selling strategies. I think they're frequently counterproductive. I'll only get out of a stock if the fundamentals or our confidence level in the end markets has changed.

Kazanjian:　*Do you pay attention to variables like insider selling?*

Wick:　Absolutely. We look at that all the time, especially after a stock has had a significant runup in price. If insiders are selling, it's certainly a signal that maybe we should take our chips off the table as well.

Kazanjian:　*How diversified do you keep your portfolio?*

Wick:　We usually run with 50 to 70 stocks, with the top 10 representing 35 to 45 percent (of the portfolio). I don't worry too much about sector weightings, except with respect to semiconductors. A very valuable lesson in 1995, and again in 2000, is not to have too big of an exposure in semiconductors. The stock price correlation among companies in the chip industry is much higher than it is for software, media, or computer hardware companies. If you have a huge exposure to semiconductors, you can literally have the whole group trade off and act almost like one stock. Therefore, even if you have 30 or 40 percent of your fund in a wide basket of semiconductor stocks, it's almost like having 30 or 40 percent of the fund in just one or two companies. I don't worry about diversification with respect to the software industry because you don't have that phenomenon there. The fortunes of Oracle, Electronic Arts, Microsoft, and Symantec are very loosely correlated with each other.

Kazanjian: *Is there a limit to the percentage you'll own of any one stock in the portfolio?*

Wick: It depends. Over the last few years, there have been fewer good ideas to choose from, so we've run with a more concentrated portfolio. We've had up to 9 percent in a single company, with the top 10 holdings accounting for 50 percent of the fund. That's about as concentrated as we've ever been.

Kazanjian: *While the technology sector came back in 2003, the last few years have been very difficult. What's your outlook for technology stocks over the next three to five years?*

Wick: I actually don't think there are a whole lot of excesses anymore. Valuations are not at crazy levels. There are plenty of tech companies that are fairly inexpensive. Certainly the IPO market is quite discriminating and has been for a few years.

I think there are a few things at work right now. One is that the electronics industry has had a pretty strong recovery over the last three years. We're back to revenue levels we had in 2000, with a growth rate in the high teens, although that is starting to decline. The growth of PC and cell phone sales will also slow down. Not that the industry will decline, just the rate of growth. In terms of cell phones, we're at a point where we're selling 600 million cell phones a year. You overlay that on 6.3 billion people and you can see that the penetration rate has gone up pretty significantly in the developed world. These things all suggest that the technology industry is getting more saturated. It's not as "growthy" a place as it used to be.

Kazanjian: *Does this mean investors should temper their expectations for returns from the technology sector going forward?*

Wick: I think they already have to some degree. In the mutual fund I manage, this is the fourth year in a row I've had huge redemptions. Investors are not throwing money at technology mutual funds. The sentiment is very negative, which is why I don't think there are a lot of excesses to be worked out. I think the tide is about to turn, though. When I look at the amount of cash on the balance sheets of these public companies, most have never had more. Profitability in the industry is pretty good, even though the growth may not be as robust as it once was. For a few companies, like Microsoft, Oracle, Intel, and Applied Materials, profitability is actually quite impressive.

Kazanjian: *So the fundamentals look good to you?*

Wick: The fundamentals are good. We won't see any significant growth until we get some sort of big new driver for the industry. I'm not sure what that might be. One that people talk about is getting movies over the Internet, which I think will probably happen. The whole way people incorporate entertainment from the Internet into their home with TV, Tivo, and the like should have impressive growth over the next few years.

Wick is also excited about the whole flat panel phenomenon and believes wireless (especially wireless Internet access) will remain a strong investment area for the next few years. While corporate information technology spending isn't growing as fast as it used to, Wick contends that technology remains a good business, and will continue to grow faster than most other sectors. "You'll still have winners and losers, namely those that get displaced by a new technology or a more able competitor with a better design," he says. "But the pendulum has swung so hard against technology stocks, it's bound to swing the other way."

PART FIVE

The FIXED-INCOME WIZARDS

DANIEL FUSS

Loomis Sayles

Dan Fuss is not only one of the most celebrated bond investors on Wall Street, he's also among the most disciplined and structured guys you'll ever meet. He gets up at the same time every day, follows the same morning routine, rides into work on the same train, and comes home about the same hour every night. He traces these strict habits partly back to his stint in the Navy and says following a regular routine assures he has plenty of time during the day for his favorite activity: thinking.

During a career that has spanned more than 45 years, Fuss has invested through many market cycles, and is by far the most experienced of all the

Masters featured in this book. He has also steered the Loomis Sayles Bond
Fund to steady, stellar returns, with only one down year since inception.

Fuss is willing to buy attractive bonds wherever he finds them around
the world. Indeed, it's not unusual to find a healthy percentage of his portfolio invested in countries outside of the United States (Canada and New
Zealand are two particular favorites at the moment).

At 70, Fuss continues to be optimistic about the outlook for fixed-income
securities. Indeed, he expects bonds to outperform stocks in the coming
years, though he has low expectations for both asset classes. He also has some
timely advice for individuals looking to buy bonds in what has increasingly
become a market dominated almost exclusively by institutional investors.

Kazanjian: *Do you really get up at exactly the same time, and follow the exact same
routine, every morning?*

Fuss: It's very true. I get up at 4:28. While I set the alarm, I really don't
have to. On Saturday and Sunday, we don't set the alarm and I still wake up
at 4:28. I'm a creature of habit. I even set out the stuff for breakfast the
night before and have the coffee ready to just pour in the water and turn
on. That frees up time for thinking. I then get dressed downstairs and start
reading the newspapers. We have a special early morning delivery. I go
through the *Boston Globe* rather quickly. I like to check the front page and
the front of the local news. I check the sports page real quick and tear out
just the hand of the bridge column. I do some shoulder exercises as I'm
scanning the news. I normally have CNBC on to see if there's anything
unusual going on that morning. The rest of the time is spent going
through the remaining papers. By the time I've brought my wife her coffee in bed at six o'clock, I'm ready to go to the office. By then I've gone
through the *Globe*, the *New York Times*, and normally Section D of the *Wall
Street Journal*. The critical part is really the front section of the *New York
Times*. That's where you pick up the background music for what's going on
in the world. You have to watch what's going on in the world to see what's
happening in the macroeconomic background. I then leave the house at
6:04 and walk to the train station no matter what the weather. The train
leaves at 6:25. I'm normally at my desk by 7:03.

Kazanjian: *Talk about structured! Did you learn this from your days in the Navy?*

Fuss: To some degree, but it traces back before that. I've always been a
morning person.

Kazanjian: *Did you go into the Navy right after college?*

Fuss: Immediately after graduating. I majored in finance with a minor in accounting, philosophy, and naval science. I then went on for three years of active duty. I started out at flight training in Pensacola. After about eight months, I got dropped because I didn't pass a physical. It was the biggest disappointment of my life. I then became a plank owner on the U.S.S. *Saratoga* and was there for two and a half years. I actually thought about staying in the Navy. But I was married and had a couple of kids so it didn't make sense. That was in the mid-1950s, which is when the Navy was going through a big cutback anyway.

Kazanjian: *What did you do after getting out of the service?*

Fuss: I went to work for the Wauwatosa State Bank, in the Wisconsin town where I grew up. I had put my savings from being a paperboy and pinsetter at the local bowling alley there as a kid. There weren't many jobs in Milwaukee in late May 1958. Milwaukee was a capital goods town smack at the bottom of a weird economic turndown, not unlike the one we just had. It was tough finding a job. I had an offer from Merrill Lynch in New York and Bank of America in California, but I didn't want to go to New York or California. So I went back to Milwaukee and wound up talking with the president of the bank, which had 40 employees. He offered me a job and I took it because he said he'd not only pay me $300 a month, but he'd also send me through graduate school at night.

Kazanjian: *What were you doing at the bank?*

Fuss: I was a bookkeeper until my section of the books was closed. Then I helped the janitor. That was a real comedown because aboard the carrier, I eventually became assistant communications officer and had 144 people reporting to me.

Kazanjian: *You really started at the bottom at the bank.*

Fuss: Literally, because bookkeeping was in the basement. The only worry I had was that the river would overflow someday and flood the basement. I went from that to being a proof operator for a little while. Then I became a savings teller and a commercial teller. I next was appointed manager of a little loan and discount department. I didn't actually make any loans. I just did the paperwork for the lending officers. It was a great experience. I liked the people but I had sort of peaked out early on in my career at the bank. There was no place to go unless somebody died. So I transferred to

First Wisconsin Trust. I was an analyst there. I didn't get a raise, but I did learn a lot, and I went to graduate school at night.

Kazanjian: *Did you analyze stocks and bonds?*

Fuss: Yes, all corporate obligations. You really got to understand capital structure in a hurry. And I also did basic reports for all of the privately held companies. The one I remember most was the Chicago Cubs. It had a two-part annual report. In the first part, [Cubs manager] Charlie Grimm reported on baseball operations, and in the second part he reported on the prospects for the team. I was very lucky to work with some good teachers who gave me a lot of leeway.

Kazanjian: *Did you go from there to Loomis Sayles?*

Fuss: No. There were a few other stops along the way. In 1963 I became assistant treasurer of a life insurance company, after they offered me twice as much money as I was making at the bank. I was responsible for the investment portfolio. I then went to Continental Illinois, to help grow a division that served as an investment advisor for insurance companies. I stayed there until March 1971. I then came out to Boston to manage the Yale Endowment, which was a mistake, but it led to good things. The Boston Company made me an offer in November of that same year, and I went over to help build an investment management operation on the employee benefit side of the firm. I came to Loomis Sayles in 1976 after being offered the position of managing the institutional department here.

Kazanjian: *When did you start focusing exclusively on fixed-income securities?*

Fuss: I actually started working on fixed-income at Wauwatosa State Bank. Before I helped the janitor, I used to run the numbers on the bank's bond portfolio for the president. As an analyst and portfolio manager, I followed both stocks and bonds. In the early days at Loomis I did both as well. But as the bond business grew in the early 1980s, I eventually dropped my coverage of stocks.

Kazanjian: *What's the primary difference between analyzing stocks versus corporate bonds?*

Fuss: Bonds are further up the line, so you have more certainty about getting paid when a company falls into trouble. But the work is pretty similar. What often gets missed is your very best credits don't have any bonds outstanding. The company you ideally look for as an investor is one that is generating cash over and above the need for reinvestment. Odds are companies like that aren't going to have any outstanding debt.

Kazanjian: *Does this mean, by definition, that you have to go down in quality these days when buying corporates?*

Fuss: That's absolutely correct. It used to be you'd get a lot of AAA's being issued. That doesn't happen anymore. For a long time, higher-rated bonds were coming out of the regulated industries, especially from telephone and power generation companies. Nowadays it's much more from the industrial sectors.

Kazanjian: *You keep a large percentage of your portfolio in below-investment-grade securities. Where do you start the process of finding bonds to buy?*

Fuss: We've got a large research operation. They do a lot of good work on the credit side, in evaluating company balance sheets and pricing. Bonds are not like stocks, where you can pick up the *Wall Street Journal* in the morning and have a rough idea of what you would pay for an issue. With corporate bonds, you just don't know what something is worth until you go check it out. You need good trading capabilities. This is not something I could do on my own. We've got a bunch of traders in all the different markets.

What I'm looking for when evaluating a bond is relative value. Relative value is far easier to find in bonds than in stocks. With bonds, by and large the terms are set in advance. You can contrast the yields for various maturities. Of course, in general 8 percent tends to be better than 7 percent and 7 percent tends to be better than 6 percent. Therefore, you can make simple comparisons and rule out areas that you're not interested in. But you also have to go beyond that and do work on the credit direction, while watching for which variables might change that. Selling and buying bonds is expensive. It doesn't show up on the statement, because it's a dealer market (meaning the commission is added into the cost of the trade). But the costs are far bigger than normal stock commissions, so that also must be factored into the equation. As a result, if your turnover goes up, your returns go down.

On the other hand, the passage of time changes the characteristics of a bond. What was a 20-year bond becomes a 15-year bond, becomes a 10-year bond, and so on. So a change in credit direction will obviously change the pricing. A move in interest rates either way will change the pricing. All these things cause change to happen. In general, however, I've found that, except at turning points in the market, the best returns normally tend to coincide with turnover somewhere between 25 and 35 percent. In other words you're turning over the portfolio every three or four years. Most bond managers would say, "That's for wimps! We turn over our portfolio two or three times a year." That's not what I do. I like to find a bond selling cheaply relative to where I figure it should sell. I don't mean one or two price points. I mean 10 or 12 price points or more. In today's market, you often have to settle for 7 or 8 price points. It normally takes a few years for this kind of disparity to work its way out in the market, and you get paid extra income for holding on during that period.

Kazanjian: *Are you then trying to capture not only the yield, but also the capital appreciation gained from buying at a discount and holding on while the spread narrows?*

Fuss: You got it. The principle is pretty much the same as with stocks. There's not really such a thing as a growing bond, as with a growth stock. Bonds, unfortunately, either implicitly or explicitly, can get called away from you by the issuer. You can get squeezed out of a bond. It's much harder to do that if you're a stockholder.

Kazanjian: *Do you buy most of your bonds on the secondary market?*

Fuss: Yes, although I will occasionally buy a new issue.

Kazanjian: *How far out are you generally looking, in terms of the time you're willing to wait for this spread to close?*

Fuss: Fairly far depending on where we are in history. I'm currently using an analytical horizon of five years. What's an analytical horizon? Simply, I want to know or have a good guess as to what a credit will look like five years from now. You say, "Nobody can know that." Well, that's true, but you can get a pretty good idea. I want to know what a company does, what its market looks like, what kind of market share it has, and who else is investing in that area. This gives me a sense of what the return on investment might look like five years from now.

Kazanjian: *How do you make projections based on that information?*

Fuss: My analysts do it by picking up on trends and being good students of their industries. Then they watch for market share changes and product pricing. Once in a while they can also learn something from management. Management unintentionally can mislead you with their enthusiasm. I have a rule that I won't talk with management. I learned that one the hard way. Once in a while, there are exceptions. But even then I will talk about what other people are doing and about things in general. With most companies, if you ask specifically about their business, they'll put on their sales hat. You can also get in trouble with the SEC. So I like to deal with secondary information and the secondary markets. I do like to get a picture of the credit all the way around. If you're investing somewhere along the semiconductor production line, for example, you want to have a reasonable understanding of what's going on in the overall semiconductor market.

Kazanjian: *That sounds an awful lot like stock analysis.*

Fuss: There is no difference. If you're analyzing a corporate bond of, say, medium grade or lower, there is basically no difference at all between that and looking at the company's stock. The major difference comes in the area of valuations. That's where you find enormous differences between stocks and bonds. I'll often look at a bond that seems to be on the cheap side and ask how that can be when the stock appears to be worth twice what I think it's worth. If the bond looks cheap compared to the stock, I'll try to figure out what I don't know about the company. What did I forget?

Kazanjian: *Presumably you're looking for a bond with a credit rating that will either stay the same or improve five years out, assuming that's your time horizon.*

Fuss: Most of the time that's exactly right. The exception comes during periods when interest rates have been going down for a long time. At that point, you'll often find your best opportunities in some of the most disappointing areas, which is dangerous. It's like crossing the street in Boston. You never know where you're going to get hit. I think we're probably past that point for another 10 or 20 years. My guess is we can look forward to interest rates going up for a long time in the United States. That's a good thing. If you're lending money, do you want to lend at 6 percent or 5 percent? All things being equal, I'll take 6. It would be a whole lot better if rates got to 7 or 8 percent. How you get there is very important, though.

Kazanjian: *How do you find these attractive bonds?*

Fuss: You really need to work with good traders in all these markets. I also like to contrast bonds across markets because subsectors of the overall bond market can get overpriced or underpriced at the same time. The covariance in bonds is a whole lot higher than it is in stocks. Not only do most bonds like to march in lockstep, they like to go to the same tavern on the same night, and order the same thing to drink. When you find a situation where that correlation breaks down, it can be your opportunity to either buy or sell at favorable prices.

Kazanjian: *The average investor doesn't have a team of traders to do this work. How can they locate these bonds?*

Fuss: Really, the only thing you can do right now is look at the bond section of the New York Stock Exchange, which doesn't carry many issues. It's tough. I couldn't do this myself. I am very dependent on both trading and research. There is no way I could cover the waterfront like they do. This is a tough game for individuals to play.

Kazanjian: *I realize you have a vested interest in the answer to this question, but are you suggesting that the best way for an individual investor to access the bond market is through a mutual fund such as yours?*

Fuss: I really believe that. It's where I invest my money. If the money is in a tax-deferred account, such as a 401(k), another option is to build a ladder of maturities. You replace the longest rung on the ladder each year until the average embedded return in the portfolio represents that of the longest year in the ladder, typically 10 years. I wouldn't play it any cuter than that. I would add to the yield and eventual return by using as many corporates as I could understand and buy at my price. But determining your price is very difficult.

Kazanjian: *You keep a decent percentage of your portfolio invested in international bonds. How do you find and analyze these foreign securities?*

Fuss: Actually, finding them is easier than in the United States. The global issues tend to be a lot bigger, and you can get far better price information. Again, you're dependent on your traders, but it's not quite as competitive as the United States is right now. On the lower end of the credit curve, there's a lot you can do with bonds in the emerging markets. The problem with the emerging markets, and many U.S. high-yield bonds, is you can run into liquidity issues. There are times when you can't buy or sell anything in the market. The times you can't sell often come when you want to be a buyer. We try to take advantage of this opportunity. After getting analysis and input from the traders, we bring a bid to an illiquid market. This illiquidity might be measured in a microsecond, which would be the case with the Treasury market, or it might be measured in 10 or 15 price points in a distressed market. If you do your buying correctly by bringing a bid and providing momentary liquidity for the seller, you can do some really good buying. You don't always have the option of doing good selling, though. That's important to understand because it's a very common misperception in the market that you're going to buy and sell at a certain point. If I buy or sell a bond in an account, that transaction gets logged and compared to the most comparable Treasury. When the bond is sold, we measure how it did relative to the Treasury. It's a lesson in humility and a score that shows us how well we're doing, and whether we're playing the game right.

Kazanjian: *So you're looking to buy during periods of weakness when others are having a hard time selling. That really does require some good trading expertise.*

Fuss: The corollary is you don't want to be in a situation where you absolutely have to sell. You want the selling to be an opportunity you take advantage of. When I buy a bond, in my mind I immediately close the market for that bond for the rest of its life. Now am I happy? If I say no, I won't buy it. I used to do that with stocks, too.

Kazanjian: *That sounds a bit like Warren Buffett. He has a similar philosophy for stocks. Given that you own so many foreign bonds, what type of work do you do in terms of adjusting for currency fluctuations?*

Fuss: Currency is the toughest variable. Unlike with quality, maturity, and coupon, you can't set your parameters with currencies. I view currencies as having commodity market characteristics. A currency is supposed to be an accepted means of exchange, a store of value, and an accounting mechanism. It keeps score for you. I try to see what the fundamentals are for the issuer of that currency. That's a good place to start. Is the country's budget in balance? Then you look at the nation as a whole and see whether it is bringing in money or sending it out. But you're wrong a lot of the time. It's a tough thing to accurately call.

Kazanjian: *Are there any countries you absolutely won't invest in?*

Fuss: A lot of them. There are only a handful that I do invest in.

Kazanjian: *Such as?*

Fuss: Essentially I invest in all of the OECD countries and most of the bigger ones. I've even gotten as venturesome as the Ivory Coast, but those are speculations.

Kazanjian: *What percentage of the portfolio do you keep overseas?*

Fuss: It depends on the account. For the Loomis Sayles Bond Fund, I normally keep up to 40 percent outside of the United States, although I'll rarely keep more than 20 percent outside of the United States and Canada combined.

Kazanjian: *Speaking of Canada, you have a decent weighting in that country.*

Fuss: We just happen to really like Canada a whole lot. The economy, political structure, and currency are all in balance. The country has a positive balance of trade and current account. This situation won't last forever, but it looks good right now.

Kazanjian: *Going back to U.S. corporate bonds, if someone is looking for stability with a higher yield than they could get at a bank, what is the lowest credit rating they should look for in the current environment?*

Fuss: Probably AAA, especially if they're going to put all that money in one bond. With the Loomis Sayles Bond Fund, I can't keep more than 35 percent of the portfolio in below-investment-grade securities.

Kazanjian: *What advice would you offer to investors who would like to buy individual bonds on their own?*

Fuss: I would stick with bonds listed in the bond section of the New York Stock Exchange. Then I'd do my homework. At least you'll know what prices in general look like as a start. Then I'd go to the library and see what they have in the way of research information. If you don't feel comfortable with that work, either use a mutual fund or go with a high-quality laddered portfolio, such as the one I previously described.

Kazanjian: *Looking out over the next few years, what do you think the overall bond landscape will look like?*

Fuss: I think it's going to get a whole lot easier for bond investors than it has been. The primary uncertainty you have with bonds, apart from credit, is that you don't know what you're going to be reinvesting those coupons at. In other words, you don't know where future rates will be. We're coming off a period of low rates. My guess is that interest rates, with fits and starts, are probably going up in the United States for quite a while—at least 10 years. A decade from now, I would expect interest rates to be comfortably above where they currently are. If that's the case, you might wonder why on God's earth you should own bonds. Won't stocks do better in that environment? No, I don't think they will. I think bonds, corporates in particular, will do slightly better. The trick is to get from one cyclical point to the next one with your capital intact. It's just the reverse of what you had for 20 some years where interest rates, with fits and starts, always went down.

Kazanjian: *But how do you protect your principal as rates rise? As we all know, the price of bonds goes down as rates rise.*

Fuss: That's the art form. The best way is with a ladder approach.

Kazanjian: *You said bonds should return more than stocks over the next 10 years. Can you quantify that with an expected return?*

Fuss: I'd guess the return from stocks might be 6 percent on average, versus maybe 7 percent for bonds.

Kazanjian: *So your expectations are low for both asset classes?*

Fuss: Right, because of where we are in the cycle. If I'm right, that interest rates are going up over the next 10 years, that's not a rosy scenario for stocks. It's tough for stocks to do well against rising rates. My guess is we'll continue to be in what I call a trading range market, where both stocks and bonds go up and down with a lot of short cycles. At the end of this, you'll see interest rates measurably above where they are now. I'd even take the 10-year Treasury up to somewhere between 7 and 8 percent, which is quite a rise. If so, you won't have PEs on stocks anywhere close to 20. You'll start looking at low double-digit or even single-digit PEs.

Kazanjian: *Given your outlook, what sort of maturities are you buying these days?*

Fuss: In the bond fund, I have shortened maturities more than ever in its history. The average maturity is around 10 years. Since we use a mix of different coupons, it's better to look at the duration, which is 5.56 years.

Kazanjian: *What's the difference between average maturity and duration?*

Fuss: Average maturity is just that. You take all the bonds, add them up, and divide so that the average maturity would be 10 years. The duration is the present value of all future cash flows. This gives you a better idea of how the portfolio looks relative to the bond world at large. Other than that duration doesn't help you. It is useful as a proxy for how much the fund might bounce around over short periods of time because of shifts in the level of interest rates.

Kazanjian: *Let's talk briefly about government bonds. What do you look for in this area of the market?*

Fuss: This area is a lot of fun, although the rewards for taking specific risks tend not to be as great as they are on the corporate side. But the things you can do with the term structure of interest rates are far more interesting than in the corporate markets. The yield curves are very clear and you can contrast them across major markets, including foreign markets. That said, the only place I'm using Treasuries now is in the very short end. I use them as a liquidity reserve. I'm riding the curve out about 16 or 17 months. You make a tiny bit more than just holding cash equivalents with basically zero risk. I also own government bonds in other countries. I especially like New Zealand, where the country is in good shape and yields are very high.

Kazanjian: *What about state municipals?*

Fuss: Right now municipals are coming back into the right part of the cycle creditwise. Certainly pricewise they're somewhat attractive, relative to Treasuries, for a taxable account. The reason I like them is that I think we're going to start seeing higher individual income tax rates in the future. Otherwise we won't be able to deal with our federal deficit. That makes municipals attractive. And state and local municipalities are doing a pretty good job with balancing their books, in contrast to the federal government.

Kazanjian: *Is there anything else you'd like to add?*

Fuss: The most important thing, in a way, is that I'm really old. And that's not a joke. I really am. And I plan on getting a whole lot older. I've seen a lot and read a lot. Over time, if you catch the direction right, you're 80 percent of the way there. As long as you have the wind at your back, you'll do reasonably well. I think the direction now is one of rising rates. I'm always checking my perceptions, because certain things could happen to change them. And I work very hard on thinking. It's like doing pushups. You've got to work on that. Thinking is very important. It's easier said than done, and it's a process that's taken a long time to develop.

Indeed, Fuss says he's always thinking, even when he's away from the office. He counts it as one of his few hobbies. After all, with six kids, five grandchildren, and one great-grandson, he has plenty to keep him busy without taking up too many outside pursuits. Fuss does like to travel and, despite his reflective and calm demeanor, loves going to parties. The reason? He enjoys being around people. That's why, he says, being a teller was the best job he ever had. It gave him a chance to constantly interact with others.

MARGARET PATEL

Pioneer Investments

A few years back, one investment industry publication dubbed Margie Patel "Queen of the Junk Heap." Junk bonds, that is. Patel has managed the Pioneer High Yield Fund to impressive gains in recent years through the savvy buying and selling of both corporate high-yield and convertible bonds.

After graduating from the University of Pittsburgh, Patel began her career as an equity analyst. This proved to be great training for her future role as a bond manager. After all, she's often analyzing smaller, riskier companies, and must examine them with the same watchful eye as a stock analyst would in determining whether the juicy yield is worth the accompanying risk of ownership.

High-yield bonds have been impressive performers of late, and Patel's fund is at the top of the pack. But what will rising rates mean for this market sector? And can these outsized returns and yields continue into the future? While Patel, 54, certainly has lower expectations for the next several years, she remains positive on the sector. She also has a plan in place to deal with the changing interest rate environment, which she believes will allow her to keep making money even in the face of a tighter money stance by the Federal Reserve.

Kazanjian: *How did you get started in the investment business?*

Patel: I was always interested in it, and got into the business out of college by taking a job with Dreyfus in New York. I then worked at American Capital in Houston. I came to Boston in 1988 to work for what was then a proprietary fund family run by Advest. When those funds were acquired at the beginning of 1998, I went to work at Third Avenue Funds in New York and started the high-yield fund I run now. The Third Avenue High Yield Fund was taken over by Pioneer Investments and became the Pioneer High Yield Fund after I joined that company in August 1999.

Kazanjian: *Did you begin your investment career analyzing stocks or bonds?*

Patel: I started off as an equity analyst. I think that's why I've always run my high-yield fund more like an equity manager would. At Dreyfus, all the analysts were stock jockeys. But when I worked in the asset management subsidiary, I got more and more interested in bonds. I saw how you could add value through research, especially in the high-yield market. While at Dreyfus, I got interested in running private institutional bond accounts, so I had the chance to run some fixed-income money using my analyst background. That's really how I got into the bond business

Kazanjian: *I'd venture to say that most folks entering the investment business are more interested in covering stocks than bonds. Bonds just don't seem as exciting.*

Patel: It's true that equities are more sexy. But the high-yield area of the fixed-income market is very equity-like in terms of volatility, risk, and efficiency. It's the same story with convertibles. The high-yield and convertible markets aren't as efficient as other types of fixed-income securities. They're not even as efficient as the equity markets because they are less liquid. One reason is that there's not an efficient shorting mechanism for high-yield bonds. If I said I'd like to buy $1 million in bonds of ABC Company, I'd have to effectively find $1 million worth of the bonds. Bonds trade over the counter individually, so on any given day or short-term time period you might not be able to find an offer or a bid for the issue you want. That's unlike equities, where all stocks almost always trade every day of the week. So because of the lack of liquidity, and because it's an over-the-counter market, I think there is more opportunity to add value in the high-yield area.

Kazanjian: *You buy a mix of fixed-income securities for your fund, right?*

Patel: Yes, I use both high-yield and convertible bonds. I have a blend of about 50–50 right now. That percentage changes over time. The key is I use an industry approach, instead of an index approach, which is what the vast majority of portfolio managers do, whether in bonds or equities. Because I'm dealing with a risky security, I look at the industry backdrop first since so much of a company's performance is really driven by the industry experience. That's even truer if you're looking at companies with a lot of debt because they have less flexibility. Even small changes can have a material effect on the bottom line. Once I've uncovered attractive industries, I then look for income opportunities in that industry. And I'm willing to own either convertible bonds or straight high-yield bonds.

Kazanjian: *What's your definition of a high-yield bond, in terms of the investment grade?*

Patel: Definitely below investment grade. BBB is the bottom-tier investment grade, so anything rated below that.

Kazanjian: *In addition to convertibles and convertible bonds, you also own some convertible preferred stocks.*

Patel: Just a couple. Basically the convertible preferreds are much more equity-like in terms of subordination. For instance, if a company goes into bankruptcy, which is something I think about, first the bondholders get their claims satisfied, then it's on to the preferreds.

Kazanjian: *How does a convertible corporate work?*

Patel: With a convertible bond, you get a coupon with a maturity just like a straight bond. Typically convertible bonds have a lower coupon rate than the equivalent straight bond. In other words, if a company were to issue a straight bond at, say, 7 percent today for 10 years, they might issue a convertible bond with a coupon rate of 2.5 or 3 percent. Why would you give up that extra income? Because with the convertible you get the right to buy shares of stock at a fixed price. So if the underlying stock is at $20, you might get the right to buy it at $28—in other words, a big premium over today's value. Therefore, if you buy a $1,000 bond with the right to buy the stock at $28, it means you get to buy 35.7 shares of stock with your one bond. On day one, that's not very attractive because you can buy the stock on the open market for $20. But you get income while you wait for the price to go up. Over time, if you're lucky and your stock goes up to $30, the bond will trade at a bigger premium over its $1,000 face value, because you have the right to buy 35.7 shares at $28 and the stock is trading at $30. That's where the value comes in. It relates to whether the underlying stock goes up. It depends on the market or the coupon rate but you may get 40 to 80 percent of the upside as the common stock goes up.

Kazanjian: *Given that, are you buying securities for your portfolio based on the appreciation potential instead of the high yield?*

Patel: I'm really looking for a combination of the two. My goal with the fund is to achieve a total rate of return. Typically high-yield funds are run to maximize high current income. But I feel that's the wrong way to do it because what ultimately winds up happening to most funds is they take too much risk in trying to get the highest current income, and wind up losing part of their principal to losses that offset that extra income. I think sometimes you're better off buying the convertible of a good company in anticipation of the potential growth payoff. You get a little less income, but you get the chance for capital appreciation. And that's really my approach. As a result, my fund's dividend yield is a little below that of a typical high-yield fund, largely because I have about half of my fund in convertibles, which have a lower current yield. But the upside is that if the underlying stocks go up, you get to share in that appreciation. As a pure bondholder, you don't get that upside.

Kazanjian: *The convertibles are interesting because you get the higher potential with much less risk than owning the stock.*

Patel: That's absolutely true. If things turn out badly and the company goes into bankruptcy, you as an equity holder could be wiped out. But a bondholder, as I mentioned, has first claim on the rights of the company. The equity holder might get zero and you, the bondholder, might get, depending on how bad it is, 50 cents or even 20 cents on the dollar. But it's still a lot more than the equity owner. If a company also has a straight bond outstanding, those typically are senior to the convertibles. In that sense, they are riskier than straight bonds. But convertibles are definitely safer than the common stock.

Kazanjian: *The high-yield market has done very well over the last few years. What does the future look like going out three to five years in the future? We're in an environment of rising rates, which makes me wonder how high-yield bonds will fare going forward.*

Patel: High-yield bonds have done well since the Fed started raising rates, meaning their yields have not increased nearly as much as Treasury yields. This reflects the fact that what's making Treasury rates go higher is that the economy's doing better. What's good for the economy is bad for Treasuries, but it's good for high-yield bonds, just like it's good for equities. A stronger economy typically means higher equity prices, and the same thing is true for straight high-yield bonds as well as convertibles. The effect a positive economy has on a company's operating results swamps much of the negative interest rate effect. As a result, high-yield bonds will typically go up in yield less than the increase in Treasuries, meaning they perform better. Plus they have higher income, which helps to offset any price decline. That's what typically happens during the early stages of a Fed tightening. For the first year and a half, high-yield bonds should outperform Treasuries of the same maturity.

Kazanjian: *What happens after that year-and-a-half period?*

Patel: What's happened historically is if the Fed keeps on raising rates, or if as rates go up some of the more marginal companies are denied access to credit, you start to see people get more worried about credit quality. That's the time when yield spreads typically widen. So if Treasury rates kept going up, you could see high-yield bonds begin to underperform Treasuries and the yield spread start to widen. Then you would have not only that negative interest rate effect, but also credit concerns related to people's fears of more bankruptcies or of deteriorating operating results. That would cause yield spreads to widen. From this point you could expect that high-yield bonds would no longer outperform Treasuries. They may do about the same or worse, depending on how tight the Fed made credit conditions. Do you see a real slowdown in the economy as a result of the tightening, and do you see a pickup in default rates so that people get more concerned about taking risks and tend to cut back their holdings in high yield? Those are the variables you'd have to look at.

Kazanjian: *Is there a particular indicator that you would look at to determine whether it was time to get out of high-yield bonds?*

Patel: I would look at two things. First, the economy: Is the economy looking like it's actually declining or it is going to roll over and begin to decelerate? Number two: What's happening to liquidity in the financial markets? Are banks beginning to cut back loans to risky borrowers, which is typically one of the primary red flags that you see? In such a case, you might also see more marginal borrowers run into trouble.

Kazanjian: *If you saw this happening, how would you react, as far as positioning your own fund?*

Patel: In advance of this, and that's what I've done this year, I would try to raise the average credit quality for starters, because if defaults go up, the riskier credits would have the highest likelihood of default. Therefore, by being in somewhat higher credits, the BB names rather than the bottom CCC-rated issues, you at least lower the statistical odds of bankruptcy. Second, I'd try to eliminate any lower-tier bonds because they would be more vulnerable to widening yield spreads, meaning their prices could go down more than the decline in Treasury bond prices as rates go up because people are now worried about risky credits. Also, the reality is that lower-rated credits have higher default rates, and therefore higher bankruptcy rates. So all things being equal, I'd want to be out of those issues that would statistically have the most likelihood of bankruptcy.

Kazanjian: *In a way it's ironic that you'd want to move to higher-quality issues as interest rates go up, because that's usually a signal that the economy is doing well, and therefore defaults should be down.*

Patel: That's what's going on right now. You're in the virtuous part of the cycle. But when you get to the point where the Fed begins to overtighten so that you start to restrict credit, you get into the negative side of that cycle where credit is denied to riskier borrowers. Typically riskier companies have a lot of debt. As interest rates go up, you raise their debt cost and they can get denied credit altogether. Sometimes you can be a risky company, but as long as people keep lending you money, nothing bad happens. If you get to that point where credit conditions get tight, that alone can precipitate increases in bankruptcies because a company needs to roll over its commercial paper or other short-term debt. It may have a bond coming due that must be paid to prevent violating some of its covenants. The company might go to the bank and ask for a little slack, and the bank may say no. Banks are cruel. That could precipitate a bankruptcy. Once you have higher bankruptcies and a slowing economy, people tend to get nervous about taking risks and it becomes self-perpetuating on the other side. If you get to that tipping point where you become more worried about losses or yield spreads widening, bond prices go down and you start to think something bad is happening and want out. We're not at that point yet.

Kazanjian: *The key is to start making these moves in your portfolio before this happens.*

Patel: Right, because then it is not yet all reflected in the market. I figure that even if yield spreads don't really widen out from here, it's worth being in better quality issues on balance and giving up a little bit of yield. And by little bit of yield I mean a percent and a half, which is nothing compared to the losses you could have.

Kazanjian: *Given the great performance of high-yield bonds in general over the last few years, don't you by default go back to regression of mean in terms of returns?*

Patel: Please don't use that word.

Kazanjian: *Which one?*

Patel: Default.

Kazanjian: *Sorry. For a moment I forgot I was talking to a bond manager!*

Patel: That would be a common sense conclusion, unless you think they've thrown out the rule books.

Kazanjian: *Do you feel that they have?*

Patel: Well, no. Historically it's really been the Fed slamming the breaks on credit that's caused the economy to slow down. The question is whether it will be different this time from the rest of recorded history. Will the Fed very gently raise rates and surprise everybody with how these adjustments are made so gradually? That's the open question. In a sense, higher rates aren't bad to me because we've had great economies when the 10-year Treasury was at 7 or 8 percent. It wouldn't be bad to have rates continue to go up for the foreseeable future because that would say to me that you have a strong economy, good demand for borrowing, and therefore the expected return on borrowed capital must be going up. So you don't mind paying 5 to 7 percent to borrow money if you believe you can reinvest it and earn an even higher rate. In a sense we could have a scenario where we have rising rates with a growing economy and stronger equity markets. Often we think that if rates go up that's bad for equities. But in the last few years we saw rates below 1 percent, and that wasn't good for equities either. Low rates are symbolic of an economy that's sick like Japan. In a sense, higher rates would signal a healthy economy, and that would be healthy for the financial markets in general, and equities in particular.

Kazanjian: *Speaking of international issues, do you buy any foreign bonds?*

Patel: No, I strictly stick with domestic securities.

Kazanjian: *In the early 1990s, junk bonds got a really bad name. But people seem to be embracing them again. Have things changed so fundamentally that we couldn't have another meltdown as we did back then?*

Patel: Yes and no. I would say it looks pretty unlikely that we'd see a repeat of that disaster. In the early and late 1990s, we had two perfect storms, and they are unlikely to be repeated again, even though we did it twice in a decade. In 1990 you had a collapse in savings-and-loan institutions that were forced to liquidate their high-yield portfolios. This resulted in one of the greatest wealth transfers we've seen in the twentieth century for the lucky people who bought anything the Resolution Trust Corporation was dumping. You also had a recession and the bankruptcy of Drexel Burnham Lambert, the leading brokerage firm in junk bonds. Later, in the fall of 1998, you had the bankruptcy of Long-Term Capital Management, which created a lot of disorder in the marketplace. In 1998 to 2000 you had the creation of a huge amount of extremely poor-quality paper that was doomed to go bankrupt, especially in the telecommunications sector. And just as you had the Internet and telecom bubble in the stock market, you had the same thing in the high-yield market. You had enormous supply to the point where telecom bonds comprised 20 percent of the universe of high-yield bonds. Those are the new telecoms with negative cash flow, no management team, very little revenue, and ultimately no profits. In addition, there was a big dropoff in the equity market, along with the Fed really tightening credit conditions after Y2K. That was followed by the collapse of the equity bubble, and the implosion of telecom and Internet stocks. All of that rolled over into the high-yield market because you had all these companies with negative cash flow and no way to roll over their debts. To top it all off, you had high-profile bankruptcies like Enron and

MCI. How quickly we forget. Then there was September 11 and the recession.

Kazanjian: *What's to say another perfect storm like that isn't on the horizon?*

Patel: Although yield spreads are narrow, the Fed is committed to restoring the economy. They're gradually raising rates, which says there should be ample liquidity to prevent the Fed from precipitating a recession by tightening up too fast. Also, unlike previous years, the economy is growing and that's a big difference. This says to me that high-yield bonds should probably do all right because you'll still have liquidity and the economy will continue to grow. An expanding economy is really the most important positive factor. Besides a slower economy and tighter credit, the other thing that often causes defaults to go up is an enormous amount of new issuance and the quality of those issues. We've really had a moderate new issue calendar, and a lot of it has just been refinancing outstanding issues at lower interest rates. You still have some poor-quality issues able to access the credit market, but it's maybe 30 percent of the size it was, and not big enough to be a precursor of a huge spike up in defaults. I think we'll see defaults stabilize at some point in the future. The odds of rates rising substantially, and spreads widening considerably, are pretty low over the next year. So things still look pretty good for the high-yield market. Incidentally, there's a close correlation between high-yield bonds and small-cap equities. If the economy is doing well, small stocks and high-yield companies often both do well.

Kazanjian: *Given that correlation, what kind of diversification are you getting by adding high-yield bonds to a stock portfolio?*

Patel: The long-term correlation between high-yield bonds and the market overall as measured by the Russell 2000 (a small-cap stock index) is about .55, which is not very high.

Kazanjian: *For a fixed-income investor, what percentage of the portfolio would you put in the high-yield bond market?*

Patel: Typically I see it as an income supplement, so 10 to 20 percent of a person's fixed income investments would be the right amount.

Kazanjian: *Should an investor who doesn't need income and who has a long time horizon even bother with owning high-yield bonds, or should they just stick with equities?*

Patel: I think high-yield bonds are still interesting, especially if younger investors can buy them in a tax-sheltered account, such as a 401(k). If you can compound the income, and not have to pay taxes on that income in a tax-sheltered account like a 401(k), it tends to be pretty attractive over time. It's also a good source of asset diversification that in general has less downside volatility.

Kazanjian: *You mentioned that when building your portfolio, you begin by looking at sectors you want to be in. How do you identify those sectors?*

Patel: I start with my economic outlook, come up with a scenario for what I expect to happen, and ask myself which industries I think would do well under that scenario. Then I particularly look for industries that are out of favor and might benefit from the economic cycle, especially those where the negatives are already factored in and I think the yield is too high for the fundamental risk that actually exists.

Kazanjian: *In essence, you're looking for value plays.*

Patel: Right. Then, because I do use an industry focus, I look at companies with leading niches and check to see whether they have high-yield bonds or convertibles available. A lot of times a company may not have high-yield bonds, but it might have convertible debt. That way I get the exposure I want in the industry, and I have more choices of companies. For instance, I can see whether the convertible is trading at a discount or around face value. If I get at least a little bit of income and the stock goes up over time, I get that share of participation I talked about earlier. Depending on how big or small the premium is, you might have participation between 30 and 80 percent. That's a wide range, but the market's pretty wide. In other words, you get something more than you would just by being in a bond. Even if you have a low equity participation, generally speaking that still more than makes up for the little bit of income you gave up.

Kazanjian: *What about with the straight high-yield bonds? Here are you looking primarily for income, or also at the capital appreciation potential?*

Patel: On the high-yield side I'm really looking more for the income, especially at this point in the cycle where bonds are trading pretty much at par (face value). There's not a lot of capital appreciation opportunity in high-yield bonds, which gives me a better opportunity in the fund because I also own the convertibles. You can buy a bond at par and it can go above par, but the upside tends to get limited because bonds typically are callable around five years from the time of issuance. That's why there's generally a limit to the price that a straight bond can go up, because pretty soon they're callable in a few years at maybe 105 cents on the dollar. That means it's pretty hard for a bond to go up much beyond that.

Kazanjian: *You mentioned you're looking for industries that are out of favor, but doesn't that mean they have more risk attached to them?*

Patel: That's right, though not as much if the price reflects the problem. Keep in mind we're not talking about fundamentals that would lead to going out of business. We're talking about situations where people are concerned about the near-term earnings or prospects of an industry. Perhaps there's a negative outlook for the next year or sometimes even less. To me, that's the nature of a company being in business. Returns don't go in a straight line. They tend to go up and down, and there are always surprises, usually unpleasant ones. Therefore, when investors get surprised, they tend to overreact. Prices tend to go down more than what a rational investor would estimate is the real fundamental risk.

Kazanjian: *How many sectors are you normally in at any one time?*

Patel: The portfolio is pretty diversified. I own close to a hundred different companies. I don't keep more than 15 percent in any narrowly defined industry.

Kazanjian: *Looking ahead, are there certain industries you're especially enamored of?*

Patel: I think basic materials is going to be a surprisingly good sector over time, and that includes chemicals, paper, packaging, forest products, and nonferrous metals. During the last several decades these industries have been plagued with low returns on capital, excess capacity, and too much competition. But I think as we move forward with global growth and see inefficient competitors closing their doors, the companies left in the basic materials sector will be highly competitive. So much inefficient capacity has been closed down, it isn't going to be built up again unless we see demand and more growth picking up very substantially. I think you'll see much better supply–demand fundamentals in basic industries than we've seen for many years. To me it's a multiyear scene that's not going to change. The other attractive area is technology. Companies in the technology space are very volatile because if demand fluctuates, prices typically go down, and product lifecycles are very short. But even with all that, the fact is that technological components are increasing for virtually every product and service we use. So it's a volatile area, but growing faster than the economy. I think that technology will still be attractive over time because it's going to continue to grow even with occasional periods of downward volatility in operating results.

Kazanjian: *Once you've identified attractive sectors, tell us more about how you choose individual issues for the portfolio.*

Patel: I look for companies with critical mass and at least three years of operating history, with enough liquidity on the balance sheet to fund their activities. I like to see a company that, by looking at the balance sheet, is pretty well covered by assets. What really drives my process is looking for companies that are leaders with sustainable revenues to improve the corporate worth and generate better earnings.

Kazanjian: *How can individuals find good high-yield bonds on their own?*

Patel: It's really become much more difficult for individual investors to buy individual bonds in the last 10 years. It used to be that bonds came out registered, meaning anybody could buy them, and they often were listed on the New York Bond Exchange or the American Bond Exchange. Today most new issue bonds and convertibles are issued under Regulation 144A, meaning they're available for purchase only by qualified institutional investors for a certain period of time, usually 60 to 90 days. Therefore, they're just not available for purchase by individuals. Even at the point an investor could buy them, they won't be able to find them because these issues don't trade on an exchange the way a lot of regular bonds used to. The number of bonds overall that trade on the exchange has really diminished. Typically all brokerage firms are getting away from the retail trading of bonds for individual accounts. Therefore, if you went to a broker, the chances are pretty low that the broker actually would have bonds available in a small enough amount for individual investors. Even if the broker could find a small quantity of bonds, because of the high transaction costs, the price of the bonds would be so high, you really wouldn't be getting that good of a deal on the yield compared to the yield offered in a mutual fund. In other words, you're better off in a fund. Even with the advantages of my professional knowledge, I never personally buy individual bonds for myself.

Kazanjian: *How do you find, buy, and sell your bonds for the fund?*

Patel: I deal directly with all the major Wall Street houses. You generally have to trade bonds in the multimillions of dollars for them to do business with you.

Kazanjian: *So are you pretty much selling your inventory to other institutions?*

Patel: Yes. Again, retail investors are generally excluded in this process.

Kazanjian: *Given that you're dealing with other professionals, how are you able to find these values? Shouldn't they also recognize the value, or lack thereof, in these securities?*

Patel: Well, that's the great thing about investing. Everybody's entitled to their opinion. Some people feel very uncomfortable buying a bond of a company with a near-term negative outlook. So if you feel the near-term outlook is negative, but the company still has good prospects and the price more than fully reflects these negative factors, you can make some attractive purchases. Also, most investors are quasi-indexers. Even if a company or industry gets pretty cheap, they may not necessarily buy a large amount of an issue because they don't want to get their weightings too different from the index. I don't use that approach, so I have holdings that are very much overweighted or underweighted compared to the index. I think this creates an opportunity because sometimes things are cheap, and if you can overweight them, you'll really benefit if you make the right decision.

Kazanjian: *If an individual were able to locate and buy high-yield bonds on his or her own, I take it diversification is very important.*

Patel: Right. And then it comes down to how many bonds you need to be diversified; I'd say at least a dozen, or preferably two dozen.

Kazanjian: *With the way you run your fund, if the high-yield market falls out of bed, will you adjust your portfolio to account for that, or should investors expect your performance to decline in line with what's happening in the overall market?*

Patel: I think I have an advantage over a pure play on a high-yield fund because I do own the convertibles. Therefore, I have a chance to invest in more sectors along with an avenue for equity appreciation if the stock goes up. That's important, especially in a market like today where the majority of high-yield bonds are trading at a premium.

Kazanjian: *What's an example of a bond you bought that exemplifies the approach you have outlined for us?*

Patel: I bought some Corning Glass convertible bonds in 2002 with a coupon of only 3.5 percent. But I got them well below 90 cents on the dollar. Because the stock went up substantially from depressed levels, the bonds are now worth about 120 cents on the dollar, or $1,200 for a $1,000 bond. So you had a relatively low coupon rate, but you got capital appreciation that more than compensated you for that.

Kazanjian: *Was that because the company itself was out of favor, and therefore other investors were looking to unload the convertibles?*

Patel: Both the stock and bonds were depressed. When the stock price went up, that ability to convert into equity has actually become worth something.

Kazanjian: *Do you therefore follow the stock market activity of companies, perhaps looking to buy bonds of companies hitting the new low list and such?*

Patel: Yes, I'll take a look. Sometimes I have companies I'm watching with the idea that if, for some reason, they disappoint or the outlook for the industry turns negative, I might consider adding to my position.

Kazanjian: *Your fund now has about $7.8 billion in assets. Does being that large impair your ability to be more flexible and liquid?*

Patel: No, and the first reason is when you're a true value player, you're buying what's relatively out of favor, and therefore more available. Second, I'm not an index fund, so if something is cheap, I can overweight it. Also, having the ability to buy not just high yield but also convertibles, I have two markets to choose from.

Kazanjian: *Looking through your portfolio, it seems like the majority of companies you own are rather small. Is that because you normally find high-yield bonds among smaller companies?*

Patel: Generally speaking, that's right. It's harder for those companies to raise money, so they might do it either through the high-yield or convertible market.

Kazanjian: *Why don't these companies just issue more stock?*

Patel: Because if the equity base is relatively small, say a market capitalization of $1 billion, raising another $200 million would result in a 20 percent increase in the number of outstanding shares. It might be very difficult to sell that much stock without really depressing the price. Therefore, if you could raise the money through a bond issue, it's more appealing.

Kazanjian: *The yield on your fund right now is around 6.75 percent. Would you expect that to change as interest rates rise?*

Patel: The yield may go up if interest rates rise over the next year, but it will go up very gradually. The only way you'd really get the benefit of the yield going up would be if a massive amount of new cash were invested in new securities at newly prevailing higher rates.

While that yield sounds good, it's important to emphasize that these higher returns don't come without risk. As Patel readily admits, this is a volatile market sector, with equity-like characteristics. But the respectable income and potential for capital appreciation offered by high-yield and convertible corporate bonds can make them an attractive income supplement for the fixed-income component of most overall portfolios.

Incidentally, Patel launched a new fund at the end of 2004 that lets her apply her strategy to stock investing. The Pioneer Equity Opportunity Fund invests in stocks across all market capitalization and style ranges, although Patel expects to primarily focus on small- to mid-cap companies.

PART SIX

INVESTING LIKE THE MASTERS

Ten Keys to Beating the Market

As you've no doubt gathered from reading these interviews, all of the Masters have a slightly different strategy for finding, buying, and selling their investments. However, there are 10 traits they all seem to share, which have helped them remain steady through a variety of market environments. I call these qualities the "Ten Keys to Beating the Market," and believe that following these rules will help you to enjoy similar success in managing your own personal stock and bond portfolio.

1. Follow a discipline that makes sense to you. One thing that comes through clearly in these profiles is how the investment strategies followed by the Masters originally grew out of their unique life experiences. Therefore, to figure out whether a value or growth approach is more appropriate for you, begin by examining your own lifestyle and temperament. "I think it's really part of one's personality and it's ingrained in you," says John Schneider, who maintains that his value orientation permeates all areas of his being. "I don't want to come off as cheap, but I don't have a fancy house or a fancy car." Adds fellow value manager Susan Suvall, "It's really the way I live my life. I don't go to Neiman Marcus to buy an outfit. I'll go to a store that has the same stuff at a discount."

It's a lesson value Master Rich Pzena learned early on. "You're either a bargain hunter or you're an optimist," he explains. "The bargain hunters are the ones where it's ingrained in you from the first day you're born because your mother's taking you to buy clothes only when they're on sale. I still have that orientation in all aspects of my life. The people who are trying to find the next Microsoft are a totally different breed."

Sarah Ketterer says even brand-new managers know what style fits them best before they even understand exactly how the investment process works. "When we interview young inexperienced MBAs, they already sort

255

of know what they want," she says. "They either want to chase growth stocks, because they're mesmerized by momentum, or they have a calmer demeanor with enough maturity to look out beyond the cycle we're in now. In house hunting, it's the difference between the person who just sees the ramshackle disaster in front, as opposed to the other who can actually look behind it all and see it renovated."

If you're always up for a good bargain, value investing may be most appropriate for you. On the other hand, if you prefer to live in the fast lane, and believe in paying up for what's most fashionable, a more growth-oriented approach could suit your personality better.

Having said that, if you buy mutual funds, instead of individual securities, it can make a lot of sense to hire the best managers from both disciplines to maintain a more diversified portfolio. More on that is coming up in key number 10.

2. Stick to your strategy, even when times are tough. The reason it's so important to follow a discipline that makes sense for you is that sticking with a given strategy is essential to long-term success. Those who consistently suffer from mediocre, or even negative, returns frequently switch from one technique to another, often following hot tips or buying on a whim. One reason that's so deadly is you never learn anything from your mistakes.

There are many approaches to investing that work, though you can really only be an expert at one. After you've figured out the best strategy for you, don't stray from it even in difficult times when it's tough sticking to your guns. For Rich Pzena, the late 1990s was the most challenging period of his investment life. While high-tech stocks with outrageous multiples were skyrocketing, his value stocks were barely treading water. But he never wavered and wound up coming back strong in the years that followed. Pzena believes the reason most investors underperform the market is because they're constantly getting sucked into whatever technique happens to be working at the moment. "They're always a day late and a dollar short," he says. "If you can stay disciplined, and there are a lot of disciplines that work, you should be able to beat the market. It shouldn't be that hard."

In a more difficult market environment, such as the one we're in right now, those who are disciplined will reap the most rewards. "I think those who succeed at investing over the next five or ten years are those who stick to their knitting, follow their disciplines, and grind it out," says Sam

Stewart. "If you're an amateur listening to tips in the clubhouse, it's going to be tough."

3. Don't be reliant on Wall Street research. Having worked on both sides of the business, Whit Gardner knows how problematic research from the major Wall Street firms can be. After all, investment banks serve two masters. On the one hand, they deal with retail clients and want to provide them with effective stock and bond recommendations. However, they also make huge fees by taking companies public and performing other investment-related services. Therefore, there is often a large incentive to make information about these investment banking clients sound more positive than it probably should be at times.

That's why Gardner, like many of the other Masters, prides himself in doing his own homework. "To do research right, you need to go directly to the companies themselves and talk with their customers, competitors, and suppliers. You need to understand from and through the eyes and ears of the CEO, CFO, and head of marketing what's creating change within the business that hasn't been properly perceived or priced into the stock."

Andy Pilara couldn't agree more. "We like to turn over as many rocks as possible," he insists.

By the same token, it's essential to always be on the lookout for new investment ideas, even in some of the most unlikely places. Paul Wick finds companies for his technology fund through a variety of sources, including paying attention to media outside of the mainstream. "My analysts certainly talk to company management of the entire food chain and sample a whole lot of companies," he says. "We also read a prodigious amount of electronic and tech industry trade publications, including *Microprocessor Report, PC Magazine, InfoWorld*, and *Business Communications Review*. This helps us to have a better understanding of the product and the industry. I think it's important not to base all of your views of the world on sell-side research."

To find ideas for his healthcare fund, David Chan gets out and talks to those most likely to use the products he's investing in. "My team and I meet with companies, go to medical meetings, talk to physicians, and do physician surveys," he says. "We try to keep abreast of what's going on in every therapeutic area and figure out where there are unmet medical needs. We look for products with characteristics that doctors would like and could use."

4. Scrutinize the numbers. While management is continuously putting a positive spin on the business and a company's potential to make more money, the numbers never lie (unless they've been fraudulently cooked, which is a whole other story). That's why many of the Masters begin reading annual reports and other company documents from the back forward, which is where all of the balance sheet items are located. For one thing, this helps them determine how much the company might be worth to a private buyer, a number that can be compared to the current share price. It also lets them know how financially secure the business is, depending on how much cash and debt are on the books.

"We want to read the footnotes," says Andy Pilara. "It's sort of like being a detective. The best compliment I received was when a CEO said to me, 'I feel like I'm talking to Detective Columbo.' Columbo asked the apparently inane questions, but at the end of the day he solved the murder. That's what we're trying to do: Ask simple questions that will lead us to an understanding of the business."

Janna Sampson says she and her colleagues "spend a lot of time tearing the balance sheet apart and going back to the most basic fundamentals of stock market analysis. We build our own earnings models and look for what we call true earnings as opposed to published earnings. We want to get rid of earnings from pension funds and other noncontinuing operations. We then adjust for option payouts and other things that can really distort operating earnings."

"We mostly want to see that the company creates more cash than it consumes," offers John C. Thompson. "We also like companies with an average return on equity of 15 percent or better over time. The higher, the better."

The more impressive the numbers, the better positioned a company is to prosper, regardless of overall economic conditions. "I look for companies with critical mass and at least three years of operating history," says Margie Patel. "I like to see a company that, by looking at the balance sheet, is pretty well covered by assets and with sustainable revenues to improve the corporate worth and generate better earnings."

Adds Sarah Ketterer, "We go through each stock and reject those that we consider to have inadequate financial strength. This is particularly critical for deep cyclicals. In order to be patient we must have financial strength."

Beyond that, you're looking for other financial statistics that might help you to determine whether there's any trouble on the horizon. "Do company insiders own stock?" asks Susan Suvall. "That's very important because you want them (management) to be on your side."

5. Valuation matters. Although in roaring bull markets a momentum approach of chasing stock prices ever higher can work, over time valuation really does matter. As you no doubt noticed, the price of a stock is an important consideration for both the value and growth Masters. "The process I learned at Fidelity was to buy companies you understand at a decent valuation," says David Ellison.

Even Sam Stewart, who generally favors fast-growing small-company stocks, pays close attention to price. "We might see a company and love it, but if it's selling at an outrageous multiple, we won't buy it," he insists. "It's hard to define outrageous, since it depends on the company's growth prospects. If it's too richly priced, we might instead put it on a watch list to buy at a later point."

Margie Patel says values can often be found in parts of the market the rest of the herd is ignoring. "I particularly look for industries that are out of favor and might benefit from the economic cycle, especially those where the negatives are already factored in and I think the yield is too high for the fundamental risk that actually exists," she notes.

Knowing even basics about PE ratios and other valuation measures is an essential ingredient to stock market success, according to John C. Thompson. "If you don't understand PE multiples and cash flows, and if you don't understand that PEs go up and down, I don't see how you can do a great job in the long term," he observes.

6. Pay attention to risk. As the Masters are often quick to point out, most investors buy stocks or bonds based on the kind of return they expect. Perhaps they anticipate a stock will double, or a bond will shower them with a generous 8 percent dividend yield. What they often don't consider strongly enough is the ensuing risk they are taking with these investments. Indeed, risk preservation and avoiding big blowups is among the most important considerations to keep in the background at all times.

"It's easy to only focus on the upside," admits Andrew Davis. "But God help you when things go wrong. And as we've seen over the last few years, things can go very wrong."

"I tell my guys, 'If you fall out of a window, fall out the basement window. Don't fall out the top floor window,'" says Andy Pilara. "Most times we go into stocks with low expectations. We're all about losing less, not making more. For the most part, when one of our companies misses its earnings, nobody cares because it's not a high-expectation stock.

"Most times we go into stocks with low expectations," Pilara adds. "Our return potential must be much greater than the risks we are taking. We're all about losing less, not making more."

One way to keep risk at bay is by sticking with higher-quality companies. "If you go into a bad stock market with a low-quality company, your bankruptcy risk is high and the market slaughters your stock," says John C. Thompson. "A risk-mitigating strategy is to stay with strong balance sheet companies. . . . Any stock can lose 10, 20, or 25 percent with random bad news. The permanent losses come when you lose 50 percent or more of your money."

Manu Daftary learned this lesson about steering clear of potential blowups early in his career. "I believe the only way you can outperform in the growth universe is to avoid negative surprises and downside volatility," he shares. "If you can truncate the downside, you'll have all the money to play on the upside, which is where all the money is made in the stock market. . . . We actually spend more time making sure we avoid the losers than finding the winners."

Adds David Ellison, "Avoid the blowups at all costs and make sure you understand what you own and the risks of those investments. Then, always reassess those risks."

7. Have realistic expectations. It's true that the stock market showered investors with amazing returns throughout the 1990s, so much so that surveys showed people expected to make at least 20 percent annually on their portfolio for the foreseeable future. Of course, we now know those numbers were unrealistic. And while the S&P 500 has historically returned in the area of 11 percent, including dividends, many of the Masters feel investors should temper their expectations looking out over the next decade.

"I'd guess the return from stocks [for the next several years] might be 6 percent on average, versus maybe 7 percent for bonds," maintains Dan Fuss, among the bearish of the bunch. "If I'm right that interest rates are going up over the next 10 years, that's not a rosy scenario for stocks. It's tough for stocks to do well against rising rates. My guess is we'll continue to be in what I call a trading range market, where both stocks and bonds go up and down with a lot of short cycles."

Sam Stewart forecasts a similar scenario. "I don't expect the markets to be as good as they've been going backward," he offers. "I think 10 or 15 years from now, the Dow may still be at 10,000."

While not all of the Masters are quite as bearish, almost all expect lower returns over the next decade than we saw in the previous one. "I think equity markets will generally offer high single-digit returns," says Sarah Ketterer. "If you get 10 percent you ought to go running to the bank."

However, she, like the rest, is quick to point out that this assessment relates to the market overall. Investors willing to do their homework to find attractively positioned and priced stocks, like the Masters, have the potential to do much better.

"If you look at the last 20 years, you had a period of declining interest rates and declining inflation. It's been the best of times for stocks," Andy Pilara observes. "I do not expect interest rates and inflation to exert such a positive influence on equities in the next few years. I believe we're in a low-return environment for most asset classes."

8. Never fall in love with an investment. All of the Masters enter their stock and bond positions with a long-term perspective, just like Andrew Davis. "Our ideal holding period is forever," he says. But the truth is there is a time to hold 'em and a time to fold 'em. Falling in love with a stock or bond and refusing to sell can be a major error.

Many of the Masters set target prices before making a purchase, in essence giving them an exit strategy at the start. "You want to sell on strength, so when a stock reaches its target, you should be disciplined about selling," says Rob Lyon. If a security goes down in price, and the fundamental reasons you bought the company in the first place have changed, that's another good reason to get out. "We follow a 20 percent rule," offers Whit Gardner. "Basically, if a stock is down over 15 percent but less than 20 percent, we try to make sure we understand what happened to cause this. We then decide whether it's an opportunity to add to our position, or whether we should leave."

Price alone isn't the only reason to sell. Even more important is whether the reason you bought the stock in the first place still holds true. "It really comes down to the fundamentals," says John C. Thompson. "Is it a good long-term company or not? If it remains a good long-term investment, we'll stick with it no matter how low the price goes."

Adds David Chan, "You buy a stock with a certain thesis in mind. The main reason to sell is because the thesis doesn't develop the way you hoped." In summing up this concept, Andy Pilara contends that, "If we don't believe it's creating value, we will sell."

9. Look for pockets of inefficiency in the market. Sam Stewart originally entered the investment business through the world of academia. He was always taught that nobody could beat the market because all information about a company is already factored into the price of a stock. But his real-life research proved otherwise. "The less widely covered a company is, the less likely it is to be efficiently priced," Stewart says. That's why he began specializing in small-cap stocks, which tend to have the least Wall Street coverage of all, and therefore the most inefficient pricing.

"I've always believed there are many pockets of inefficiency in the market," says Rob Lyon. "These inefficiencies can be found in really big companies that are not well followed. Sometimes they are spinoffs of even larger companies; other times they're complex multi-industry companies that fall through the cracks, or those with some pretty serious baggage."

Whit Gardner looks for these inefficiencies by seeking companies with positive changes on the horizon that other investors don't yet know about. This pursuit of pockets of inefficiency is one of the reasons Rob Lyon has such a large percentage of his portfolio invested in European equities. "We think Europe is less efficiently priced than the United States," he shares. "The analyst community is smaller and the market isn't picked over as widely."

10. Diversify, diversify, diversify. This might be the most overstated investment rule of all, but it's amazing how few people adhere to it. "What does diversification do for an investor?" asks Sarah Ketterer. "It lowers risk, which I define as volatility of return. Why do we care about volatility? Because returns that fluctuate less allow one to sleep better at night. A calm investor is less likely to make a poor decision because they will have returns that are consistent and more predictable."

I'm always surprised when people show me their "diversified" portfolios, which contain 20 similar technology stocks, or 5 growth funds that all look alike. Paul Wick has learned the importance of diversification within industries even in running a sector-specific technology fund. "If you have a huge exposure to semiconductors, you can literally have the whole group trade off and almost act like one stock," he says. "Therefore, even if you have 30 or 40 percent of your fund in a wide basket of semiconductor stocks, it's almost like having 30 or 40 percent of the fund in just one or two companies."

True diversification means owning an array of different stocks, bonds, or mutual funds spread among a variety of industries and sectors. As Riad Younes points out, "There is a saying that there is no free lunch in the market. In reality there is only one free lunch and that is diversification. It's a free insurance. . . . The more you're diversified, the more you reduce your risk, and it doesn't cost a thing."

Another good reason for diversification, says Younes, is there's no reason not to have it in your portfolio. "Why should you have a small menu to choose from?" Younes observes. "When you start with a smaller universe, you start with a suboptimal universe."

Plus, assuming you're investing through funds instead of individual stocks, it also makes sense to own pieces of both growth and value, since these styles are generally in vogue at different times. "Value has its day, and then growth has its day," Susan Suvall explains. In the case of funds, the trick is to find the best managers for each of these styles, all of whom are disciplined and follow the rules outlined in this chapter. Then, let them go to work making money for you.

GLOSSARY OF FREQUENTLY USED INVESTING TERMS

alpha   Excess return provided by an investment that is uncorrelated with the general stock market.

asset allocation   Act of spreading investment funds across various asset categories, such as stocks, bonds, and cash.

behavioral finance   A field of study that combines finance and psychology in an effort to predict the behavior of markets or particular securities.

beta   A coefficient measure of a stock's relative volatility in relation to the Standard & Poor's 500 index, which has a beta of 1.

bid price   The highest amount a buyer is willing to pay for shares of a stock.

book value   What a company would be worth if all assets were sold (assets minus liabilities). Also, the price at which an asset is carried on a balance sheet.

bottom-up investing   The search for outstanding individual stocks with little regard for overall economic trends.

cash ratio   Ratio of cash and marketable securities to current liabilities. Tells the extent to which liabilities could be immediately liquidated.

contrarian   Investor who does the opposite of the majority at any particular time.

convertible bond   Security that can be exchanged for other securities of the issuer (under certain conditions), usually from preferred stock or bonds into common stock.

cost of capital   The opportunity cost of an investment. In other words, the rate of return that a company or investor could earn at the same risk level as the investment being considered.

credit risk   Possibility that a bond issuer will default on the payment of interest and return of principal. Risk is minimized by investing in bonds issued by large blue-chip corporations or government agencies.

current assets   Balance sheet item equal to the sum of cash and cash equivalents, accounts receivable, inventory, marketable securities, prepaid expenses, and other assets that could be converted into cash in less than one year.

current ratio   Current assets divided by current liabilities. Shows a company's ability to pay current debts from current assets.

debt-to-equity ratio   Long-term debt divided by shareholders' equity. Indicates how highly leveraged a company is.

distribution   Dividends paid from net investment income plus realized capital gains.

diversification   Spreading risk by putting assets into several different investment categories, such as stocks, bonds, and cash.

dividend   Distribution of earnings to shareholders.

dividend discount model (DDM)   Procedure for valuing the price of a stock by using predicted dividends and discounting them back to present value.

dividend yield   The cash dividend paid per share each year divided by the current share price.

dollar cost averaging   The process of accumulating positions in stocks and mutual funds by investing a set amount of money each month, thus buying more shares when prices are down, less when they are up.

fair market value   Price at which an asset is or can be passed on from a willing buyer to a willing seller.

institutional investor   Organization that trades a large volume of securities, like a mutual fund, bank, or insurance company.

intrinsic value   Estimated worth of a company; often determined by a series of valuation models.

market capitalization or market value   Calculated by multiplying the number of shares outstanding by the per share price of a stock. One can also categorize equities into several different classes, including micro-cap, small-cap, mid-cap, and large-cap. The general guidelines for these classifications are as follows:

> **micro-cap:** market capitalizations of $0 to $500 million.
>
> **small-cap:** market capitalizations of $500 to $2 billion.
>
> **mid-cap:** market capitalizations of $2 billion to $5 billion.
>
> **large-cap:** market capitalizations of $5 billion or more.

Nasdaq Composite   An index of the National Association of Securities Dealers weighted by market value and representing domestic companies that are sold over the counter.

net current assets   Assets calculated by taking current assets minus current liabilities. Also referred to as working capital.

price-to-earnings ratio (PE)   Price of a stock divided by its earnings per share.

price-to-book ratio (PB)   Shareholders' equity divided by the number of outstanding shares. If under 1, it means a stock is selling for less than the price the company paid for its assets, though this is not necessarily indicative of a good value.

price-to-cash flow ratio   A stock's capitalization divided by its cash flow for the latest fiscal year.

price-to-sales ratio   A stock's capitalization divided by its sales over the trailing 12 months.

private market value   The value of a company if each of its parts were owned and/or sold independently.

return on equity (ROE)   Measure of how well a company used reinvested earnings to generate additional earnings. Equal to a fiscal year's after-tax income divided by book value, expressed as a percentage.

Standard & Poor's Composite Index of 500 Stocks (S&P 500)   An index that tracks the performance of 500 stocks, mostly blue chips, and represents almost two-thirds of the U.S. stock market's total value. It is weighted by market value.

shareholders' equity   Total assets minus total liabilities of an individual company. Also known as net assets.

stock   Represents ownership in a corporation. Usually listed in terms of shares.

top-down   Investment strategy that first seeks to find the most optimal sectors or industries to invest in, and then searches for the best companies within those sectors or industries.

technical analysis   Method of analyzing securities by relying on the assumption that market data, such as price charts, volume, and open interest, can help predict future—especially short-term—market trends.

turnover   For a company, the ratio of annual sales to inventory. For a mutual fund, the number of times a year that a manager turns over the securities in a portfolio.

INDEX

Seligman Frontier Fund, 210
Seligman Growth Fund, 210
Seligman High Yield Bond Fund, 210
Seligman Tri-Continental Fund, 211
Sell-side approach, 18, 121–122, 179, 186
Semiconductor industry, 211–212, 220, 262
Shareholder value, 84
Shilling, Gary, 68
Short sales, 12–14, 172, 180
Silicon Valley, 217
Slowing economy, 242–243
Small-cap equities, 245
Small Cap Financial Fund, 206
Small-cap funds, 201, 210
Small-cap stocks, 7–10, 21–22, 42–44, 47–50, 79,
    84–85, 90, 116, 119–120, 129–130, 160,
    173, 262
Smith, Monica, 69–70
Smith, Morris, 197
Software industry, 221
Sony, 58
South Sea bubble, 154
Southwest Airlines, 128
Spinoffs, 72, 262
Spot rate, 148
Spread compression, 202
Standard & Poor's ratings, 56
Stansky, Bob, 197
State municipal bonds, 236
Steinhart, Michael, 83
Stephens, Paul, 84
Stewart, Samuel:
    America's Best Growth Company (ABGC),
        40, 46
    DuPont Analysis, 45
    earnings growth, 43
    economic forecasts, 260–261
    educational background, 39–40
    exit strategy, 44, 47–48
    on inefficient markets, 262
    investment strategy, 256–257
    onion peeling, 46
    portfolio diversification, 47
    professional background, vii–viii, 39, 41
    small-cap stocks, 42–44, 47–50
    stock selection strategy, 41–45
    on valuation, 46–49, 259
    Wasatch Advisors, 40
    Wasatch Heritage Growth Fund, 50
Stock buybacks, 128, 143
Stock market bubbles, 116
Stock market crash of 1987, 71, 72, 94
Stock options, 72
Stock screening, 20, 44–45
Stop-loss orders, 12, 25
Sun Microsystems, 104

Supply and demand, 8, 77–78, 85–86, 163, 189,
    192, 247
Suvall, Susan:
    buy-side approach, 122
    on cash, 124
    on down markets, 124, 127
    earnings forecasting, 125–126
    educational background, 120
    exit strategies, 128–129
    fund management, 120, 122–123
    investment style, 130–131
    macro perspectives, 126
    managerial quality, 128
    market capitalization, 124–125
    personal investments, 129–130
    portfolio diversification, 126–127, 129–130,
        263
    professional background, viii, 119–123
    research methods, 259
    on sell-side approach, 121–122
    stock selection process, 125–126
    success rate, 130
    on valuation, 120, 125
Sykes, 47
Symantec, 221
Sysco, 33

Taft Broadcasting, 70–71
Tax legislation, 1986, 189
Tax shelters, real estate, 189
TCW Galileo Value Opportunities Fund, 120
Technical analysis, 26
Technology bubble, 126, 213
Technology industry, 103
Technology mutual funds, 221
Technology sector, 207, 209–210, 247–248. See
    also Wick, Paul
Technology stocks, 8, 60–61, 209, 211–215,
    256
Telecom bubble, 244
Templeton, John, 7
Tenet Healthcare, 10
Terminology, 265–267
Terrorist attacks, economic impact of, 191,
    245
Thompson, John C.:
    aggressive growth, 61
    on bear markets, 61–62
    educational background, 52–53
    exit strategy, 58–59, 261
    free cash flow, 54–56
    holding period, 58
    investment process, 54–58, 61
    portfolio diversification, 60–62
    professional background, vii–viii, 51–54
    research methods, 258

About the Author

Kirk Kazanjian is a nationally recognized investment expert, mutual fund analyst, bestselling author, and lifelong entrepreneur. He spent several years as an award-winning television news anchor and business reporter before moving into various roles within the investment industry. Among other things, Kazanjian is the former Director of Research and Investment Strategy for two leading investment firms, where he performed investment manager research and due diligence, oversaw the creation of new investment programs, and developed strategies for managing client assets.

In addition to *The Market Masters*, Kazanjian has written many other personal finance books, including *Wizards of Wall Street, Growing Rich with Growth Stocks,* and *Value Investing with the Masters.*

Kazanjian regularly offers investment advice on CNBC, Bloomberg, plus many other radio and television stations across the country. He has been featured in numerous publications, including *Barron's, Entrepreneur, The Christian Science Monitor,* and *USA Today,* and is a popular speaker and teacher on investment topics.

The author welcomes your comments and feedback. He can be reached through his web site at www.kirkkazanjian.com.